THE GRIMOIRE OF ARTHUR GAUNTLET

Published by Avalonia

BM Avalonia
London
WC1N 3XX
England, UK

www.avaloniabooks.co.uk

"The Grimoire of Arthur Gauntlet"
Being a complete transcription of Sloane MS 3851, with
introduction and notes by David Rankine.

Copyright © David Rankine 2011

ISBN-13: 978-1-905297-38-2

First Paperback Edition, June 2011
Design by Satori

The cover illustrations are drawn from Sloane MS 3851, with
the kind permission of the British Library in London.

British Library Cataloguing in Publication Data. A catalogue record
for this book is available from the British Library.

David Rankine is an esoteric researcher and occult author who first started exploring the practices and history of the Western Esoteric Traditions in the 1970s. His work has contributed towards a resurgence in the interest in medieval and renaissance grimoires in the 21st century. Through works such as *The Veritable Key of Solomon* and other books in the Sourceworks of Ceremonial Magic series with Stephen Skinner, his work has significantly furthered the corpus of primary texts available to students of the grimoires. His work with Sorita d'Este, including books such as *Hekate Liminal Rites* and *The Cosmic Shekinah,* have brought him recognition for his work in mythology, mysticism and magic around the world. David lives in Wales, near the internationally reknowned town-of-books Hay on Wye in the United Kingdom.

If you enjoy *The Grimoire of Arthur Gauntlet,* you may also find the following titles by the same author of interest:

David Rankine
Climbing the Tree of Life (Avalonia, 2005)
The Book of Treasure Spirits (Avalonia, 2009)
Heka – Egyptian Magic (Avalonia, 2006)

David Rankine, with Sorita d'Este
Practical Qabalah Magick (Avalonia, 2009)
Practical Elemental Magick (Avalonia, 2008)
Practical Planetary Magick (Avalonia, 2007)
The Isles of the Many Gods (Avalonia, 2007)

David Rankine, with Paul Harry Barron
The Book of Gold (17th century Psalm Magic), (Avalonia, 2010)

David Rankine, with Stephen Skinner
The Grimoire of St Cyprian (Golden Hoard Press, 2009)
A Collection of Magical Secrets (Avalonia, 2009)
The Veritable Key of Solomon (Golden Hoard Press, 2008)
The Goetia of Dr Rudd (Golden Hoard Press, 2007)
The Keys to the Gateway of Magic (Golden Hoard Press, 2005)
The Practical Angel Magic of Dr John Dee (Golden Hoard, 2004)

For more information on these and other titles see:
www.avaloniabooks.co.uk

The Grimoire
of
Arthur Gauntlet

A 17th century London Cunning-man's book of charms, conjurations and prayers

Includes material from the Heptameron, the Arbatel, the Discoverie of Witchcraft; and the writings of Cornelius Agrippa and William Bacon

Edited by David Rankine

Published by Avalonia
www.avaloniabooks.co.uk

Acknowledgements

I would like to thank the British Library for their kind permission to reproduce the manuscript Sloane MS 3851 which forms the basis for this book.

A huge thank you must be made to Yuri Robbers for his excellent work in translating the Latin parts of the text. Additional thanks go to Iris Sala for her work on parts of the Latin.

Furthermore, I would like to also thank Joseph Peterson for his assistance with texts and advice, particularly regarding Folger Vb.26 and Additional MS 36674; Jerry Buterbaugh for helping me track down some of the obscure texts I needed to consult; Stephen Skinner for ongoing discussion of the grimoires and their provenance; Dan Harms for first making me aware of Folger Vb.26.; Andrea Salgado-Reyes for proof-reading and checking the book.

I would particularly like to thank Sorita d'Este, for her invaluable assistance and encouragement with this project from start to finish.

Introduction

The early seventeenth century was a time of change in England and particularly so in London. London was growing rapidly at this time, with a population of around a quarter of a million people in 1600, just over 6% of the English population of around four million. This rapid growth in population was mirrored by the increase in magical texts being made available in both manuscript and printed form.[1]

At this time England was a political powder-keg, with ongoing disputes between King Charles I and Parliament. In 1629, Charles I dissolved Parliament and ruled without a government for eleven years, an act known alternatively as The Personal Rule or The Eleven Years Tyranny.

During this period medicine was still in its infancy and had not fully divorced itself from magic, with barber surgeons competing with cunning-folk for custom. Major medical authorities drawn upon by seventeenth century physicians and surgeons included charms in their writings, as can be seen in the works of figures such as Gilbertus Anglicus (thirteenth century), John Gaddesden and John Arderne (fourteenth century), and Thomas Fayreford (fifteenth century).[2] Conversely, sixteenth and seventeenth century

---

[1] E.g. the 1650s saw the first English editions of Agrippa's Three Books of Occult Philosophy (1651) and Fourth Book of Occult Philosophy (1655), Paracelsus' Of the Supreme Mysteries of Nature (1656), Ars Notoria (1657), Fama Fraternitas (1652), Causabon's True and Faithful Relation (1659), Kircher's Oedipus Aegypticus, and the second expanded edition of Scot's Discoverie of Witchcraft. More than a quarter of the known Key of Solomon MSS date to this period (33/124).

[2] See e.g. Sloane MS 56, Sloane MS 1067, Additional MS 33996, Harley MS 2558.

magical texts[3] often contained instructions for conjurations and charms to assist in the practice of *'physick'* (medicine).

Such texts were often sought and used by cunning-folk, men and women who provided a range of magical services to anyone who paid them. Such services included a wide range of possibilities including healing people and farm animals, recovering lost or stolen goods, protection from witches, curses and evil spirits; gaining love, and locating hidden treasure. To achieve such diverse results, cunning-men and women drew on numerous techniques and sources, often creating books of practice of charms and conjurations they found effective.

The Witchcraft Act of 1604 introduced by King James I (1566-1625), had been aimed at cunning-folk as well as witches, and covered such deeds as, *"Witchcrafte Inchantment Charme or Sorcerie to tell or declare in what place any treasure of Golde or silver should or had in the earth or other secret places, or where Goodes or Thinges loste or stollen should be founde or become; or to the intent to P[ro]voke any person to unlawfull love."*[4]

However the Witchcraft Act was largely ignored in many parts of England, particularly the capital. Davies (2003:17) observes that *"The ecclesiastical courts in London, a city that abounded with magical practitioners, were apparently the earliest to lose interest in cunning-folk and popular magic, with hardly any relevant cases after 1600."*[5]

England was largely Protestant, with a degree of intellectual suspicion expressed by contemporary writers such as John Melton in his famous work *Astrologater* (1620) towards magical conjuration *"with its hallowing, fumigations and consecrations, was strongly reminiscent of the Roman Mass."*[6]

It is during this period that the Sloane MS 3851 manuscript, the cunning-man Arthur Gauntlet's book of practice, which forms the corpus of this book was written. It probably dates to the 1620s or early 1630s, as the evidence I will present demonstrates.

---

[3] In this context text refers to both grimoires and books of secrets.

[4] *Witchcraft and Society in England and America, 1550-1750*, Gibson, 2003:5-7.

[5] *Cunning-Folk: Popular Magic in English History*, Davies, 2003:17.

[6] *Religion and the Decline of Magic*, Thomas, 1971:319.

Arthur Gauntlet & Sarah Skelhorn

The only known published literary reference to Arthur Gauntlet was by the famous astrologer William Lilly (1602-1681) in his autobiography, written around 1668.[7] The quote from Lilly provides some significant peripheral information which can help us create at least a sketchy picture of Arthur Gauntlet.

"I was very familiar with one Sarah Skelhorn, who had been Speculatrix unto one Arthur Gauntlet about Gray's Inn Lane,[8] a very lewd fellow, professing physick. This Sarah had a perfect sight, and indeed the best eyes for that purpose I ever yet did see. Gauntlet's books, after he was dead, were sold, after I had perused them, to my scholar Humphreys: there were rare notions in them. This Sarah lived a long time, even until her death, with one Mrs. Stockman in the Isle of Purbeck, and died about fifteen years since."[9]

It seems curious that Lilly should describe Sarah Skelhorn (called Sarah Shelborne in the introduction) so positively as such a good seer, and yet be negative about Arthur Gauntlet. Lilly's single reference to him as a *'lewd fellow'* stands out and labels Gauntlet without allowing any opportunity for defence of his character or further consideration. However it is clear from Lilly's writings that he was quick to denigrate anybody who he felt was not a respectable practitioner of astrology or the magical arts by his standards. I suggest that the fact that Arthur Gauntlet should have such a good speculatrix or seer combined with the heavily angelic and moral nature of Gauntlet's manuscript may mitigate Lilly's unqualified negative remark about his character.

Another document would seem to support Lilly's view, until we consider that it was written in 1889, and seems to repeat verbatim Lilly's words, with some embellishment. How accurate this information is must be a matter of speculation. Nevertheless I have included it here to provide all the available information:

"It was so also with Sarah Skelhorn, the speculatrix of Dr Gauntlet of Gray's Inn Lane, a very loose liver. On leaving the Doctor's service Sarah became engaged by Mrs Stockman, with whom she lived in the Isle of

---

[7] "Wrote by himself in the 66th year of his Age", The Life of William Lilly, Davies:1774:1.

[8] This street is now called Gray's Inn Road.

[9] The Life of William Lilly, Davies, 1774:149.

Purbeck until her death, seventeen years later, seeing visions for her mistress and her mother, the Lady Beconsfield."[10]

We can deduce something more about Arthur Gauntlet through another mention of his name, in MS Laud Misc 19. This manuscript contains an early ownership inscription of Arthur Gauntlet, and was in William Laud's possession in 1636. This manuscript includes a *"Treatise, based on and including extracts from Hilton's Scale, describing the way of meditation and the mystical experience".*[11]

Considering the nature of Walter Hilton's *Scale of Perfection* offers some revealing insights. Hilton (c.1343-1396) discusses such topics as the form of spiritual visions and how to induce contemplation through meditation, prayer and Scripture. The *Scale of Perfection* was written as an instructional guide for women who had taken vows or committed to a religious life, and as such may have been of interest to, for example, a female skryer such as Sarah Skelhorn.

There are some clues in the text which suggest that Arthur Gauntlet was a very capable practitioner, who did not just rely on material from earlier sources, or had access to someone else who was. The magic circles found at fo.114v-115 have some very interesting features which are not seen in other grimoires, and which would seem to be the result of experience being applied. Thus we see the circles having a larger and more spacious diameter of fourteen foot, not the standard nine foot found in many grimoires drawing on the *Heptameron*.

It is also significant that in light of his conjurations being largely of angels; Gauntlet uses a second smaller circle for the crystal to be positioned in, and for angelic manifestation. The shape of this is in contrast to the constraining triangle used with demons found in the *Goetia*, or the pentagram used with faeries found in Sloane MS 3824. However a circle would make sense for angels as a perfect shape representing the divine and not seeking to dominate them as one would need to do for demons.

Another interesting feature of this manuscript is that the one magical tool emphasised is the wand. There is a consecration of a wand given, as well as charms which require the use of a wand.

---

[10] Current Opinion Vol 3, Wheeler & Crane, 1889:153.

[11] The Index of Middle English Prose Handlist XVI, Ogilvie-Thomson, 2000:1.

Considering the emphasis on the sword in many grimoires, this suggests a more practical and simplified approach with a more transportable and inconspicuous tool.

If we make the tentative assumption that MS Laud Misc 19 passed directly from Arthur Gauntlet's hands, being sold on after his death, and that it went directly into William Laud's possession from Gauntlet, then it suggests a date of death around 1636. Now Lilly gives us a death date of 1653 for Sarah Skelhorn, writing that she had died *'about sixteen years since'* (the publication of his autobiography in 1669) we can place this around 1653. The other reference to Sarah Skelhorn reproduced in *Current Opinion* says she died seventeen years after leaving Gauntlet's service, which would also give a date of 1636 (i.e. 1653-17). Therefore we can suggest that Sarah Skelhorn left Gauntlet's service when he died, in 1636.

It is noteworthy that after Sarah Skelhorn left Arthur Gauntlet's service, she took service with a woman, for whom she would skry into the crystal. As has already been mentioned, from 1636-1653, Sarah lived with Mrs Stockman in the Isle of Purbeck. In his autobiography, Lilly mentions Mrs Stockman asking Sarah to skry for her to determine whether her mother, Lady Beconsfield, was at home, before going to visit her. [12]

One of the last pieces of information Lilly provides about Sarah Skelhorn suggests she was at times irritated with her gift, describing her frustration with seeing angels everywhere she went. Lilly commented that, *"Sarah told me oft, the angels would for some years follow her, and appear in every room of the house, until she was weary of them."*[13]

Lilly also describes how Sarah began her skrying practice, continuing with the same for Ellen Evans, daughter of the Welsh astrologer who trained Lilly himself:

"This Sarah Skelhorn, her call unto the crystal began, 'Oh ye good angels, only and only, &c'. Ellen Evans, daughter of my tutor Evans, her call unto the crystal was this: O Micol, O tu Micol, regina pigmeorum, veni, &c" [14]

---

[12] The Life of William Lilly, Davies, 1774:150.

[13] The Life of William Lilly, Davies, 1774:150.

[14] The Life of William Lilly, Davies, 1774:149. The Latin conjuration, "O Micol, O you Micol, queen of the pigmies [fairies], come", contains a name for the Fairy Queen found in Sloane MS 1727, an undated C17th MS. The

The emphasis on female skryers, as well as women using their services, and the probable ownership of Sloane MS 3851 by Ann Savadge (as I will subsequently demonstrate) places a far greater emphasis on the place of women in magic in the seventeenth century than has previously been credited.

William Laud

That a book containing spiritual material belonging to Arthur Gauntlet should end up in the hands of William Laud (1573-1645) is very interesting. William Laud was the Bishop of London from 1628-33, and it may be possible that he and Arthur Gauntlet met or even knew each other. This would provide a possible explanation for why Laud should end up with one of Gauntlet's books, particularly considering the religious nature of its contents.

By the end of his life Laud had risen to the position of Archbishop of Canterbury. He was beheaded during the English Civil War for his support of King Charles I and his vehement opposition to much of Puritanism, with great exception being taken to some of his ideas which were considered too *'catholic'*, such as reintroducing stained glass windows and statues, and moving the altar from the middle to the east.

Captain Bubb

The tangential references to his contemporaries in Lilly's autobiography give us some idea of when Arthur Gauntlet may have been practising magic and physick. Captain Bubb is mentioned by Lilly, and also by Arthur Gauntlet on fo.8v of Sloane MS 3851, so the two were probably acquainted, and may well have been moving in similar circles.

After describing the sale of William Hart's books in 1634,[15] Lilly went on to describe how *"In Lambeth Marsh at the same time lived one Captain Bubb, who resolved horary questions astrologically; a proper handsome man, well spoken, but withal covetous, and of no honesty"*[16]

---

possibly derivative name Mycob for the Fairy Queen in found in Sloane MS 3824 (1649).

[15] The Life of William Lilly, Davies, 1774:36.

[16] The Life of William Lilly, Davies, 1774:38.

Lilly specifically identifies Captain Bubb as having been pilloried for falsehood, which enables us to find out more about Bubb.

It seems clear that Captain Bubb had influential associates, as Boas (1928:161) notes that *"In Times Literary Supplement 12 Jan [1928], Bertram Lloyd identifies The Juggling Captain in 'The Fair Maid of the Inn', v.ii, with a Captain Bubb to whom S[amuel]. Rid dedicated The Art of Juggling (1614) and who was pilloried in 1618 for telling fortunes."*[17]

The comedy *The Fair Maid of the Inn* was first performed in 1626, and had been written by the famous playwright John Fletcher (1579-1625) and some of his collaborators. John Fletcher was one of the most popular and influential playwrights of his day, along William Shakespeare and Christopher Marlowe.

Juggling and sleight of hand have long been associated with magic, so the dedication of a book on juggling to Captain Bubb again emphasises the extent of his connections. The first edition of *The Art of Juggling or Legerdemaine* was published in 1612, and it is interesting to note that a number of the tricks in it are drawn from material given in Scot's *Discoverie of Witchcraft* (1584), one of the main published works of the period which made grimoire material available.

In the latter half of the seventeenth century there is a reference to a Captain Bubb in a parliamentary context, as being one *"who also stands for a Member"*,[18] i.e. acted for a Member of Parliament.

John Searle

Another person mentioned by Arthur Gauntlet is John Searle, in the heading *"A Prayer to God for good Success in Matters written by John Searle Practitioner in Surgery And in Astronomy Ano 1594:"* (fo.6-7). The combination of prayer with surgery points to a John Searle who was a choirman for a year, and was appointed as a minor canon in Westminster Abbey in 1594, holding this post for ten years.[19]

---

[17] Elizabethan Drama, Boas, 1928:161.

[18] The House of Commons, 1660-1690 Vol 1, p185

[19] Westminster Abbey Reformed: 1540-1640, Knighton & Mortimer, 2003:101.

This was probably the same John Searle who had a licence from Cambridge university in 1607 to practice chirurgery,[20] and who published an ephemeris from 1609-1617 with three treatises attached, being (1) on the use of an ephemeris, (2) on the fixed stars and (3) four sections on astrology.[21] The early date of the prayer, 1594, suggests the prayer may have been passed on to Gauntlet or circulated amongst his peers.

William Bacon

An interesting inclusion by Gauntlet is the piece entitled, *"The Roman Secret touching the Spirit called Sathan by which the Romans did understand of things present past and to come: By W. Bacon"* (fo.109v-111). The only other references I have located to William Bacon regarding esoteric matters are the pieces called *'To discover witches'*, *'To staunch blood'* and *'To help one that is bewitched'* which are found in Sloane MS 3846 at fo.95v-98; and *'The Experiment of W. Bacon to Destroy Witches'* in Bodleian e. Mus 173 at 37v.

Both Sloane MS 3851 and Sloane MS 3846 were part of the library of the angel magician Lord Jekyll (see below for more details). When Lord Jekyll died and his huge library was sold, both these manuscripts were purchased by Sir Hans Sloane and formed part of the collection he bequeathed to the British Library.

These pieces were probably written by the astrologer William Bacon (1577-1653), whose book *A Key to Helmont* (published posthumously in 1682), was a work which rejected Paracelsian medicine and promoted the study of chemistry as essential to medicine.[22]

It has been suggested by Klaasen (2011:9) that William Bacon may be a corruption of Roger Bacon (1214-1292), the medieval natural philosopher,[23] to whom several texts were attributed, however this seems unlikely to me. Not only are there several pieces in different manuscripts, suggesting the name was not miscopied, but the William Bacon pieces are short pieces (unlike e.g. the *Nigromancia* attributed to Roger Bacon) which have a certain consistency in their material. Furthermore Roger Bacon's known

---

[20] Surgery.

[21] Athenae Cantabrigiensis Vol 2, Gray, 1861:530.

[22] The Chemical Philosophy, Debus, 2002:503.

[23] Three early magic rituals to spoil witches, Klaasen, 2011, 1.1:9 fn39.

writings emphasised a more scientific approach, for he *"rejected many of the magical beliefs of his day, though he gave credit to astrology and alchemy ... because ... they seemed to him to be justified by experience."*[24]

John a Windor

The prayer at fo.39v, which begins *"O Domine Jesu Christe Rex Glorie per virtutem illorum qui hoc nomen Hermelie"* is also found in Sloane MS 3846 with a description of its circumstances, also mentioned by Lilly in his autobiography.[25] Lilly states that the prayer was said to have been copied by the scrivener (scribe) John a Windor from one of John Dee's books of conjurations, which he saw open in a window whilst visiting him at Mortlake.

If this is true then the prayer obviously dates to the late sixteenth or more likely early seventeenth century (pre Dee's death in 1608/9). Dr John Dee (1527-1609) was an astrologer, mathematician, cartographer and magician of huge importance. As Queen Elizabeth I's astrologer and occasional advisor, he contributed a number of very significant suggestions to the Queen which contributed to the expansion of English power overseas.[26]

Much of Dee's material was lost, after being hidden in a cabinet he owned. The papers were discovered in 1662, decades after Dee's death, and with the chest having passed through the hands of several owners. Unfortunately the family's maid used about half of the papers for kindling, resulting in the loss of a substantial portion of Dee's magical writings.

I will quote the description from Sloane MS 3846 in full, as if this is true it is a very important and significant example of Dee's material which was lost, not being reproduced in any of the known works of Dee:

"John a Windor declareth at Newbury in County Court, being once brought before Mr Justice Wallop, & accused for using unlawful arts, among the depositions taken before him, by Mr Oliver Withers his Clark,

---

[24] Roger Bacon: The Father of Experimental Science and Medieval Occultism, Redgrove, 2003:16.

[25] The Life of William Lilly, Davies:1774:145.

[26] See The Queen's Conjuror, Woolley, 2002 for more information about the life of Dr John Dee.

there is this following Call, which he said, being once at Dr Dee's house at Mortlake he saw lie in a Window, & which he soever since used."[27]

John a Windor is an interesting character, who Lilly describes as having *"many good parts, but was a most lewd person"*.[28] Lilly also indicates that Windor was a practising magician; and that because he *"was much given to debauchery, so that at some times the Dæmons would not appear to the Speculator; he would then suffumigate: sometimes, to vex the spirits, he would curse them, fumigate with contraries."*

The debauchery offending the dæmons is indicative of the purity expected for effective conjuration. More significantly the wording indicates that John a Windor was performing conjurations for money, hence the presence of a *'speculator'* desiring to see dæmons.

A contraction of two of the lines was reproduced by Lilly in his autobiography, being, *"Per virtutem illorum qui invocant nomen tuum, Hermeli, mitte nobis tres angelos"*. This was later used in novels, including *Brambletye House* by Horace Smith by an astrologer performing an angelic conjuration;[29] and by the character of John Dee himself in *Agnes de Mansfelt* by Thomas Grattan in 1836.[30]

Lilly also mentions that Oliver Withers *"brought up a Windor's examination unto London, purposefully for me to peruse"*.[31] The interconnection of the community of astrologers and magicians of the time is repeatedly emphasised in his autobiography, showing how easily it would have been for material to be transmitted between practitioners.

As the example of the prayer in this MS is in Arthur Gantlet's handwriting, this would suggest that either John a Windor made up his story, or that somehow Gauntlet got hold of the prayer from John a Windor, or another person who had copied it from John a Windor.

---

[27] Sloane MS 3846, fo.113v.

[28] The Life of William Lilly, Davies:1774:145.

[29] Brambletye House; or Cavaliers and roundheads, Vol 3, Smith, 1826:228.

[30] Agnes de Mansfelt: a historical tale, Grattan, 1835:277.

[31] The Life of William Lilly, Davies:1774:145-6.

How old is Sloane MS 3851?

It has been suggested that Sloane MS 3851 dates to 1696, however a number of factors demonstrate that this is a mis-dating, and that it is somewhat older. The alleged date reference is written next to the word *hore* ('hour', Latin), which immediately brings it into question.

The number 1696 may rather refer to the 19th hour, as 1696 = 1+6+6+6, with the middle 6 being written upside-down. This would be entirely in keeping with the peculiar numeration found throughout Sloane MS 3851, e.g. 6 being comprised of three upside-down 2's in the *Of Perfumes* section (fo.113-114).

The first tangible factor that demonstrates the manuscript must be from an earlier date is that Elias Ashmole's handwriting is found spread throughout Sloane MS 3851. Elias Ashmole died in 1692, which immediately pushes the possible date of Sloane MS 3851 back several years.

As I will show in the next section, there is material in Sloane MS 3851 which is derived from Folger Vb.26(1), which dates to around 1580. An example of this material derived from Folger Vb.26(1) is seen in fo.130-132, in the conjuration to have conference with familiar spirits, which also includes a group of fairy beings called the seven fairy sisters. The use of these names may help in dating Sloane MS 3851, as it predates the set of names for the seven fairy sisters found in the 1640s in Sloane MS 3825 (1641) and Sloane MS 3824 (c.1649).[32]

As I have already demonstrated, a provisional date of death of 1636 for Arthur Gauntlet seems likely. Therefore the date of Sloane MS 3851 must be 1636 or earlier. In the same paragraph of his autobiography that he mentions Sarah Skelhorn, Lilly observes that, *"Gauntlet's books, after he was dead, were sold, after I had perused them, to my scholar Humphreys: there were rare notions in them."* [33] From his other comments, it is clear that Lilly is referring to John Humphreys. Elsewhere in his autobiography Lilly introduces Humphreys, saying, *"In the year 1640 I instructed John Humphreys, master of that art, in the study of astrology"*.[34]

---

[32] These names are Lilia, Rostilia, Foca, Folla, Africa, Julia, Venulla.

[33] The Life of William Lilly, Davies, 1774:149..

[34] The Life of William Lilly, Davies, 1774:50.

Lilly was again uncomplimentary about Humphreys, describing him as *"a laborious person, vain-glorious, loquacious, fool-hardy, desirous of all secrets which he knew not"*.[35] However, from the sequence of mentioning the death of Gauntlet and the disposal of his books, followed by writing about the death of Sarah Skelhorn, we can assume this taking possession of the books must have occurred between 1640 and 1653, as Lilly looked at them before Humphreys bought them.

We know from the 1614 dedication to Captain Bubb that he may have already been practising astrology and magic. As this is the earliest reference to Captain Bubb, and Arthur Gauntlet refers to one of his charms, it provides a range of 1614-1636 as the likely date of writing of Sloane MS 3851.

Of course Sloane MS 3851 contains earlier material from grimoires dating back to at least 1580. Indeed some of the charms existed in earlier forms as far back as the fourteenth century, and obviously became corrupted or mutated with the passing of time.

The Material in Sloane MS 3851 from other Grimoires

Some of the other material contained in Sloane MS 3851 also needs to be discussed to further set the context and provenance of the material collated by Gauntlet. One consideration which stands out is that the work he translated from other languages is from foreign editions or manuscripts, being noticeably different to the later English editions. Indeed the English editions of the works he collated material from were all published subsequent to Arthur Gauntlet's death.

The material drawn from the *De Occulta Philosophia* of Cornelius Agrippa is a translation from German or Latin and not a reproduction of the English edition which was published in 1651. Likewise the *Heptameron* and Agrippa's *Fourth Book of Occult Philosophy* were only published in English in 1655, after Gauntlet's death, and the material included from them has been translated from the original and is noticeably different to the 1655 Turner translation.

The version of the *Arbatel* included by Gauntlet is unique, not only in that it is a different translation to Turner's later published

---

[35] The Life of William Lilly, Davies, 1774:52.

version in 1655, but it is the only known version which includes the diagram of the Seal of Secrets (with Aphorism 27) which is a hugely important image. This suggests that Gauntlet's copy of the *Arbatel*, irrespective of the omissions and mistakes it contains, was probably derived from a manuscript copy not generally available, and not the first published 1575 Latin edition.

The conjuration of Oberion at fo.115v-116 is clearly derived from the material found in Folger Vb.26(1). As well as having very similar conjurations, Vb.26(1) has two images of Oberion (at fo.185 and fo.186) with the sun and moon on his right and left sides and the names of his four counsellors around him (with their seals), Scorax, Carmelion, Severion and Cabereon. These are the names subsequently used in the conjuration provided by Arthur Gauntlet in Sloane MS 3851.

Sloane MS 3846 also includes 'The invocation of Oberion concerning Physick &c' (fo.102v-108), showing another point of commonality between these two Sloane manuscripts. Reading the description of Oberion given in Vb.26(1) it is easy to see why a cunning-man would seek the assistance of the King of the Fairies:

"He appeareth like a king with a crown on his head, he is under the government of the ☉ and ☽, he teacheth a man knowledge in physick, and he showeth the nature of stones herbs and trees and of all metal. He is a great and mighty king, and he is king of the fairies ..."[36]

Indeed we see precedents for the conjuration of Oberion in a court record from 1444 which describes a man being pilloried for summoning a *"wicked spyryte the whyche was callyd Oberycom"*.[37] A likely precedent to this specific conjuration which also predates Vb.26(1) by many decades was recorded in the Archiepiscopal Register of York in 1510. Here reference was made to a group of treasure-seekers conjuring *"a certain demon, Oberion"* along with *"four others, whereof Storax was one"*. Clearly Storax and Scorax are the same, and the three unnamed others can be presumed to be Carmelion, Severion and Cabereon. The group included the former lord mayor of Halifax and the church Canon who owned the grimoire containing the conjuration,[38] showing again how both

---

[36] Folger Vb.26(1) fo.80, 1577-1583. I have modernised the English somewhat for convenience.

[37] The Anatomy of Puck, Briggs, 1959:114.

[38] Witchcraft in Old and New England, Kittredge, 1929:208, 519n.

important people and church officials sought the aid of spiritual creatures when it suited them.

Another instance of material derived from Folger Vb.26(1) is seen in fo.130-132, in the conjuration to have conference with familiar spirits, which also includes the seven fairy sisters. A slightly corrupted version of the conjuration from Arthur Gauntlet is found in *A Collection of Magical Secrets* (Wellcome MS 4669), a text which dates to 1796 and was bound in with a copy of the *Key of Solomon*.[39] In this text the conjuration is entitled *'To Have A Familiar Spirit Called Ebrion at Your Disposal'*.[40] Oberion has become Ebrion, and Cabereon has become Kaberion, but these are minor changes. What is more notable is that it is a French manuscript, and so the invocation has crossed the language barrier, though the actual conjurations are in Latin.

Another spiritual creature that is found in this manuscript and only has a precedent in Folger Vb.26(1) is the demon called Baron. The conjuration in Sloane MS 3851 is clearly derived from Folger Vb.26(1), as may be seen in both the text (in English here, Latin in the Folger) and the sequence of characters, with those in this manuscript being based on those in Folger Vb.26(1).

The *Key of Solomon* was the most copied set of grimoire families of the Renaissance period, and so it is unsurprising that there should be material from one of the manuscripts in this work. The spirit curse at fo.111 is copied straight out of Additional MS 36674, a sixteenth century collection of manuscripts which includes a *Key of Solomon* text that is one of the earliest known examples of this family of grimoires. Also bound into this manuscript were copies of the *Heptameron* and Agrippa's *Of Occult Philosophy* from the *Fourth Book*.

This particular manuscript also had an interesting history, with the component sections including the *Heptameron* and Agrippa's *Of Occult Philosophy* passing through the hands of several notable people. These texts (including the *Key of Solomon* and some notes by the astrologer, physician and magician Simon Forman) were all owned by the poet Gabriel Harvey (1545-1630), the friend and occasional mentor of Edmund Spenser. Harvey and Spenser were no strangers to the magical world of the time, as seen by references in their letters to their acquaintance figures such as Philip Sidney

---

[39] See The Veritable Key of Solomon, Skinner & Rankine, 2008.

[40] A Collection of Magical Secrets, Skinner & Rankine, 2009:42-46.

and Edward Dyer, who were at the time pupils of Dr John Dee.[41] Harvey noted in the manuscript of the part of it containing the *Heptameron* and Agrippa's *Of Occult Philosophy* that:

"This torne booke was found amongst the paper bookes and secret writings of Doctor Caius, master and founder of Caius Colledg[e]. Doctor Legg gave it to Mr Fletcher, fellowe of the same colledge, and a learned artist for his time"[42]

Doctor John Caius (1510-1573) was physician to both Queen Mary and Queen Elizabeth I, though the latter dismissed him from her service in 1568 due to his adherence to Catholicism. He is perhaps best known as a pioneering naturalist and the co-founder of Gonville and Caius College, Cambridge University. Doctor Thomas Legge was his successor, and the Mr Fletcher he passed the manuscript on to is not John Fletcher the playwright mentioned above, but John Fletcher (1566-1613), a talented mathematician, physician and astrologer.[43]

That notes by Simon Forman (1552-1611), the most infamous astrologer and physician of the Elizabethan Age, should also be contained in Additional MS 36674 demonstrates again the way material was sold or passed on between practitioners. It is interesting to note that Forman was based in Lambeth, where subsequent figures such as Captain Bubb would be based. The whole of Additional MS 36674, which includes a great deal more miscellaneous material as well as a draft of Dr John Dee's *Heptarchia Mystica*, was later owned by Baron John Somers and his brother-in-law Sir Joseph Jekyll, who also owned Sloane MS 3851, the manuscript which forms the basis of this book.

In the Latin section of Psalm use in Sloane MS 3851 we see the exact same charms for eleven of the Psalms (17, 18, 34, 38, 42, 47, 50, 57, 76, 90, and 98) as are found in the seventeenth century French Psalmic work, *The Book of Gold*.[44] Two further charms (second charm for 50, 114) are simplified versions of those found in *The Book of Gold*, and four charms (7, 7, 66, 95) bear no resemblance to those found in that work. Of the Psalm charms, only one is derived from

---

[41] The Occult Philosophy in the Elizabethan Age, Yates, 1983:96.

[42] Additional MS 36,674, C17th.

[43] Biographical History of Gonville and Caius College 1348-1895 Vol 1, Roberts & Gross, 1901:95

[44] The Book of Gold, Rankine & Barron, 2010.

those in *Sepher Shimmush Tehillim* (18), so there is no clear evidence of derivation from that text.[45]

That there are so many examples of the same charms in this manuscript (*The Grimoire of Arthur Gauntlet*) suggests that they were either copied from the manuscript of *The Book of Gold* (Lansdowne MS 1202), or that both manuscripts were copied from an earlier (and as yet unknown or destroyed) manuscript. This latter option seems quite likely, as *The Book of Gold* is written in French, and the Psalm material in *The Grimoire of Arthur Gauntlet* is in bad Latin, which may well indicate copyist's errors. This would then suggest that if there was an earlier manuscript it was written in Latin, and the scribe of Lansdowne MS 1202 translated it into French, which fits with the fact that *The Book of Gold* was bound with a French copy of the *Key of Solomon*. As with *The Book of Gold*, the Psalm numeration in the *Grimoire of Arthur Gauntlet* is based on the Greek (Septuagint) system.

Material copied into and from Sloane MS 3851

Fo.	Copied From:	Date	Copied In:
9		1692	Book of Receipts and Chirurgery – Lady Ayscough
10-29v	Unknown Arbatel	C16th-17th?	
39v	Sloane MS 3846	C17th	
56-58	Folger Vb.26(1)	1580/1649	Sloane MS 3824
61-74v	Heptameron	C15th-C16th	
75-91	Of Occult Philosophy 4th Book – Agrippa	C16th	
94v-96	Discoverie of Witchcraft - Scot	1584	
98-99	Folger Vb.26(1)	1580	
99-107	Discoverie of Witchcraft - Scot	1584	
102v-108	Sloane MS 3846	C17th	
111	Additional MS 36674	C16th	

---

[45] The Book of Gold, Rankine & Barron, 2010:57.

112v-114v	3 Book of Occult Philosophy - Agrippa	1510/1533	
115v-117		1796	Wellcome MS 4669
117v-119	Lansdowne MS 1202[46]	C17th	
125	A Right Profitable Book for All Diseases	1582	
125	A Book of Experiments out of Dyvers Authors	1622	
125-127		1692	Book of Receipts and Chirurgery – Lady Ayscough
130		1692	Book of Receipts and Chirurgery – Lady Ayscough
130-132	Folger Vb.26(1)	1580	
137-139		1692	Book of Receipts and Chirurgery – Lady Ayscough
145	A Book of Experiments out of Dyvers Authors	1622	
146v		1696	Miscellanies Upon Various Subjects – John Aubrey

Who Owned This Book?

Tracing the ownership of Sloane MS 3851 demonstrates the way in which such works were sought and used by practitioners of magic and the cunning-arts. Although most of the text of Sloane MS 3851 is in Arthur Gauntlet's hand, there are also sections where additional material has been added, or comments made, in other noticeably different styles of handwriting. Having stated that the majority of the text is in Arthur Gauntlet's hand, it should be stated that this is not an absolute fact but rather a logical assumption

---

[46] Alternatively the Book of Gold in Lansdowne MS 1202 and this section of Sloane MS 3851 may both be derived from an earlier unknown manuscript.

based on the comments made by Elias Ashmole (1617-1692) in Sloane MS 3851 itself, and the inferences from William Lilly's autobiography about Gauntlet's books.

There are three sections in the book where Elias Ashmole's handwriting is found. These occur at the beginning, where Agrippa is quoted and Arthur Gauntlet is identified as the author of the book (fo.2-2v), in the perfumes section where Ashmole has added a piece from Agrippa on a page which has a paragraph written by Gauntlet at the top (fo.114), and the toothache charm at the end of the book (fo.146v).

The toothache charm was specifically mentioned by a friend of Ashmole's, the writer and antiquary John Aubrey (1626-1697) in his *Miscellanies Upon Various Subjects*. He gives the charm word-perfect to the copy in this manuscript and with the comment that it was *"out of Mr. Ashmole's manuscript writ with his own hand"*.[47] This clearly shows Ashmole owned the manuscript at some point after Gauntlet's death. John Aubrey's name is mentioned in Sloane MS 3846, with 3 pages of notes *'Excerpted from Mr Aubrey's collection of dreams'*.[48]

Ashmole became close friends with William Lilly after they met in 1646, with the two often conducting magical experiments together. Ashmole was fascinated with angelic communication, as his records show, and he was introduced to a number of astrologers and cunning-men by Lilly. Whether this number included Arthur Gauntlet we cannot know, but Ashmole certainly managed to get hold of his book and identified the handwriting as belonging to Gauntlet. Ashmole purchased Lilly's library from his widow after his death for the significant sum of £140 (this would equate to around £19,000 in 2011), but this did not include Arthur Gauntlet's work, which as previously mentioned had been sold to John Humphreys.

Here I am making an educated guess, as the very last page of the book has the curious inscription *"Ann Savadge in Rosemary Lane"* written on a blank page in Ashmole's hand. I propose that this is the name of the person from whom Ashmole acquired the book, as he would have been keen to detail such information, a fact verified by his recording of Arthur Gauntlet's handwriting at the front of the manuscript.

---

[47] Miscellanies Upon Various Subjects, Aubrey, 1696.
[48] Sloane MS 3846, fo.114v-115v.

The identity of Ann Savadge in Rosemary Lane is a mystery. There was an Anne Savadge married to a mariner called Richard Babson on 19th December 1642 in Stepney. Babson died at some point after May 1649, leaving Anne Savadge with two living children Margaret (b. 12 September 1643) and Thomas (b. 11 May 1649). They also had a daughter called Mary in 1645 who died aged 9 months.

To have possessed the book Ann Savadge would logically have been interested in magic, or more likely a practitioner. As there are two unidentified hands in the book it is likely that one of them is hers, which would make her a practitioner, possibly even a cunning-woman. With Gauntlet having worked with a woman as his speculatrix, it seems appropriate that his book should have subsequently been used by another female magician.

The only Rosemary Lane in London is in Mortlake, which is not only where Dr John Dee lived, but curiously was mentioned by Lilly in his autobiography and was also associated with the alleged witch Sarah Griffith in 1704.[49] Lilly described how *"One Sir Thomas Jay, a Justice of the Peace on Rosemary Lane, issued out his warrant for the apprehension of Poole"*.[50] The astrologer William Poole evaded capture due to the death of Jay, and Lilly subsequently gave a woman called Alice How to him in marriage. As Lilly recorded that John Humphreys had purchased Arthur Gauntlet's books, then it is likely that he sold this volume on to Ann Savadge, being more of a dabbler or *'nibbler'*[51] as Lilly called him, than a serious practitioner. In July 1704, *"Sarah Griffith of Rosemary Lane, was swum in the New River Head. She apparently swam like a cork"*.[52]

In Sloane MS 3846 there is a note which refers to the table of contents being written *"in the hand of Lord Somers' catalogues"*.[53] The table of contents in Sloane MS 3851 is in the same hand, indicating that the book passed through the hands of Lord Somers.

---

[49] A Full and True Account of the Discovery, Apprehending, and taking of a Notorious Witch, who was carried before Justice Bateman in Well-Close on Sunday, July the 23. Together with her examination and Commitment to Bridewell, Clerkenwell, London, 1704.

[50] The Life of William Lilly, Davies, 1774:38.

[51] The Life of William Lilly, Davies, 1774:38.

[52] Urbanization and the Decline of Witchcraft: An Examination of London, Davies, 1997:600.

[53] Sloane MS 3846 fo.3.

Baron John Somers (1651-1716) rose to become the Lord Chancellor of England in 1697, and was President of the Royal Society from 1699-1704. He was also an angel magician who collected numerous manuscripts of grimoires and magical practices, including many of the manuscripts which he would bequeath to his brother-in-law Joseph Jekyll.

Sir Joseph Jekyll (1663-1738) was Master of the Rolls, and married the second sister of John Somers. Like Somers he was an eminent lawyer, and he also shared his passion for magic. Jekyll gathered a huge collection of magical manuscripts including a number of the writings of Dr John Dee, as well as many of his brother-in-law's treasures. When Jekyll's huge library was sold in 1740, it took sixteen days to auction it. From the reference to the manuscript being *"Lot 378 in Jekyll's Sale, 1739/40"* we know it had passed from Somers to Jekyll.

One of the most prolific buyers at the epic Jekyll library sale was Sir Hans Sloane (1660-1753), an old friend of John Somers. Sloane purchased many of the magical manuscripts in the auction, and doubtless tried out some of the material he acquired. His interest in magical material is seen in the correspondence between Sloane and Somers dated 1710.[54] Sloane's shelfmark is found on the first page of the manuscript, which along with the rest of his collection was left to the British Library on his death and formed the basis of the invaluable Sloane collection.

So on the basis of all this information I suggest the provenance of this manuscript is from its originator Arthur Gauntlet, to John Humphreys, to Ann Savadge to Elias Ashmole, to Baron Somers, to Lord Jekyll, to Hans Sloane and then to the British Library.

Based on all the conclusions I have already outlined, I suggest that the two unknown styles of handwriting in the manuscript are probably those of Ann Savadge and John Humphreys. As has already been discussed, John Humphreys was more of a dabbler, and for this reason I feel the second handwriting is more likely to be his.

The material in this second handwriting covers pages on the antimonial cup, making optic glass and toothache. As such it is perhaps more likely to have been written by an astrologer (hence optic glass) dabbling in physick (toothache and the antimonial cup).

---

[54] Sloane MS 4042 fo.159, & Sloane MS 4061 fo.27-33.

This would then make Ann Savadge the author of the material in the first hand, which includes advice on conjuration, use of some of the Psalms for healing, and other charms.

A number of the charms from this book, particularly on or between fo.9, fo.125-127, fo.130, fo.137-139, were reproduced by Lady Ayscough in her *Book of Receipts and Chirurgery* (1692).[55] Some of the charms reproduced by Lady Ayscough were subsequently copied and reproduced by Charles Dickens in 1852 in an article called *Old Household Words* in *Household Words Volume 5*, pp80-83. Dickens also makes a point of mentioning Agrippa, saying, *"Cornelius Agrippa, a name held in great veneration by our ancestors, has written a great deal to the same purpose as the above. One or two extracts from his 'Occult Philosophy' will show what sort of wisdom he encouraged."*[56]

---

[55] Wellcome MS 1026.

[56] Old Household Words, Dickens, 1852:82.

Contributors

Folio	Hand
1	Baron Somers catalogues
2-2b	Ashmole
3-29b	Arthur Gauntlet (Main hand)
30	Unknown hand (possibly Ann Savadge)
31b-113b	Arthur Gauntlet
114	Ashmole (Agrippa piece)
114b-116	Arthur Gauntlet
117-120b	Unknown hand
121-125b	Arthur Gauntlet
125b-126	Unknown hand
127-127b	Unknown hand 2 (possibly John Humphreys)
128-132b	Arthur Gauntlet
133b	Unknown hand
134-145	Arthur Gauntlet
145b	Unknown hand 2
146b	Unknown hand
148	Ashmole

Notes on the Manuscript

The following conventions have been used in reproducing this manuscript:

When words are in bold in this document, they were in red in the original manuscript, and italics in this document indicate the words were in bold in the original manuscript. Where words are underlined, they were underlined in the manuscript.

Page numbers within the manuscript are indicated by a number within normal brackets, e.g. (3). Thus a number indicates that the text following it is on that numbered page.

Where a contraction is given, it may be expanded with the rest of the word in square brackets, but this was not part of the original manuscript. Many words, particularly in Latin, were written in an abbreviated form, and where this occurs, the words are given in full in the text, e.g. the letter *ū* represents *um*, so modū = modum.

Likewise where Roman numerals have been used for numbers, the number is given in square brackets afterwards for convenience, e.g. iii [3]

Where symbols for weights and measures were used in the original manuscript, I have replaced these with the term they describe, e.g. ½ for ß.

Whenever text is given in Latin, as it was in places in the original manuscript, the English is footnoted to provide a convenient translation of the material. In some instances the words appear to be gibberish, and may be mis-copied or corrupted *voces magicae*.

Having studied the original manuscript in the British Library, I can confirm that it is faded and stained in places, making it extremely difficult to read some of the words and images. As well as reproducing all the original illustrations, examples of pages of the original text are provided throughout the book to demonstrate both the different styles of handwriting found in the manuscript, and the difficulty in reading some of the faded or stained words.

Sloane MS 3851 – the Manuscript

MS.B: ~~1510~~
3851[57]
XVII C

**Lot 378 in Jekyll's
Sale, 1739/40** [58]

---

[57] This shelfmark on the MS demonstrates its ownership by Sir Hans Sloane.

[58] The number of the lot assigned to this book in the epic 16 day auction of Sir Joseph Jekyll's book collection.

1.

Instructions of Ptolomy. fo. 1

Instructions of Cyprian — fo. 1.2.

Darles Prayer — fo. 4.

Prayer of thy Genius, and Several Spells — fo. 6. o

Magick of the Ancients (Arbatel) — fo. 8.

Signū Pentaculum Salomonis — fo. 34. 8.

Spells Experiments Conjurations et — fo. 35.

4th Book of the hidden Philosophy writ by forn. Agrippa fo. 84

Invocations — fo. 101.

Wm Barons Roman forret other spells — fo. 119. 6.

The Book of the 7 Images — fo. 145.

Charms for divers diseases — fo. 157.

To have Conference with Spirits — fo. 157.

Experiments — fo. 163.

1 - Contents Page of Sloane 3851, the handwriting suggests it was added by Baron Somers or someone who worked for him

Instructions of Ptolomy. fo.1[59]

Instructions of Cyprian – fo.1.2

Searles Prayer – fo.4

Prayer of thy Genius, and several Spells – fo.6b

Magick of Arbatel (the Ancients) – fo.8

Signum Pentaculum Salomonis – fo.34b

Spells Experiments Conjurations etc – fo.35

4th Book of the hidden Philosophy writ by Corn. Agrippa – fo.84

Invocations – fo.101

Wm. Bacon's Roman Secret & other spells – fo.119b

The Book of the 7 Images – fo.145

Charms for diverse diseases – fo.151

To have Conversure with Spirits – fo.157

Experiments – fo.163 (2)

---

[59] Note that the numbering is not consistent with that in the book, e.g. the Arbatel starts at fo.10 not fo.8.

Bodwell.

2

Cornelius Agrippa.

Dies mies, ieschit, benedo=effett
Dovima finitemauf: 3 tynio .

_____

Ante operis inceptionem :

_____

Actiones nostras quæsumus domine aspirando
prævenias et adiuvando prosequeris vt
cuncta nostra oratio et operatio a te semper
incipiat et per te coepta finiatur . per
Christum dominum nostrum :
Et me junctis manibus in modum crucis dicis
Benedicta sit sancta et individua
nunc et semper per omnia
corum ambo : hæcq dicas etiam post
perfectionem operis :

17 ♃ 507/475
6:30 ♈
♂ ♃

2 - Latin Page showing Elias Ashmole's handwriting. The faded seal near the bottom of the page is a British Library mark, and the meaning of the sequence of letters and numbers is unknown.

Leadwell

Cornelius Agrippa

Die smies, ieschet, bene doeftett[60]

Dovima emitemans: 3 tymes[61]

Aub operis inceptionum[62]

Actiones nostrus quae sumus domine aspirando provemient et ad invando prosequare ut cuncta nostra oratio et operatis a le Sempur incipial et per le coepla finiatur per Christum dominum nostrum[63]

Tumi iuncti manibus in modum crucis dailo[64]

23 enedicla pil semcla A ni (dividing?)[65] nunc A Semper per omnia feoculum[66] Corum amdu hoecque dicere alium pop perfectioni opera[67,]

i7 x$^{U\ 102/495}$

6:30 cd

f d

---

[60] "On my day, ieschet [barbarous name?] may he receive benediction."

[61] "Utter these words of power: 3 times."

[62] "After the beginning of the work."

[63] "Our actions shall arise from the highest Lord we must aspire to, and we shall attend to that which we must overcome, so that we may always begin all our speech and works [all we say and do], and may, by beginning, finish them by/through Christ our Lord."

[64] "Then the shadows/wraiths shall be joined [bound] by means of the cross."

[65] The word 'dividing' is written overhead in English, then followed by an illegible word due to staining.

[66] Illegible word due to staining.

[67] "23: by saying this they shall be joined as twins, and dividing [illegible word due to staining; perhaps meaning "never"?] now and forever through all the centuries, each heart bound to the other by saying this for the perfection of the work." The 23 may refer to Psalm 23.

*This Book in the handwriting of one Mr Arthur Gauntlet,
who professed Physick, and lived about Gray's Inn Lane.*[68]

---

[68] This note is in the writing of Elias Ashmole and identifies Arthur Gauntlet as the author of the manuscript.

Instructions of Ptolomie[69]

1. **In what day** thou wilt begin to work Thou shalt make Invocation for them thou wilt call.

2. **Thou must** make clean thy hands and feet before the sight of the signs And characters of Solomon.

3. **Thou must** make clean thy hands and face and pare thy nails both of Hands and feet.

4. **Thou must** bathe thy self in a bath of Laurel and other sweet herbs.

5. **Then clothe** thy self with clean Clothes.

6. **Thou shalt** abstain from all carnal lusts 3 days before.

7. **Thou shalt** call and name the Spirit that thou would attain every day for the 3 days before, **As followeth.**

8. **O thou** Spirit N I require thee by the virtue of God almighty that thou appear thy self unto the time and place appointed of my calling upon thee.

9. **This** must be done in the morning when the Sun is up And in the Evening before the Sun goes down.

Instructions of Cyprian

There be 6 especial things to be observed in this work whereof if you neglect but one It is doubtful you shall not obtain your purpose.

1. **The** Master must have a firm faith And doubt not in his work for he that Doubteth to obtain his petition Prayeth with his Mouth Not with his heart

2. **He** must be secret And betray not the secrets of his Art but to his fellows and to them of his counsel

3. **He** must be strong minded severe and not fearful.

4. **He** must be clean in conscience Penitent for his sins never willing to return to them again so far forth as God shall give him grace.

5. **He** must know the reigning of the Planets And the times meet to work.

---

[69] Ptolemy.

6.   **He** must lack none of his Instruments He must speak all things plainly and distinctly He must make his Circle in a clean Air and One time.

Whoso observeth these 6 Rules By Gods grace shall not miss but obtain his purpose. (3)

Exclusion of all evil things maledictions colligations[70] incantations Bewitching Enchantments either be devices or otherwise which we know Or those which we know not:

Autor est St. Cyprianus: co: ~[71]

---

verse Jesu esto mihi Jesus:[72]

Our help is in the Lord And in his holy name. O Lord hear our prayers. The Lord is with us. Amen. So be it. +

I call upon thee and invocate thee O Omnipotent God which art King of all Kings Eternal Governor of all the world uncorrupt unspotted undefiled Invisible wonderful most farbeles[73] unreprehensible Almighty Ruler Great and Holy + Adonay + Eloy + Sabaoth + God of Gods And father of all Glorious and most renowned virtues The truth it self High King Father of our Lord and Saviour Jesus Christ give thy benediction and blessing unto me thy servant And unto all things that are about me belonging and appertaining unto me.

Also I call upon thee Oh Omnipotent God King immortal which sittest upon the Cherubim and Seraphim unbind me unloose me O Lord. If any misdeeds any maledictions bindings Enchantments or Charms are used or done against me Or if any evil tongue have evil spoken or bewitched me Or Enchanted me Or if any evil things which may be hurtful unto me Is put under the foundation of my House Or in the entrance thereof Or in my bed Or in my Chamber Or in any part of the building of my House Or in the Dunghill Or in the Field Or in the way Or in the Street Or in

---

[70] A colligation is a conjunction, alliance or bringing together.

[71] "The author is St Cyprian".

[72] "Jesus turned around [or 'reversed'] will be Jesus to me."

[73] Farbele is an old word meaning colours.

the Garden Or in the Fire Or in any of my monables[74] and Goods Or in any other place whatsoever That I can now call to mind Or to my remembrance. Unbind them unloose them O Lord and permit not any evil tongue hereafter to hurt me Or any way to indamage[75] me **AG**[76] thy humble servant Or any thing which is mine And is either now Or shall hereafter Or at this present time ought to be appertaining or belonging to me + Amen. (4)

I conjure you all harms which either done now or shall be done hereafter be they known or unknown + I Conjure you Devils and unclean Spirits by him which is to be feared honoured and Glorified And by his reverent name + Adonay + Eloy + Sabaoth + That you hurt me not nor approach near unto me **AG** being the servant of God Or to any thing that is appertaining or belonging unto me Or shall be hereafter Or ought now to be appertaining or belonging unto me. But away and fly from me. And Light you all upon their heads which have made you come hither sent you hither Or directed you hither Of what calling Or what kind of person Or persons soever they be. + + +

I call upon you yon virtues of Heaven which stand before the seat and throne of God in Heaven And I beseech you for to defend me **AG** the servant of God from all the slights and subtleties of evil Spirits And all things whatsoever are mine and appertaining unto me + Also I beseech you yon virtues and powers of Heaven to defend me **AG** The servant of the everliving God from all evil perils and dangers from all unjust men from envy From all infirmities From all bewitchments Enchantments Maledictions or Charms And from all Devilish temptations From all kind of Maledictions and from all evil which is either known Or at this time present I cannot call to my remembrance + + +

I Conjure you all harmdoers Or all you wicked Spirits which are hurters of Mankind by + I conjure you by the Omnipotent God which is a mighty and a true God which hath divided Light from darkness and also the Heavens giving unto them their due portions And hath ordained the Earth as a strong Turret or Pillar + I Conjure you by him Which spake to Moses in the Mount Sinai when he gave the law and Commandments to the Children of Israel And

---

[74] Things held in common, a legal term sometimes used in wills of the period.

[75] Endamage, or cause damage to.

[76] AG = Arthur Gauntlet.

filled them with water out of the hard stony rock and gave them Manna instead of Meat + Also I Conjure you by the reverent name of God and by the most dreadful father of our Lord and Saviour + Jesus Christ + And by the fear of one chief King + Jesus + Christ + who shall come again at the last day to judge both the quick and the dead and the world by fire. + **Amen.** + + +

I Conjure you evil Spirits whosoever you be that are hurtful and pernicious either in body or in soul Already done or to be done hereafter either bound or enchanted sent of others Or come of your selves which are contented to hurt by any slights wiles or arts or by any maledictions or by any other hurtful means or pernicious ways either night at hand or afar off + Tremble and fear Great Mighty and Strong is the name of the Lord + By the which I Conjure you that you hurt me not nor approach near unto me **AG** which am the servant of God Or to any thing which is appertaining unto me Or shall be hereafter Or ought to be now at this present belonging to me **AG** But away and fly ye far from me And Light you all upon their heads which have either caused you come hither Or have directed you hither Or have sent you hither what soever Or whosoever they be + God is peace + God is Charity + God is justice + God is light and light of light + God is virtue + God is with us + Amen +++

We will not fear nor be sorrowful because God is our father Let us fear the Lord or God And reverence him only + To whom be all honour virtue power and Glory both now and ever more + For whoso calleth upon the name of the Lord shall be saved + *Allelujah* + *Allelujah* +

3 – Symbol sequence following from Allelujah in preceding text

Pater noster &c

Ave Maria &c

Credo in Deum Patrem &c

Then say the :54: Psalm :

Then the :71: Psalm :

Then the :6: Psalm

Then the :8: Psalm

Concluding At the end of every Psalm with **Glory** be to the Father &c.

Then say the Prayers following.

Let us Pray. (5)

Oh God which doth direct and govern the heart of the faithful by the illumination of the Holy Spirit Give us grace by the same spirit to do those things which are lawful and right And always in his consolation to rejoice Through the Father and Son And the Holy Ghost And in the unity of the three persons Grant to thy servants we beseech thee O lord to rejoice in a perpetual quietness both of body and soul And by the Glorious intercession of the blessed virgin St Mary to be always delivered from present sorrows and to be in Joy and everlasting Gladness. **Amen**

Oh God which dist in wonderful order dispose the functions and offices of Angels and Men be favourable and near unto us And grant that whatsoever is disagreeing to thy most holy will in Heaven The same may always be separated from us on Earth And by thy help we may be defended and Guarded from the same. **Amen**

Oh Omnipotent God everlasting which hast granted to thy servants in the confession of the true faith to understand the Glory of the everlasting Trinity And in the power of the Majesty to worship the unity Grant we beseech thee That by the certainty of the same faith we may be defended from all adversities through Jesus Christ our Lord and Saviour. **Amen** So be it +

Then say the Gospel for Ascension day which beginneth at the 14 verse of the 16 Chapter of St Mark And endeth at the 20 verse of the Same Chapter. **viz.**

Jesus appeared unto the eleven as they sat at meat and cast in their teeth their unbelief and hardness of heart because they believed not them which had seen that he was risen again from the dead And he said unto them Go ye into all the world and preach the Gospel to all Creatures. He that believeth and is baptised shall be saved But he that believeth not shall be damned And these tokens shall follow them that believe In my name they shall cast out Devils. They shall speak with new Tongues They shall drive away serpents And if they drink any deadly thing it shall not hurt them They shall lay their hand on the sick and they shall recover. So then when the lord had spoken unto them He was received into Heaven

And is on the right hand of God And they went forth and preached everywhere The Lord working with them And confirming the word with Miracles following.

Thou art my helper and my refuge O Lord Jesus Christ In thee only have I trusted and in no other Neither will at any time hereafter trust in any other besides thee Help me therefore O most mighty God which art + Alpha + et ω + The first and the Last whose virtue and aid I most humbly desire And heartily require. Have mercy upon me O my God have mercy upon me Even as thou wilt And as thou knowest And even as it seems expedient unto thy most Godly wisdom. So Lord God help me **Amen** So be it. +

+ **The word** is made flesh + And shall dwell in us + Amen + Jesus + Christ + virgin + Mary + St + John + Evangelist +++

Then say the :64: Psalm :

Then the :91: Psalm Pg. 35[77] **Glory be to the Father &c**

Look upon me thy servant I beseech thee O my Lord God and have mercy upon me thy humble servant I beseech thee O Lord my God For whom our Lord and Saviour + Jesus + Christ + Spared not to be Committed into the hands of the hurtful And to suffer most extreme and exceeding pains and torments upon the Cross + Amen + fiat + fiat + fiat

---

A Licence to depart

In his name that you came Go again. The Father with me The Son with me And the Holy Ghost betwixt us And be for ever **Amen.** (6)

A Prayer to God for good Success in Matters written by John Searle Practitioner in Surgery And in Astronomy   Ano 1594 :

[78]**O most mighty** high and incomparable God + Father of our dear sweet and Loving Lord Jesus + Creator and maker of the world with all things therein contained. And Man which thou hast created and made out of the Earth after thine own Image. And hath set him as a King to rule and Reign over all other of those thy

---

[77] This insertion "Pg. 35", refers to the folio number in the original version of the MS where Psalm 91 is found.

[78] The probable identity of John Searle is discussed in the Introduction.

creatures which thou by thy most ineffable word hast created in this world. And have given him power and authority over all beasts and fishes and all other creatures which thou hast created and made as well sensible and unsensible to rule and guide according to thy blessed will and appointment + Mighty God we thy humble servants But penitent sinners which do acknowledge and confess all our wicked filthy and detestable sins before thy most mighty and heavenly Majesty which have not spared to blaspheme thy holy and sacred name By swearing with lying and vain words without any conscience or fear thereof and most specially by committing of so many wicked and abominable sins That if thou wert not a loving and a kind father we should presently be consumed before the face of the Earth. Yet Oh sweet God we call for mercy And humbly crave pardon for our former wicked sins and vile offences that thou wilt vouchsafe to bend thy merciful ears to hear our prayers And to forgive our odious sins + O merciful Father forgive us + Oh sweet Son forgive us + Oh Holy Ghost forgive us + Oh Father + Oh Son + Oh Holy Ghost + Three persons and one most mighty God + we humbly earnestly and heartily desire thee to have mercy on us And grant that this thing which we take in hand may be well brought to pass without any hurt or prejudice to me or any of my fellows being thy servants Or any other creature which thou hast made + Most Loving Father we beseech thee to bridle the stout stomachs of those obstinate Spirits that will not bow and dutifully obey to thy desire word and holy name.

We most reverently desire thee + O most **blessed** Trinity + Three blessed and one deity + To give us victory and mastership of and over those Spirits (Or that Spirit) which we intend to command and call for to appear to us By three most mighty and Strong names + Agla + On + Tetragrammaton + Oh all ye holy and renowned blessed orders of Angels Be ye helpers to our desires and work that we intend by God's permission this present time to put into practice. O ye Arch-Angels which are appointed by the most mighty + Jehovah + to rule and reign in most joyful manner before his most mighty Majesty we earnestly desire you to be aiders to us in our desires that we by God's power take in hand this present day to do O all ye mighty and holy orders of Heaven we most heartily entreat you all to be comforters to us in this our matter That we by the help and powers of the most mighty and Glorious high God do purpose to exorcise this present time O all ye blessed Apostles Patriarchs Prophets Confessors Martyrs and all Holy Saints we beseech you all to be furtherers and aiders to us in this one business and pretended purpose To have the speech of that Spirit (or those Spirits) whom we command by the most mighty high and ineffable name of the almighty and holy + Adonay + Lord and King of all creatures whatsoever either in Heaven Or in Earth The Sea and under the Earth At whose Voice Heaven Earth and Hell do quake tremble and fall

Then read the 51 Psalm pag: 50[79]

Then the 91 Psalm pag: 35

Concluding at the end of each Psalm with

Glory be to the Father &c. **Then say**

Most Mighty and renowned King of all Kings Father of all Glory and renowned Majesty we invocate and call upon thee beseeching thee that thou wilt vouchsafe to prosper us in this one enterprise – giving us victory and Mastership of and over that Spirit (or those Spirits) which by thy most mighty holy names we intend to command and call desiring thee for thy sweet and well beloved Son + Jesus Christ + Sake who suffered his most precious blood (7) to be shed And his blessed body to be grievously wounded and macerated upon the Cross for to redeem us miserable sinners from the bondage of wicked Sathan. + That thou wilt licence permit and suffer that Spirit (or those Spirits) peaceably to appear to us affably and gently to speak to us. And without all deformity or ugly shape neither to fright fear trouble or hurt me nor any of my fellows nor any other creatures either sensible or unsensible. + Grant this we beseech thee O most mighty Governor whose power is Invincible, whose might is incomparable, whose Love is Inseparable, And whose wonderful works are innumerable For the tender love of that immaculate and unspotted Lamb that taketh away the sins of the world. To whom be all renown Glory Prayer rule power might dominion rule and authority world without end + Amen + fiat + fiat + fiat +

& Ausi Soyt il[80]

---

[79] This and the following page reference refer to the original numbering in this MS.

[80] "And so be it".

That thou wilt vouchsafe to give leave and license to suffer and permit Those Holy Angels of thine And those Spirit as in thy most holy and blessed name we thy humble servants shall this day call for our help and comfort, Peaceably to appear to us. Affably and gently to speak to us. And faithfully Justly truly and willingly to answer our demands without any falsehood fraud guile deceit or delay. Grant &c.

A Licence to depart

Get you to the place predestinated which our lord Jesus Christ hath ordained for you until I shall call you again under pain of damnation And I do Conjure you that when I shall call you again either in the house or in the field In the night or in the day at any time or in any place I conjure you suddenly to appear in obtaining the blessing of your prince So be it.

In Hic nomine[81] Amen x⁺x⁺x⁺ the 22 May 1696 hore[82]

In the name of our lord Jesus Christ + And in the power of the highest + The Father + The Son + And the Holy Ghost + I do make the sign of the Holy + upon me That the Spirit which is coming may not hurt me Nor yet offend me grievously Nor yet any way molest me nor yet mine And that they may not be able to do it but that + Jesus Christ + being my helper And defender to preserve me whom all Heavenly things and all Helly things do cast under + So be it + fiat + fiat + fiat + Amen +

Save me good Lord and I shall be saved for because thou art mine and my Joy all the days of my life + Agios + Athanatos + Christ doth bind + Christ doth reign + Christ doth overcome +

---

[81] "In this name".

[82] "Hore" means "hour", and this placement is relevant as it refers to the figure of 1696; 6's are sometimes reversed are written like 9's in this MS, so this may signify 19 (=1+6+6+6) hours, or 7.00pm. Some have taken this as a date and used it to date the MS, but as I have already shown in the Introduction, the MS is undoubtedly considerably older, probably dating between 1614- 1636.

Shordi[83] + Christ doth bless thee + And against thy enemies that is coming to thee he doth help thee + So be it + fiat + fiat + fiat + Amen.

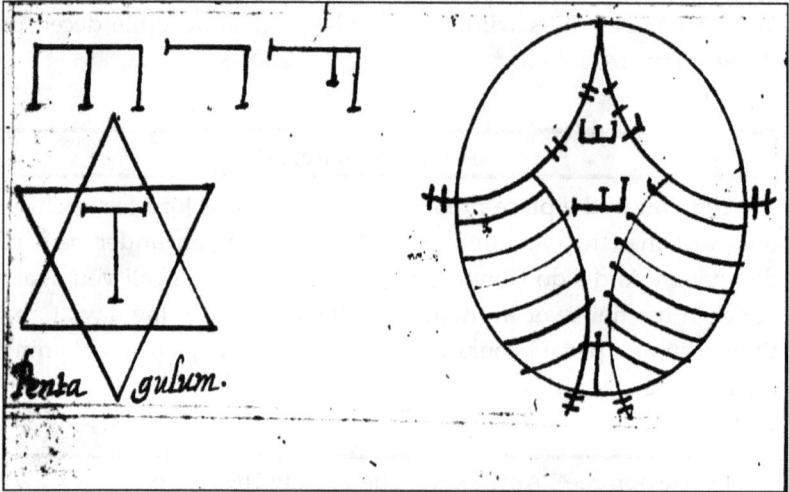

4 – Stylised Figures, including the Pentagulum, not linked to any specific charms

---

[83] This may be a corruption or mis-copying of the divine name Shaddai.

5 - *Sigils of the planets. The column on the left are listed respectively the Latin names for Saturn, Jupiter, Mars, the Sun, Venus, Mercury and the Moon, all written in red ink which appears faded.*

A Prayer for thy Genius:~:

I AG with bended ♥ and knee with all hearty humiliation do most earnestly desire of Jacob's God that great יהוה to grant me his holy permission That I may have resolution and answer in writing or otherwise with my good Genius whereby I may accomplish such actions as may resound to the -good of my Neighbour my soul's comfort and God's glory + In nomine Patris + et Filii + et Spiritus Sanctus + Amen. +

O God of mercy and might
direct me AG in the right

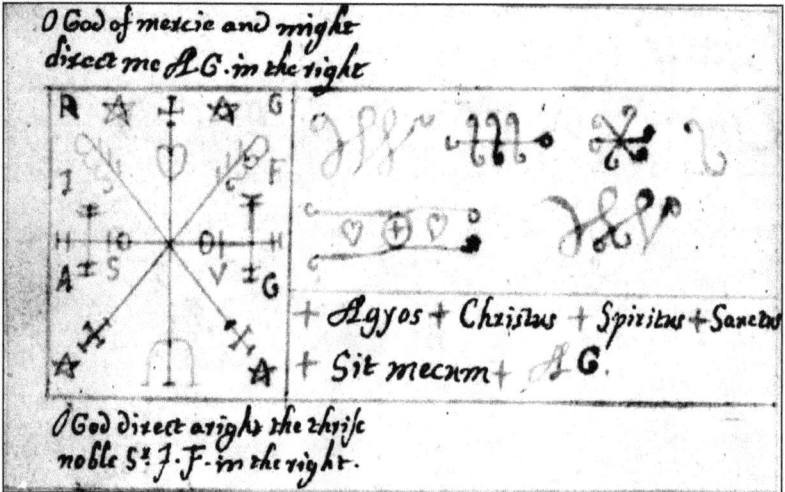

6 - *Solomonic style charm with sigils and divine names. The initials JF and AG may be read across the centre of the charm.*

O God direct aright the thrice
noble Sir J.F. in the right.[84]

---

[84] This may refer to the playwright John Fletcher, who was acquainted with Captain Bubb.

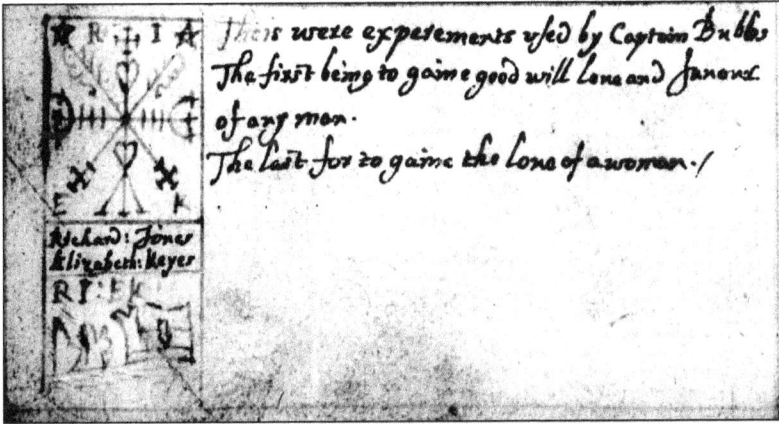

7 - *A Solomonic style charm and a simple love charm, described below. The initials of the male client RJ (Richard Jones) and the woman he desired EK (Eliabeth Keyes) are included in the love charm.*

These were experiments used by Captain Bubbs[85]

The first being to gain good will love and favour of any man.

The last for to gain the love of a woman. (9)

Whoso carrieth this writing about him shall not perish by fire nor by flame in wars Nor be grieved with the falling sickness.

+ Adonay + Jesus + Ethey + Sabaoth + Tetragrammaton + Saday + Jesse + Agla + virtus + Sara + Semel + Gebal + Guttan + Anamisapta + Gevet + Mortem + Qui fugerit tune mors est + capta in dicitur anampsa.[86]

Against enemies write these Characters In virgin parchments Or in thy right hand Bear them with thee And no evil shall hurt thee.

a. So q. m n x x r t q. t o u

---

[85] This is Captain Bubb Fisk, mentioned by Lilly and discussed in the Introduction.

[86] "He that fled is dead + captured by saying the name itself."

To make money spent to return Make a purse of a Mole's skin and write in it Belzebub, zetus Caiphas[87] with the blood of a Bat And lay a good penny in the highway for the space of 3 days and 3 nights And after put it in the purse. And when you will gain it Say vade et vene.[88]

To make one sleep at Table write their Characters in virgin parchment with a white Knife And put them under the Table.

.i.o.o.o.f.k.u.n.m.b.r.u.

St Leo the 12 [3] Pope of Rome[89] wrote this letter to King Charles[90] And said who that beareth it upon him shall not dread his Enemies to be overcome nor with no manner of Poison to be hurt nor in no need misfortune nor with no thunder he shall not be smitten nor lightning nor in no fire be burnt suddenly nor in no water be drowned Nor he shall not die without shrift Nor with Thieves to be taken Nor with no false money to be damned Also he shall have no wrong Neither of Lord nor Lady. Also if a woman travail of Child lay this writing upon her womb she shall be soon delivered by the grace of God ~~~. These be the names of God and Christ.[91]

---

[87] The name of the Jewish High Priest who presided over the death of Jesus.

[88] "Go and come". This charm is reproduced by Thompson, 1927:254, and also in a recent Cyprian book, São Cipriano, O Bruxo (capa aço), Coletânea, 2007:216.

[89] Pope Leo III was pope from 795-816 CE.

[90] This refers to Charlemagne, King of the Franks from 768 CE, and Holy Roman Emperor from 800-814 CE.

[91] The original charm is longer and has a longer list of animal names. It is reproduced in Verbal Charms in British Folk Medicine, Forbes, 1971:302. I have included it for comparative purposes:

"Trinitas + Messias + Agios + Iskyros + Otheos + Emanuel + Sabaoth + Adonay + Athanatos + Kyros + Theon + Panton Craton + Ysus + Sapiencia + Virtus + Tetragrammaton + Anamsapta + Oleo [oil] + Caritas + David + Daniel + Ego sum alpha et omega [I am Alpha and Omega] + Paracletus + Mediator + Angnus [lamb] + Ovis [sheep] + Vitulus [calf] + Serpens [serpent] + Aries [ram] + Leo [lion] + Vermis [worm] + Patris puritatis + Flos mundi + Imago + Janua + Viua lux + Splendor + Princeps + Oliva + Sol pacis + Dominus + Deus + Pater + Filius + Spiritus sanctus + Primogenitus + veritas + Summus + Bonus + Totus Amen + Iheus, fili virginis, Miserere

+ Mesias + Sother + Emanuel + Sabaoth + Adonay + unigenitus + virtus + via + veritas + Homousion[92] + Origo + Bonitas + Dietas + Elysoy + Fons + Pater + Principium + Primus + Novissimus + Ego Sum + Qui vexturus + um + vita mundus + α + ω + virgo + Agnus + Onus + vitulus + Aries + Leo + vermis + Rex + Pater + Filius + et Spiritus Sanctus + Sancti + amen +

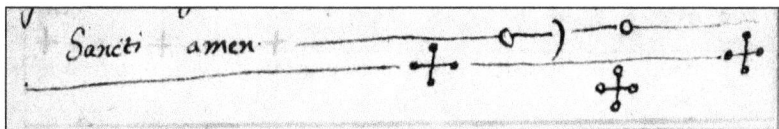

8 - *This is the final line of this name sequence, continuing directly after Sanctus.*

To make any man to go unhurt upon Sword or any Sharp thing whatsoever: ∞:

Dicas Conjure te per istam orationem sequentem meluet Dalatel Conjuro te per Patrem et filium et Spiritum Sanctum ut sis in ita nurmlis sicut hac manie.[93]

For worms

Jobe is sick and like to die and have in his body worms. There the black doth eat the flesh The Red doth suck the blood The white doth gnaw the bone, void worms from Jobe every one. Say this three times. + In the name of + the father + and of the Son + And of the Holy Ghost + Amen + (10)

Of the Magick of the Ancient,

Being the chief study of wisdom:~:

In all things consult with the Lord And do not think speak or do anything which God shall not counsel thee

mei peccatoris [Jesus, Son of the Virgin, have mercy on me, a sinner] + Amen."

[92] "Of the same substance" (Greek), a term used to describe God as the trinity, first used by the Gnostics but adopted by the Nicene Council in the 4th century.

[93] "Say I conjure thee by the following speech that was chosen, Dalatel. I conjure thee by the Father and the Son and the Holy Ghost, so that you shall manifest in this place immediately and so that you shall remain here."

He that goeth about as a slanderer discovereth a secret.

But he that is of a faithful heart concealeth a matter:~:

Arbatel of his Magick: Or the Spirit of the Ancients

As well of the Magicians the People of God As of the Heathen ~ wife men set forth for the illustration of the glory and Philanthropies of God: Now first brought out of darkness into light against the Cocomages[94] and condemners of God's gifts unto the profit and delight of all those that truly and piously are delighted with the Creatures of God and use them with giving of thanks unto God's honour and profit of their Neighbours:~:

It hath Nine Tomes of Seven times Seven Aphorisms[95]

---

[94] This should read "caco-mages", i.e. evil mages (from the Greek caco = evil).

[95] There are numerous minor grammatical differences between this version of the Arbatel and the original. I have only noted where significant differences occur as this is not the main focus of this work.

The manner [...] of the [...]

1. The first [...] is called an Isagoge or a booke of the Institutions of Magick Because it containes :49: Aphorismes the most generall precepts of all Arte.

2. The second is a Microcosmicall Magick: what Microcosme-worketh by his Spirit from the birth Magically That is what is effecteth by spirituall wisdome and how.

3. The third is Olympicall Magick How a man worketh and suffers by Olympicall spirits.

4. The fourt is Hesiodes and Homers Magick which teacheth works by the spirits Caled Calodivills As if they were not enimies to Mankinde.

[...] is the Romane or Sibilline magick which worketh with [...]ending Spirits and lords which is distributed throughout the world This is the doctrine of the Druids.

[...] is Pithagoras his Magick which only workes with Spirits to whome the doctrine of Arts is given. As Naturall Philosophy The art of Phisick Mathematicke Alchymy and the like arts.

[...] is the Magick of Apollonius and the like ioyning with the Romane and Microcosmicall But that it hath this peculias That it hath power over the Spirits which are enimies to mankind

[...] sort is the Magick of Hermes which is the Egiptian magick And it is not farr from divine Magick This produceth Gods of every kinde which dwell in the Temples.

[...] wisdome is that which dependeth of the word of God alone And is caled Prophetticall Magick or wisdome.

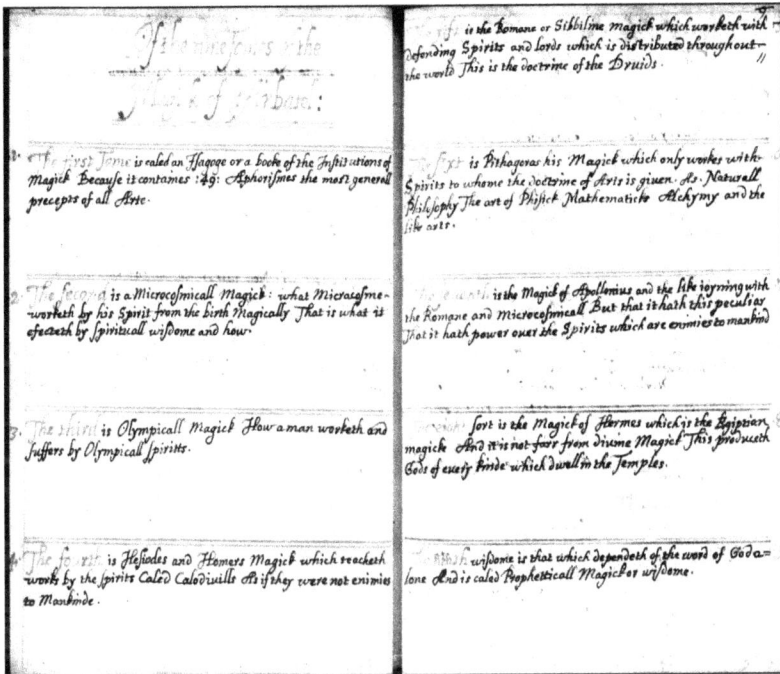

9 - The introduction to the Arbatel, written in the hand of Arthur Gauntlet, given on the following page.

Of the nine Tomes of the Magick of Arbatel:

1. **The first Tome** is called an Isagoge or A Book of the Institutions of Magick Because it contains :49: Aphorisms the most general precepts of all Art.

2. **The Second** is a Microcosmical Magick: what Microcosms work by his Spirit from the birth magically. That is what it effecteth by spiritual wisdom and how.

3. **The third** is Olympical Magick How a man worketh and suffers by Olympical Spirits.

4. **The fourth** is Hesiod's and Homer's Magick which teacheth works by the Spirits called Calodevils[96] As if they were not enemies to mankind. (11)

5. **The fifth** is the Romane or Sibylline Magick which worketh with defending Spirits and Lords which is distributed throughout the world This is the doctrine of the Druids.

6. **The Sixth** is Pythagoras his Magick, which only works with Spirits to whom the doctrine of Arts is given. As Natural Philosophy The art of Physick Mathematics Alchemy and the like arts.

7. **The Seventh** is the Magick of Apollonius and the like joining with the Romane and Microcosmical But that it hath this peculiar That it hath power over the Spirits which are enemies to mankind.

8. **The eighth** sort is the Magick of Hermes which is the Egyptian Magick And it is not far from divine Magick This produceth Gods of every kind which dwell in the Temples.

---

[96] This should read 'cacodevils'.

The ninth wisdom is that which dependeth of the word of God alone and is called Prophetical Magick or wisdom.

The Book of Arbatel of Magick The first tome Called Isagoge:~:

In the name of the Creator of visible and invisible things who revealeth mysteries out of his treasuries and his secrets to those, And fatherly and out of his clemency doth enlarge them unto us without measure. Let him grant unto us by his only begotten Son our Lord Jesus Christ the Spirits his ministers the revealers of secrets that we may write the book of Arbatel of the chiefest secrets which is lawful for man to know and to use them without offence to God. Amen.

The first Septem of Aphorisms

Aphorism the first:

Who So would know secrets let him know how to keep secrets secretly and to reveal revealed things. To seal sealed things And not to give holy things to dogs. Nor to cast Pearls before swine.[97] Observe this Law and the eyes of thy mind shall be opened to understand secrets And thou shalt hear divinely revealed what soever thy mind hath desired. Thou shalt have also the Angels and Spirits of God to prompt thee. And the Spirits following mysteries in nature as much as any human mind can desire.

Aphorism:2:

In all things call upon the name of the lord for without calling upon God by his only begotten Son[98] thou canst receive nothing either to think of or to do, use the Spirits given to thee as ministers and servants without rashness and presumption with due reverence toward the lord of spirits as the ambassadors of God. And that thou pass the remainder of thy life peacefully unto the honour of God And the profit of thy neighbours. (12)

Aphorism:3:

Live to thy Self and thy learning Avoid the friendship of a multitude. Be covetous of time. Be beneficent to all, use thy gifts, watch in thy vocation. Let the word of God never depart from thy mouth.

Aphorism:4:

Obey those that admonish thee well. Flee all procrastination. Accustom thy self unto constancy and gravity in thy words and deeds. Resist the temptations of the Tempter by the word of God. Fly worldly things, seek heavenly. Respect not thine own wisdom, but in all things have an eye unto God according to the Scriptures, when we know not what we should do, O God we lift up our eyes

---

[97] Matthew 7:6.

[98] John 14:13.

unto thee and expect thy help, for where human safeguard is wanting to us, there the help of God is present as Philo saith.

Aphorism:5:

Love the Lord thy God with all thy heart with all thy forces and thy neighbour as thy Self[99] And the Lord shall keep thee as the apple of his eye[100] and shall deliver thee from all evil[101] and replenish thee with his good and thy soul shall desire nothing which shall not in time be given to it as well for the health of body as mind.

Aphorism:6:

Whatsoever thou shalt learn repeat often and print it in thy mind And thou mayest learn much not many things Because the human mind cannot contain all things unless it be he who is divinely regenerate. To him nothing is so hard or so many double which he cannot unfold.

Aphorism:7:

Call upon me in the day of tribulation and I will hear thee and thou shalt honour me[102] saith the Lord. But now all ignorance is a trouble of the mind. Call therefore upon the Lord against thy ignorance and he will hear thee. And remember that thou givest the honour to God. And say with the Psalmist. Not unto us O Lord not unto us but to thy name give the glory.[103]

The Second Septem: Aphorism:8:

As the Holy Scripture witnesseth That God giveth names to things or persons And also distributeth with those names the same forces and certain offices to them out of his treasuries. So the characters and names of the constellations have no force by reason

---

[99] Luke 10:27.

[100] Psalm 16:8.

[101] Matthew 6:13, Luke 11:4.

[102] Psalm 49:15.

[103] Psalm 113:9.

of figure or pronunciation but by reason of virtue or office which God or nature hath ordained to such a name or character For there is no virtue or force either in Heaven or in Earth or in Hell which descendeth not from God to give who not favouring and permitting nothing which he hath can be turned in to act.

Aphorism:9:

That is the chiefest wisdom that is in God. Next that which is in the Spiritual creatures. Then that which is the corporeal. Fourthly that in nature and things natural The Apostate Spirits follow these and are referred to the Judgement of the last day Sixthly the ministers of the princes in Hell, and obeying God. Seventhly the Pygmies[104] do not possess the lowest place And those which dwell in the Elements and Elementary things. It is convenient that all the differences of the wisdom of the Creator and the Creature should be known and discerned. That what we ought to take for our own use of everything might remain sure to us. And how we should know that to done indeed For every Creature is made for the profitable end of man's nature and for his service as holy Scripture testifies And as reasons and experience proves. (13)

Aphorism:10:

God the Father Almighty Creator of Heaven and Earth And of all things visible and invisible Propounds him self plainly unto us in his word: And as a Father that tenderly loveth his Son teacheth us what is profitable, And what not, what to be avoided, what to be embraced. And also allureth us to obedience with his chief proposed benefits Corporeal and Eternal. And hindereth purposed pains from them which are commodious for us. Therefore do thou read and practice his word being conversant therein night and day That thou mayest be happy and blessed for evermore. Do this and thou shall live as the Sacred writ hath taught.

---

[104] A term sometimes used to describe Earth Elementals in human form, though in this work it seems to be used for fairies instead.

Aphorism:11:

The quaternary number is Pythagorical

Therefore here we place the ground of all wisdom after the revealed wisdom of God in Sacred writ And unto the considering the purpose in nature.

Constitute the number[105]

Aphorism:12:

In the Acts of the Apostles saith the Spirit to Peter after the vision: Go down and doubt not for I have sent them After this manner all Disciplines have been delivered. Even by the holy Angels of God As it appeareth by the monuments of the Egyptians. And these after were depraved by men's opinions And the impulse of evil Spirits who sow Tares in the Children of distrust. It is manifest out of St Paul and Hermes Trismegistus. And there is no other reason of restoring arts then of the doctrine of the holy Spirits of God for true faith cometh by hearing.[106] But because thou mayest

---

[105] The MS has the remaining half of the page blank, possibly originally to have the rest of the aphorism filled in later as most of it is missing. The missing section as given in other versions of the Arbatel is:

"Appoint therefore to him who solely dependeth upon God, the wisdom of every creature to serve and obey him, nolens volens, willing or unwilling. And in this, the omnipotency of God shineth forth. It consisteth therefore in this, that we will discern the creatures which serve us, from those that are unwilling; and that we may learn how to accommodate the wisdom and offices of every creature unto our selves. This Art is not delivered, but divinely. Unto whom God will, he revealeth his secrets; but to whom he will not bestow any thing out of his treasuries, that person shall attain to nothing without the will of God.

Therefore we ought to desire tên pneumatikên epistêmên [the spiritual science] from God alone, which will mercifully impart these things unto us. For he who hath given us his Son, and commanded us to pray for his holy Spirit, How much more will he subject unto us the whole creature, and things visible and invisible? Whatsoever ye ask, ye shall receive. Beware that ye do not abuse the gifts of God, and all things shall work together unto you for your salvation. And before all things, be watchful in this, That your names be written in heaven: this is more light, That the spirits be obedient unto you, as Christ admonisheth."

[106] Romans 10:17.

be certain of the truth and mayest not doubt whether the Spirit that speaketh with thee pronounce true or false. Let it depend on thy faith in God that thou mayest say with Paul I know whom I believe. If that a little sparrow may not light on the ground without the will of the father which is in Heaven. How much more (O thou of little faith) will God not suffer thee to be deceived If thou dependest on God and stickest to him only.[107]

Aphorism:13:

The Lord liveth and all things that live live in him and it is true יהוה who is given to all that they be what they be And only with his vocal word by his Son hath brought forth all things that are out of nothing as they are He Calleth all the stars And all the Host of Heaven by their names. Therefore to whom God shall reveal the names of his Creatures he shall know their true forces. And the nature of things. The order and policy of the whole creature visible and invisible. It remaineth also that he receive power from God to bring forth forces in nature And the universal creature Came hid from the ableness into the act from darkness into light. Therefore thy whole scope ought to be this That thou keep the names of the Spirits. That is their offices and powers and that they may be subjected and addicted to thee in office and ministry Even as Raphael was given to Tobias that he might heal his Father deliver the Son from dangers[108] And bring forth his wife unto him. (14)

So Michael the fortitude of God governed the people of God. Gabriel the messenger of God was sent to Daniel, Mary, Zachary John Baptist's father. And he is also given to thee if thou desire it, who may teach thee what things thy mind hath longed after in the nature of things, use thou his ministers with fear and trembling of thy Creator of thy redeemer and sanctifier To wit of the father, The Son, And the Holy Ghost, and do not overslip any occasion of learning And of watching in thy vocation, And thou shalt desire nothing of necessary things.

---

[107] Matthew 10:29-31, Luke 12:6-7.

[108] Book of Tobit 3:17.

Aphorism:14:

Let thy Soul live for ever forever by him which Created thee. Call thou upon thy Lord God And serve him only. This shalt thou do if thou consider with thy self unto what end thou wast Created And what thou owest to God, what to thy Neighbour. God requireth this of thee, That thou honour his Son And that thou keep the word of the Sun in thy heart. And if thou shalt honour him Thou has done the will of thy Father which is in Heaven Thou owest also duty of humanity toward thy neighbours And that thou mayest bring all that come to thee to the honouring of the Son. This is the law and the prophets In temporal things thou oughtest to call upon God as thy father That he would give all the things necessary for this life But thou oughtest to help thy Neighbour with God's gifts whether they are spiritual goods or corporeal.

Thus thou shalt pray

O Lord the builder and Creator of Heaven and Earth And of all things visible and invisible I thine unworthy Servant Being commanded by thee Do call upon thee by thine only begotten Son our Lord and Saviour Jesus Christ That thou wilt give unto me thine holy Spirit who may lead me into thy truth And unto all thy goodness Amen.

Because I desire with a true desire the Arts of this life And to know perfectly our necessaries which are overwhelmed with such darkness and blurred with such infinite opinions of Men. That I may see I cannot follow mine owns strength nor theirs If thou teaches me not: Give me one of thy Spirits which may teach me those things which thou would have us learn and know unto thy praise and honour and profit of our neighbour. Give me also a docile and Capable heart That what thou shalt teach me I may perceive easily and lay them up in my mind that they may be brought forth as out of thy deep Treasures unto all necessary uses and give me grace that I may use such thy gifts humbly with fear and trembling Through our lord Jesus Christ with thy holy spirit. Amen.

The Third Septem: Aphorism:15:

Those are called Olympical Spirits which inhabit in the firmament and in the Stars of the firmament And their office is to discern destinies and fatal chances And to administer according as God hath pleased and permitted them: For no Spirit neither the bad nor the good destiny which sitteth in the helping place of the highest can hurt. But every of the Olympical Spirits teacheth or effecteth what this Star portends to whom it is addicted. Notwithstanding without God's grant. The power deducteth nothing into act. For it is only God which giveth them the ability and effect: Of all things they obey God the Creator above the heavens the Sublunary heavens and infernals Therefore obey thou this God being Captain, what thou undertakes, undertake and all happiness and good wishes be allotted to the end of thy endeavours: For as much as the history of the whole world testifies and daily experience shows. There is peace to the Godly. No peace to the wicked saith the Lord.[109]

Aphorism:16:

There are seven Governs or Olympical differences of Offices with which seven God would have this universal frame of the world to be administered. But their visible Stars are as followeth.

Aratron: Bethor: Phaleg: Och: Hagith: Ophiel: Phul:

---

[109] Isaiah 48:22 & 57:21.

Aphorism:16:

(15)

10 - List of the Olympic Spirits, reproduced below.

Aratron:		:49:	
Bethor:		:32:[110]	
Phaleg:	Is President of:~:	:35:	Visible Provinces
Och:		:28:	
Hagith:		:21:	
Ophiel:		:16:[111]	
Phul:		:7:	

As there are in the whole universe :186:[112] Provinces the which are administered by :7: Governors, All which are plainly expressed in Astronomy But in this place how their Princes and Potestates are brought to conference is to be expressed. Aratron appeareth on the first hours of the Sabbath and giveth answers from his provinces and provincials most truly. And likewise so do the rest in order on

---

[110] This has been miscopied and should be 42 not 32. The number of provinces should decrease by 7 each time.

[111] This has also been miscopied and should read 14 not 16.

[112] Another copyist's error, this number should be 196. The incorrect numbers in the table total 188, so this is a distinct error.

their days and hours. Also every one goeth before other 490 years. The beginning of the single Anomaly was 60 years before the birth of our Saviour and the Bethor began to administer and ended in the year of our Lord 430, whose successor was Phaleg who ended in the year of our Lord god 920. Next Och who ended in the year of our lord 1410 from which time Hagith reigneth till the year 1900.[113]

Aphorism:17:

The Princes of the Governors are called out Magically. Simply in that time in which day and hour they govern either visibly or invisibly by their names and offices which God hath given them. And his Character being proposed whom they themselves either have Confirmed or Given.

Now followeth their Characters

And what things they are which they do with their own liberal will::

The Characters of Aratron:~:

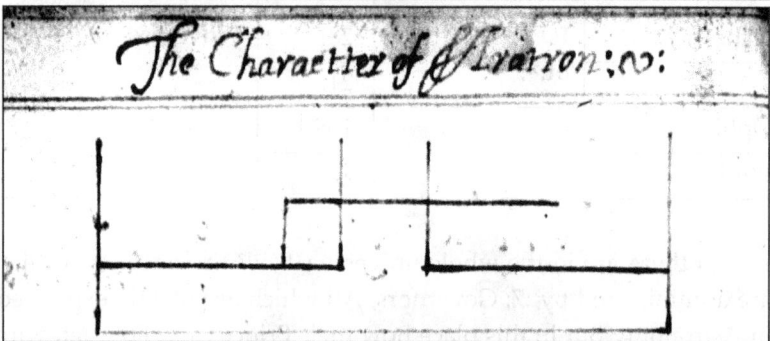

11 - The Seal of Aratron, Olympic Spirit of Saturn

The Governor Aratron hath in his power which he maketh naturally that is in the same manner and for disposed subject. All those things which in Astronomy are ascribed to Saturn's forces, whatever he will he can turn into a Stone in a moment as a creature or plant retaining the same objects of Sight. He converteth Treasure

---

[113] And Ophiel now rules until 2390 CE.

into coals and again coals into Treasure. He giveth familiar with a definite power. He teacheth the arts of Alchemy, Magick and natural Philosophy. He bringeth the Pigmies being men of low stature and your hairy men that are like beasts into the perfect form of men. He maketh a thing invisible. He maketh an unfruitful thing fruitful and giveth long life. He hath under him 49 Kings, 42 Princes, 35 nobles, 28 Dukes, 21 servants standing before him, 14 familiars, 7 messengers. He commandeth 36000 legions now a legion is 490

The Character of Bethor

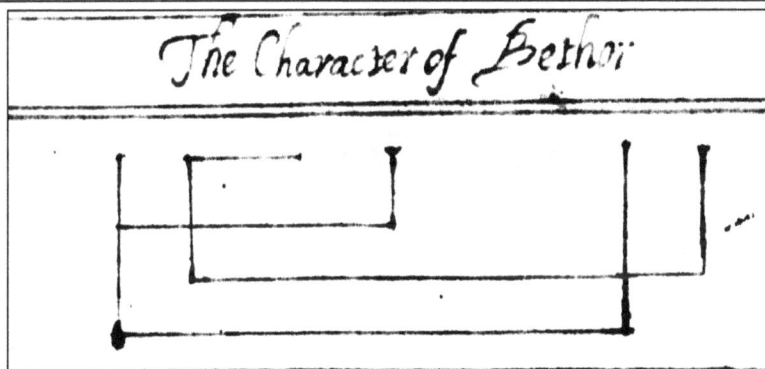

12 – *The Seal of Bethor, Olympic Spirit of Jupiter*

Bethor governeth those things which are ascribed unto Jupiter. He cometh quickly being called, who is dignified with his Character he is carried to great Honour. He objects treasures.[114] He maketh the Airy Spirits to (16) agree who give true answers. He transporteth from one place to another many things. He giveth precious stones and wonderful medicines in their effects. Also he giveth familiars in the firmament. He is able to prolong life 700 years if God will. He hath under him 42 Kings, 35 Princes, 28 Dukes, 21 Counsellors, 14 Servants, 7 Messengers, 29000 legions of Spirits.

---

[114] Other texts read 'opens' rather than 'objects' which makes more sense and suggests this may be a translation or copying error.

The Character of Phaleg:[115]

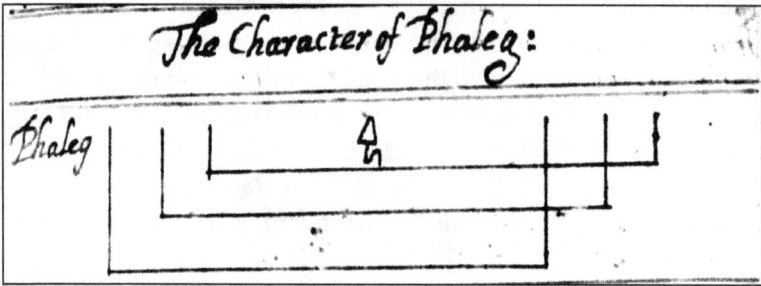

13 - The Seal of Phaleg, Olympic Spirit of Mars

Phaleg is attributed to Mars He is the prince of peace to whom whose character is given he exalteth to high dignities in the wars.

The Character of Och:

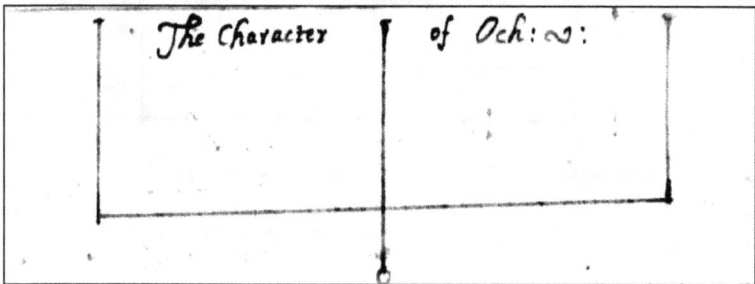

14 - The Seal of Och, Olympic Spirit of the Sun

Och governeth the Sun. He giveth 600 years with firm health, he enlargeth great wisdom. He giveth most excellent Spirits. He teacheth perfect Physick. He turneth all things into most pure Gold and precious stones. He giveth Gold and a purse flowing with Gold. To whom he giveth his character he maketh him to be worshipped of the Kings of the world. He hath under him 36536 legion of Spirits, only he administereth to all things. All his Spirits serve him by hundreds.

---

[115] Although all the other headings here are in red, this one is in black, for no specific reason.

The Character of Hagith:

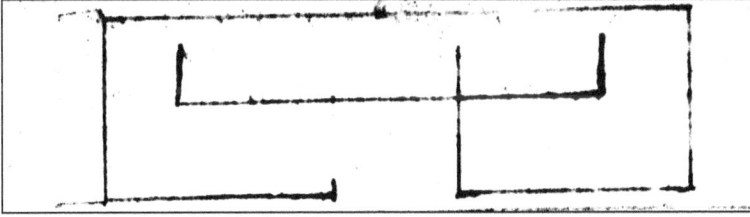

15 - The Seal of Hagith, Olympic Spirit of Venus

Hagith governeth Venus whom he will maketh most fair dignifying him with his Character and adorning him with all comeliness. He turns Copper in a moment into Gold And contrarily Gold into Copper. He giveth spirits who faithfully serve those they are addicted unto. He hath 4000 Legions of Spirits

The Character of Ophiel:

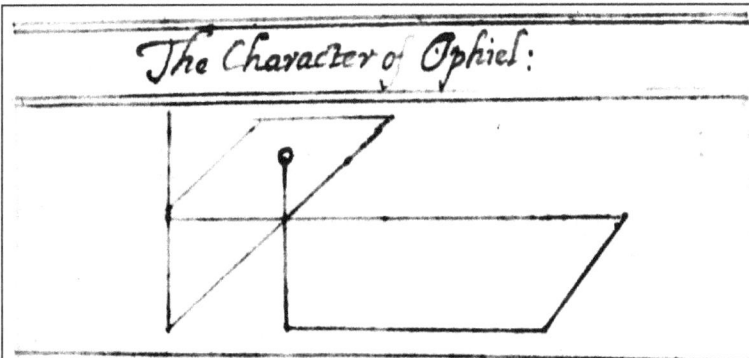

16 - The Seal of Ophiel, Olympic Spirit of Mercury

Ophiel is governor of the mercurials. His Spirits amount unto 100000 of Legions. He giveth familiar Spirits easily. He teacheth all arts. And whom he honoureth with his character he maketh to be able to turn quicksilver in a moment into the Philosopher's Stone.

The Character of Phul:co:

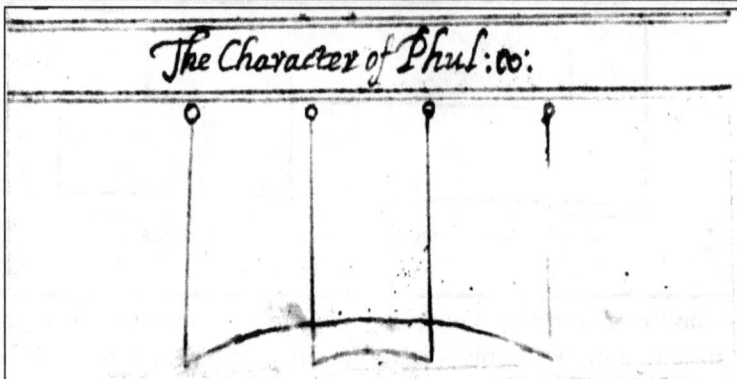

17 - The Seal of Phul, Olympic Spirit of the Moon

(17) **Phul** governeth the Moon. He changeth all metals into Silver in a moment. He healeth the Dropsy. He giveth watery Spirits and them which serve men in corporeal and visible form. He maketh one to live 300 years.

Most general Precepts of this Secret:~:

1. **Every Governor** worketh with his Spirits one way naturally to wit in the same manner. Otherwise of his free will. If he be not hindered of God.

2. **Secondly** he is able to do all things which he doth naturally in a long time in a fore disposed manner. So Och the prince of the Sun in long time prepareth Gold in the mountains. In less time by Chemical art. Magically in a moment.

3. **A true and divine magician** may use all the creatures of God, And the office of the Governors of the world unto a beck. Therefore the Governors of the world obey them and being called they come and follow their commands. Notwithstanding God is the author. As the Sun stood still for Joshua[116] **They** send indeed their Spirits to mean Magicians who obey them only some determinate business **But** they hear not false magicians but object them being deluded by Devils and they cast them into diverse perils God permitting As Jeremiah testifies of the Jews in his eighth chapter.

4. **In all the Elements** there are 7 Governors with their hosts who are moved by equal motion with the firmament And always the inferiors depend of the superiors. As it is taught in Philosophy.

5. **Man is ordained a Magician** from the womb of his mother that would be a true magician. Others that have taken upon them this office are unhappy. To this agreeth that which John Baptist saith No man can receive any thing to himself unless it be given him from above.[117]

6. **Every character** is given from this Spirit In every reason he hath his efficacy in this business in which it is given in a prefixed time but we must use him the hour and day of the planet in which it is given.

7. **God liveth** and thy soul liveth, Keep thy covenant with him which thou hast with the Spirit the revealer in God That all things may be done which the Spirit promiseth thee.

---

[116] Joshua 10:12-13.

[117] John 3:27.

Aphorism:18:

Some names of the Olympical Spirits are delivered by some men but such only in efficacy which have made known to everyone by the revealer the visible or invisible Spirit And these names are delivered to everyone as they are predestinated thereunto. Therefore they are said to be Constellated and seldom they have power beyond 40 years. Therefore it is the safest way for young Arts men that without names they work by the only office of the Spirits And if they be foreordained into this Magick the rest of the Arts required offer themselves of their own accord. Only pray for constant faith and God will grant all things in fit time.

Aphorism:19:

Heaven and his Inhabitants offer themselves to men of their own accord in form of Spirits and their offices to them that are invited By how much the more thou dost desire them they will be present. But what wicked Spirits do come from the envy of the Devil and how they have allured those men unto themselves as being sinners unto due punishment. Therefore whosoever desireth to be familiarly conversant with the Spirits let him keep himself from all enormous sins and pray diligently for the custody of the highest and let him break through the snares of the Devil and his impediments and hindrances. For he myself shall be Appointed and commanded of God to serve a true Magician. (18)

Aphorism:20:

All things are possible to him that believeth and is willing all things are impossible to the unbeliever and unwilling. There is nothing hindereth[118] more than the wavering mind lightness unconstancy facility Drunkenness Lusts Disobedience to God's word. It behoveth a Magician therefore to be a man Godly honest Constant in words and deeds with a firm faith toward God Prudent And Covetous of nothing but wisdom and those things which concern divinity.

---

[118] The word "hindereth" is repeated here a second time, I have omitted it for ease of reading.

Aphorism:21:

When thou wouldst call the Olympical Spirits Observe the rising of the Sun on Sunday of whose nature thou desirest the Spirit And say this prayer following And by thy faith thou shalt obtain thy desire.

Almighty and Eternal God who hast Created Heaven and Earth the Sea and all things therein To thy praise and honour And to the service of Man. I beseech thee that thou wouldst send thy Spirit A of the Sun's order unto me that he may inform me and teach me what I shall demand of him: Or that he may bring me medicine against the Dropsy &c. But not my will but thine be done Jesus Christ thy only begotten son our Lord. Amen.

But thou shalt not weary the Spirit above a whole hour unless he be familiarly addicted to thee.

Because thou camest pleasingly and quietly unto me and hast answered me to my demands I give God thanks in whose name thou camest And now go in peace to thine orders And return unto me when I shall call thee by thy name or by thine order or office which is given thee of thy Creator. Amen.

Ecclesiastes. C.5. V.1. Be not rash with thy mouth nor let thy heart be hasty to utter a thing before God for God is in the Heavens and thou on the earth Therefore let thy words be few for a dream cometh by reason of much business[119]

The Third[120] Septem: Aphorism:22:

We call that a Secret that no man can find out by human industry without revelation whose knowledge lyeth hid in the Creature hidden of God which notwithstanding is revealed to the Spirits unto their due use And these secrets are either concerning divine things, Natural or Human things. Search out therefore a few and the choicest whereby thou shalt command the more.

---

[119] This quote from Ecclesiastes 5:2-3 is not in the original Arbatel, though it is in Turner's 1655 edition.

[120] This should read "Fourth", a mistake found in all the Arbatel texts.

Aphorism:23:

First know the nature of the Secret whether it may be performed by Spirits in the form of a person Or by separated virtues Or by human organs or howsoever or no. This being deprehended[121] Ask of the Spirit who knoweth that Art And whatsoever the Secret is that he will tell thee briefly And pray to God that he would inspire thee with his Grace whereby thou mayest be led unto Secrets to thy desired end unto his praise and honour and to the profit of thy Neighbour.

Aphorism:24:

There are Seven chief Secrets:

1. **The first is** the Curing of all diseases in the space of 7 days either by characters or by natural things Or by the Superior Spirits with the help of God.

2. **The Second is** to know how to be able to produce life at pleasure unto what age soever to wit a corporeal life and natural. This our first Parents had.[122]

3. **The Third is** to know how to have obedience of the Creatures in the Elements which are in form of Personal spirits. Also in form of Pygmies of Saganes[123] of the Nymphs of the Dryads Of Silvatick[124] men.

4. **The Fourth is** to be able to confer with the intelligences of all visible things and invisible And to hear of every thing what is before it in dignity.

5. **The fifth is** to know how to be able to govern ones self unto the end perfixed[125] of God.

6. **The sixth is** to know God and Christ And his holy Spirit This is the perfection of our Microcosm.

7. **The seventh** is To be regenerated that he may be King of Henoch[126] the inferior of the world. (19)

---

[121] An old word meaning "detected" or "discovered".

[122] This refers to the extreme life spans described for Adam and the first people in Genesis.

[123] Also called Saganae, the Spirits of the Four Elements.

[124] "Sylvatic" means "of the woods", so here it is "men of the woods".

[125] Another way of writing "prefixed".

The which is of an Honest and Constant mind may learn the Seven Secrets of the Spirits without offence to God.

The mean Secrets are also : 7: in number :~:

---

1.   **The first** The changing of metals which is called vulgarly Alchemy – Truly it is certain it is given to very few and not without a peculiar gift. For it is not of him that runneth Nor of him that willeth But of God that showeth mercy.

2.   **The second is** Metallical cure of disease either by the magnets of precious stones or by the use of the Philosopher's Stone or the like

3.   **The third is** to be able to do marvellously in Astronomy and the Mathematics and to administer business for Heaven and the like

4.   **The fourth is** to exhibit the works of natural Magick whatsoever they are.

5.   **The fifth is** to know all Philosophical workings for visions.

6.   **The sixth to** know all Arts from the very ground of them which are exercised by the hand And gift of the Body.

7.   **The seventh** to know all Arts from their ground which are exercised by the Angelical nature of man.

The lesser secrets are also : 7: in number:

---

1.   **The first** to do a thing diligently Stoutly valiantly or nimbly.

2.   **The second** to ascend from low degree to dignities and honours. To found a new family which may raise thee to great dignity and honours.

3.   **The third** to excel in warfare and happily to bear great matters to be the head of A head of Kings and princes.

4.   **The fourth** to be a good father of a family in Country or city.

5.   **The fifth** to be a painful[127] and fortunate Merchant

---

[126] City in the writings of St Augustine named after the son of Cain, whose citizens were dedicated to the earth and satisfied with its pleasures.

[127] Other versions give "industrious" here, which makes more sense!

6.   **The sixth** to be a Philosopher, Mathematician, Physician, Aristotlican, a Platonian a Ptolemian an Euclidean, of Hippocrates skill or Galen's.

7.   **The seventh** To be a divine one skilled in the Bible a Scholar learned and skilled in all the writers of Divinity both old and new.

Aphorism:25:

We have told you what a secret is How many kinds of them there are How many subdivisions of those kinds It remains now that we tell you how we may follow the things which we know.

1.   There is but one only true way to all secrets, That is, that thou have thy recourse to God the author of all good. As Christ teacheth, First seek the kingdom of God and the righteousness thereof And the rest shall be administered unto you.[128]

2.   **Also** take heed that your hearts be made not heavy through Gluttony and Drunkenness and with the cares of this life.[129]

3.   **Also** commend thy cares unto the lord And he shall do it.[130]

4.   **Also**, I am the lord thy God teaching thee profitable things govern thee in the way wherein thou walkest.[131]

5.   **Also** I will give thee understanding and teach thee in the way wherein thou shalt walk, And will guide thee with mine Eye.[132]

6.   **Also** see which are evil know you to give good things to your Children how much more shall your Heavenly father give his holy Spirit to them that desire him.[133]

7.   **Also** If you will do the will of my father which is in Heaven – ye shall be verily my Disciples And we will come unto you and make our abode with you.[134]

---

[128] Matthew 6:33.

[129] Luke 21:34.

[130] Psalm 54:23.

[131] Isaiah 48:17.

[132] Psalm 31:8.

[133] Matthew 7:11.

[134] John 14:23.

These 7 places of holy Scripture If thou wilt be led from the letter to the Spirit or Act Thou canst not err but obtain the desired mark. Thou shalt not wander from the scope and God himself by his holy Spirit shall teach thee profitable and true things. Also he will give thee his ministers the Angels that they may be thy companions thy Doctors and helpers in every secret of the world And he shall command every creature that it obey thee That thou mayest say with the Apostles joyfully That the Spirits are obedient unto thee Lastly that which is the chiefest thing of all thou shalt be sure that thy name is written in (the book of Life) or in Heaven.[135]

Aphorism:26:

There is another way and more common that things may be revealed to thee Also I give thee knowledge that the secrets from God or by Spirits (who hath a secret in his power) or by dreams or by strong imaginations or impressions have him revealed or by the constellations at one's nativity By the heavenly intelligences. After this manner those Heroic men of fame have done As almost all your learned men of this world, Plato, Aristotle, Hippocrates, Galen, Euclid, Archimedes, Hermes Trismegistus the father of Secrets with Theophrastus and Paracelsus (20) in whom were all the forces. And unto this Secret Homer, Hesiod, Orpheus, Pythagoras are to be referred for these men had the gift of foreseeing of secrets. Hitherto we may refer the Nimphidicals[136] as the sons of Melusine and Achilles, Aeneas, Hercules begotten by the Gods. Also Cyrus, Great Alexander, Julius Caesar, Lucull, Sylla and Marius.

This is a Canon or principle that everyone must know his own Genius and that they temper him according to the word of God. And take heed of the snares of the evil Genius Lest thou be thrown into the calumnies of Brutus and Marcus Antonius. Refer hither the book of Jovian Pontane[137] concerning fortune and his Eutich.

---

[135] Luke 10:20.

[136] Male Nymphs.

[137] John Jovian Pontanus was a 15th century Italian poet and scholar.

The third way is an honest and diligent Labour In which without some divine power nothing worthy of greatness or wonder can be followed or effected – As it is said -

Thou canst not speak or do anything without Minerva the Goddess of Learning.

We Abhor your Cacomagicians who by unlawful superstition make themselves fellows with the Devils And some things God suffereth them to do. That they should be carried into the place of punishment by the Devils. Even as some evils are done by the Devil the Author As the holy scripture testifies of Judas. Hither we may refer all your Idol worshippers wherein evil Spirits in Ancient time used yea and in our age also. And the abuse of Lotts which manner of thing the Jews dealt much with all. To this also belong the Charanticall calling out of dead men's spirits as Saul with the witch of Endor And one Lucan a dead knight that was thus raised. And the witch that told the event of the Pharsalical battle and the like.

Aphorism:27:

Make a Circle Place A in the centre, BCE in the East, CD[138] in the North, DE in the west and EB in the south. Divide each quarter into 7 parts which maketh 28 parts Then divide again every part by 4 being 112 parts in all And so many true secrets there are to be revealed.

And this Circle being thus divided is the seal of the secrets of all the world which from one A in the centre (that is) from the one indivisible God is spread abroad into the whole universal creation.

The Prince of the Eastern secrets sits in the middle and hath one very side, 3 Peers or nobles the which peers have under each of them 4, And the Prince himself retains 4.

After this manner the rest the quadrangle of Secrets have their princes and peers which have their 4 Secret apiece.

But the Study of all wisdom is in the East.

The west is for force and strength.

The South for culture and Husbandry.

The North for a Rugged and hard life.

---

[138] This looks like CB corrected to CD by overwriting, which would agree with the other Arbatel MSS.

Therefore the chief Secrets are to be commended to the East, the mean for the South, The lesser Secrets to the west and North.

The use of the Seal of Secrets is this. That thou mayest know from whence Spirits or Angels are brought who teacheth their Secrets delivered them of God. And they have their names derived from their offices and virtues even as God hath distributed to every of them his gift. One hath the power of the Sword delivered him Another of the Pestilence, Another hath power given him to afflict people with famine and scarcity As he is ordained of God, Others are overthrowers of Cities, As those 2 who were sent to destroy Sodom and Gomorrah and the neighbouring places about As holy Scriptures testify.[139] Some are watchers over kingdoms, Others keepers of private men's persons, So that every man may easily form to himself their names in his own mother tongue Therefore he that will, Let him desire an Angel of Physick, Or a Philosophical Angel, Or a Mathematical Angel, Or an Angel of Civil Law, Or an angel of natural or supernatural wisdom. Or whatsoever else he be. (21)

And let him also seriously with great fervency with faith and constancy And without doubt what he desireth He shall receive of God the Father of all Spirits.

This faith goeth beyond all Seals and Subjects them to the will of Man.

To this faith belongeth the Characteristic calling out of Angels which depends also only of the divine revelation. But without faith before spoken all things lie in obscurity and darkness.

But if anyone will ask them in faith and memory and simply as from God the Creator to the creature to whom such virtue or Spiritual essence is given, He may use them without offence to God.

But let him take heed that he fall not into Idolatries and snares of the Devil who holdeth forth his poisonous baits and doth easily deceive the unwary. And he himself is not taken but only by the finger of God And brought to serve man, But not without temptations and tribulations as he hath commandment that he should bruise the heel of Christ or of the woman's seed. Therefore we ought with fear and trembling to be conversant in divine mysteries and with great reverence towards God. And to be

---

[139] Genesis 19.

conversant with the spiritual offences with gravity and justice. And take heed to thy self of all lightness,[140] Pride, Covetousness, vanity, Envy and ungodliness. For such a one must he be that handleth such divine mysteries, unless he will miserably perish

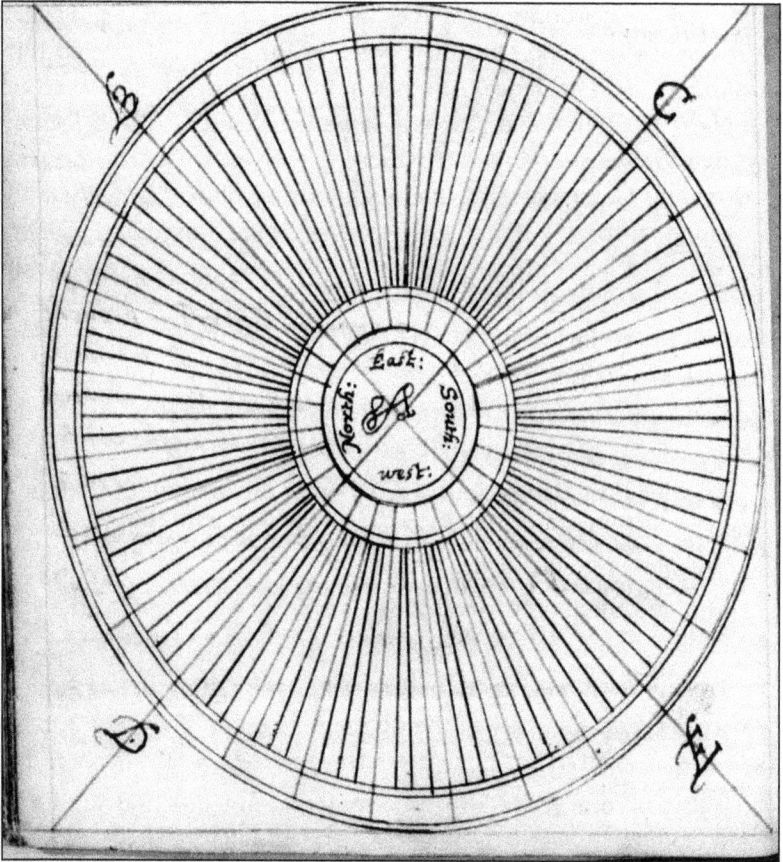

18 - The Seal of Secrets. This is mentioned in all versions of the Arbatel, but only given in this MS

Aphorism:28:

Because all good is from God alone good of whom those things we would desire It behoves us in Spirit and truth and with a single heart to pray for them. The Conclusion of the Secret of secrets is this, That everyone would be stirred up to pray for that he desireth And he shall not have a denial. Let no man despise his own

---

[140] I.e. levity.

prayers. For of whom God is desired he can give and enlarge And he will enlarge, we must acknowledge the author of whom we ask humbly our desires. The clement and good father loves the Sons of desire (as Daniel) And quickly heareth them when we shall be able to overcome the hardness of our hearts by prayer. But he will not have us to cast Holy things unto Dogs.[141] He will not have his treasures to be condemned or defiled of us. Therefore do thou most diligently read and read again the first Septem of Secrets And institute and direct thy life and all thy thoughts unto those precepts And all things shall be given thee in the Lord whom thou trustiest.

The fifth Septem: Aphorism:29:

That we may in order proceed in our study of Magick to general precepts, we come now unto the particular explication of the premises.

The Spirits are the ministers of God's word And of the Church and her members, And they are either serving the creature in corporeal things, Partly to the health of the body and mind partly unto destruction. And there in no good nor evil done without a sure and determinate order and Government. He that desireth a good end let him follow it. He that desireth an ill end – Let him also follow it: And that very quickly of the divine punishment and of the turning away from the divine will.

Even as everyone confers his own scopes with the word of God And as he were at the touchstone to judge between good and bad. And let him know what is to be avoided, what to be desired. Even as he hath appointed and defined with himself Let him follow it earnestly not with procrastination posting off[142] from day to day If thou meanest to hit the ordained mark.

Aphorism:30:

Whoso desireth riches the glory of this life Magistracy, Honours, Dignities, Kingdoms (and that Magically) Let them follow them everyone for his fate and industry and Magical science. As the Melesine history testifies. And of that Magician who appointed that no Italian by no means should obtain the everlasting

---

[141] Matthew 7:6.

[142] I.e. delaying.

Kingdom of Naples. And he effected that he that did reign in his age should be troubled from his seat. Such is the power of the watchful and vigilant Angels of the Kingdoms of the world.

Aphorism:31:

Call out the Prince of the Kingdom and desire the right of him And ask what thou wilt and it shall be, as long as that Prince again Shall not be absolute[143] from obedience by the succeeding Magician. Then the Kingdom of Naples may be restored again to the Italians. If any Magician would call him out who hath instituted this order and appointed him unto the recanting his deed. Also he may restore the lost Cleivodie[144] by Magical treasure The Book the Gem And the Magical Horn the which being had One may easily (if he will) institute himself Monarch of the world. But that Jew chose to live among the Gods until the latter judgement day before he would choose the transitory goods of this world. But that man's heart is blinded that understandeth (23) nothing concerning the God of Heaven and Earth or thinketh more But enjoyeth the delights of immortal things unto his eternal destruction. And he shall be called out more easily than the Genius of Plotinus in the Temple of Isis

---

Aphorism:32:

Likewise the learned Romans out of the books of the Sibyls after the same manner instituted themselves lords of the world as history testifies. But lesser Magicians are given to the Peer of the Prince of the Kingdom. Therefore whoso desireth a lesser office or dignity let him call out the Prince's Peer And it shall be done to his desire.

Aphorism:33:

But whoso desireth only such dignities as riches, Let him call out the Prince of Riches or one of his nobles And it shall be done to his desire. In that kind wherein he would wax rich, Either with Terrestrial goods, Or with Merchandise, Or with the gifts of

---

[143] I.e. absolved.

[144] Unknown meaning – possibly derived from clavo-die – "key of God"?

Princes, Or with the Metallic Study, Or with the Chemical, So that he may after this manner be made rich and obtain his desires.

Aphorism:34:

Every calling out of a Spirit is of one kind and form and this hath been lately a common reason with the Sibyls and the chief Priests. At this time it is lost through ignorance and ungodliness in the whole world. That which remaineth is depraved with Superstitions and infinite lies.

Aphorism:35:

The human mind is the only effecter of wonderful works so that the will join herself to what Spirit she will. Being conjoined she produceth what she will. Therefore we must proceed in Magick warily lest Mermaids and other Monsters deceive us – who likewise desire the Society of the human mind. Therefore always lie thou hid under the wings of the Highest lest thou offer thy self to be devoured by the roving lion. For whosoever desireth worldly things, doth escape very hardly the snares of Sathan.

The Sixth Septem: Aphorism:36:

Take heed that you mingle not together Experiments with Experiments, But let it be single and only on experiment. For God and nature hath ordained all things unto a sure and destinated end. As for example, They who cure with Simple Herbs and roots of all men they cure most happily. After this manner the chiefest influences or virtues actually lie hid in the constellations names and Characters, in Stone and the like which are in place of a miracle.

Also the very words themselves being pronounced presently they make both visible and invisible creatures to obey as well those of this our world As those in the waters, Air, under the Earth, and Olympical, the Supercelestial, infernal, And lastly Those in the divine world also.

Therefore we ought to study Simpleness and the knowledge of such simples as are delivered us of God. Otherwise by no other reason or experience can things be laid hold on.

Aphorism:37:

Everything hath his place allotted it decently. Order, Reason, Manner, which easily rendereth all learning of the Creatures as well visible as invisible. (24)

The order is this. That some are Creatures of Light, Others of darkness. Those that are of darkness are subject to vanity because they have thrown themselves down headlong into darkness, by reason of rebellion. Their Kingdom partly is very fair In caducal[145] and transitory things, Because it cannot consist without some virtue, And without some chief gifts of God. Partly their kingdom is very foul and horrible to be spoken, That it aboundeth with all vice and sins, with Idolatry, Contempt of God, Blasphemies of the true God and his works, with the worshipping of Devils, Disobedience towards Magistrates, with seditions. It is full of Murders, Thefts, Tyrannies, Adulteries, unlawful lusts, rapines, Lies, perjuries, And with desire of Reigning in this mixture the Kingdom of darkness consists But the Creatures of light Command as the members of Christ[146] with eternal truth and grace of God. And they are lords of this world, Also the govern the lords of darkness. Between these and those there is an everlasting war According as God hath ordained this strife unto the last Judgement day.

Aphorism:38:

1. **Magick is twofold.** In the first division thereof, The one sort is of God which he giveth to the creatures of light. The other is like unto it, But it is the gift of the creatures of darkness. And this magick is twofold, The one tending to a good end, As when the prince of darkness endeavours to do well to the creature. (God helping forward) The other to a bad end. As when God permitted such to be deceived Magically unto the punishing the bad and unto their hurt, Or else commandeth such to be thrust into perdition.

2. **The second** division of Magick is that one sort perfecteth his works by visible instruments through visible things. The other sort is which perfecteth his work in Invisible

---

[145] I.e. obsolete.

[146] I Corinthians 6:15.

Instruments through Invisible things. Another Magick worketh with commixt[147] things as well manners as Instruments and effects.

3.   **The third division** is Some Magick is performed by invocation of God alone. And this is partly prophetical and Philosophical, Partly like that Theophrastus used. Another is that which worketh through ignorance of the true God with the princes of the Spirits. Such is the work of the Mercurials.[148]

4.   **The fourth division is,** That some exerciseth his Magick from the highest God by good angels descending in the place of God. Such was Balam's magick. Other Magicians exorciseth[149] with the Peers of the evil Spirits, And such were they who wrought with the lesser Gods of the nations.

5.   **The fifth division is,** That some men work openly with the spirits face to face which is given but to very few. Others work by dreams or other signs, As they of old did wrought by Auguries and Hosts.

6.   **The sixth division is,** That some work by immortal Creatures, Others by mortal as the Nymphs, Satyrs, Pigmies, And the like of other elements.

7.   **The seventh division is** That the Spirits serve some of their own accord without Art, And some they will scarce serve being called out by Art.

If all these divisions of Magick That is most excellent which[150] dependeth only of God. The next to that, That which the Spirits serve in of their own accord, The third that which is proper to Christians which dependeth on the power of Christ which he hath in Heaven and in Earth.

---

[147] I.e. mixed together or blended.

[148] Another name for alchemists.

[149] Exorcise is being used here in its original sense, i.e. as conjure.

[150] The word "which" is duplicated here.

Aphorism:39:

There is a sevenfold preparation, That we may learn the Art of Magick.

1. **The first is** That we may day and night meditate how one should ascend to the true knowledge of God. As well by the revealed word (25) from the beginning As by the seal of creation and Creatures and by the wonderful effects which visible and invisible Creatures of God do show.

2. **Secondly** it is required that a man descend into himself and that he study especially to know himself, what mortal thing he hath in himself and what immortal And what is the property of every part, what the diversity.

3. **Thirdly,** that he learn by his immortal part to worship love and fear the Eternal God and to adore him in spirit and truth, And to do those things with his mortal part which he knoweth to be grateful to god and profitable to his neighbour.

   These are the three chief and first precept of Magick to which whosoever shall prepare himself, unto true Magick or divine wisdom to the coveting and following of the same that he may be counted worthy the knowledge thereof, whom the Angelical creatures shall obey not only obscurely but also manifestly and face to face.

4. **Fourthly** Seeing that everyone is called from the womb of his mother that he should be occupied in a certain kind of life, Therefore it is requisite that everyone should thoroughly know whether he be born into Magick or no And into what kind of Magick which everyone shall perceive which readeth these things and judged them easy and by experience shall find in himself good success. For such and so great gifts are not given but to the poor in Spirit & humble.

5. **Fifthly** he must note whether he can perceive the Spirits assisting him manifestly in the greatest businesses that are to be undertaken. Because if he shall find them to be such assistants, It is manifest he is made a Magician by the ordinance of God, that is, such a person which useth the ministry of the spirits unto the effecting of excellent things. But here he may sin, either by negligence or by ignorance, or by contempt, or also by too much superstition. Also he may sin by unthankfullness towards God whereby many excellent

men have drawn upon themselves destruction, and he may sin by rashness and stubbornness. And lastly he may sin when the gifts of God are not had in that honour and esteem as is required and as they ought to be.

6.   **Sixthly**, A Magician hath need of faith and silence that no secret especially may be made which the spirit revealeth to him as Daniel was commanded to keep secret secrets.[151] For some things are sealed that is not brought forth into public. So neither was it lawful for Paul to utter those things he saw in Revelation.[152] No man would believe how much is placed in this one only precept.

7.   **Seventhly**, very great righteousness is required in a Magician to come, that is, that he should not undertake anything that is either ungodly, irreligious or unjust, yea that he admit not any such thing into his mind. And by the holy of God he shall be defended from all evil.

Aphorism:40:

When a man shall perceive some incorporeal agent about himself either by some outward sense or inward Then let him govern himself according to these :7: rules following that he may pursue after his magical end.

1.   **Let this be the first law,** That he know that such a Spirit is ordained him of God. And that he think himself to have him to be a viewer of all his actions and thoughts Therefore let him direct all his whole life unto the prescribed order set forth in the word of God.

2.   **Secondly,** let him always pray with David. Take not thy holy spirit from me, and confirm me with a principal spirit,[153] And lead us not into temptation but deliver us from all evil.[154] I beseech thee O heavenly father give not power to the lying spirit, As thou gavest to Ahab that he should perish,[155] But keep me in thy truth. Amen.

---

[151] Daniel 8:26.

[152] II Corinthians 12:4.

[153] Psalm 50:13-14.

[154] Matthew 6:13.

[155] I Kings 22:20-23, II Chronicles 18:19-22.

3.   **Thirdly,** let him accustom himself unto the proving and trying of the Spirits, As the Scripture exorteth. For of thorns (26) Men gather not Grapes.[156] Let us try all things and hold fast that which is good and laudable. And let us avoid that which is repugnant to God's will.

4.   **Fourthly** let us be very far from superstitions. That is meant to be Superstition in this place, To attribute the duty to things in which there is no divine thing. Also it is a choosing of the will to worship God otherwise than he hath commanded. Such are all your Ceremonies of Satanicall Magick who Impudently would be worshipped as God.

5.   **Fifthly,** the worshipping of Idols is to be avoided which with their own proper motion bindeth the divine power to Idols or other things where they are not placed of the Creator, In the order of nature, Many such things the evil magicians effect.

6.   **Sixthly,** the crafty deceits of the devil is to be avoided whereby he will imitate the power of the creation and creator that he might bring forth things with a word. Things which are not as though they were, which is only incommunicable of the omnipotent God and the creature.

7.   **Seventhly,** we must stick to the gifts of God and his holy spirit That we may know these things and worship God with all our heart and with all our forces.

Aphorism:41:

We come here to the :9: last Aphorisms of this Tome wherein we will conclude the whole Isagogical Magick God's mercy helping us forward.

Therefore it is to be observed before all things what we understand by a Magician in this work.

We would have him to be a magician to whom by the grace of God the manifest spiritual essence serve unto the knowledge of the whole universal. And in these contents of nature's whether they be visible or invisible This description of a magician is evident and is universal.

---

[156] Matthew 7:16.

The evil or cacomagician is he whom by God's permissions the evil Spirits serve unto temporal and eternal hurt bewitching men and turning them from God. Such a one was Simon Magus mention of whom there is made in the Acts of the Apostles[157] and in Clement whom St Peter commanded to be put into the Earth seeing he would command himself to be lifted up into the Air as a God by wicked Spirits.

All those are to be referred into this order who are noted in the hours of the 12 tables.[158] And their evil deeds are also noted But we will mark the subdivisions and kinds of either Magick in this Tome following. It shall be sufficient in this place that we have made distinction and difference of Good Science and bad. Seeing that the first man desired possession of them both to his hurt, As Moses and Hermes show.

Aphorism:42:

We must know in the second place that a Magician is a person predestinated unto this kind of work from the womb of his mother. Neither hath anyone assumed anything to himself of such things unless he hath been called to this work divinely unto a good end from Grace, unto an ill end that the Scripture might be fulfilled. Offences must come but woe to that man by whom they come.[159] Furthermore as we have warned before let us live in this world with fear and trembling.

Notwithstanding we deny not some kinds of both Magick to be followed by some with Study and diligence if he be admitted But unto those chief kinds he shall never aspire unto. Yea if he desire those things he will be violated in body and soul without doubt Such are they who are transferred by (27) cacomagical work unto the mountains of Horeb,[160] Or are swallowed up with Some Solitudes to whom many evils happen even to bodies and minds, Or at length are deprived of their mind, As such things happen to many by use when as they are left of God, And delivered to Sathan.

---

[157] Acts 8:9-24.

[158] The Roman legal text Duodecim Tabularum, of 451 BCE.

[159] Luke 17:1.

[160] The Divine location where Moses received the commandments according to Deuteronomy, also sometimes given as being another name for Mount Sinai.

The Seventh Septem: Aphorism:43:

God liveth and his works remain in that state wherein he would have them for he would we should use them with his liberty unto the obedience of his commandments. He hath proposed (to them that obey,) his rewards, But to them that disobey; his deserved punishments.

Therefore they have known the Spirits by free will through pride and contempt of the Son of God. And they are referred to the day of wrath.[161] There is a very great power left to them in the creation, But notwithstanding it is Limited And always they are compelled by the bridle of God to keep their bonds but a magician of God which sounds the wisdom of God or the informed of God by the hand of God is brought forth to all eternal good, and mean things, or also chief corporeals.

Great is the power of Sathan by reason of man's great sins. And therefore great things have been done by Satanicall magick, yea greater things than anyone will believe.

And although they subsist in their limits notwithstanding they are beyond all human capacity, for as much as they aim at the corporeal and transitory things of this life as many histories of the Ancients testify, And we have daily examples. For conclusion both kinds of magick differ among themselves. This passeth over into eternal goods and useth temporal things with thanksgiving, That is Solicitous about eternal things but applieth himself wholly to corporeal that he may enjoy freely all his lusts and delights unto the contempt of God And of his wrath.

Aphorism:44:

The passing over the common life of men unto the Magical life is nothing else but sleeping from the same life unto the same life watching for what things happen in common life to ignorant and unskilful men. They happen much more to the learned and willing.

A Magician understandeth when his mind thinketh of himself when it deliberateth, reasoneth, constitutes, and defines something to be done. He observes when his thoughts wander from the assisting separated essence, And proveth by what order that assistant essence is separated.

---

[161] Job 21:30.

But a man unfulfilled in magick is carried as a beast is with affections up and down, And knoweth not by the word of God to overthrow the counsels of his enemies And to forekeep himself from the snares of the Tempter.

Aphorism:45:

The chief precept of Magick is to know what everyone ought to receive unto his use from the assisting Spirit, And what to refuse. For the Psalmist saith, wherewithal shall a young man cleanse his way By ruling himself according to thy word.[162] To keep therefore the word of God lest the evil one should catch it from thy heart is the chief precept of wisdom. It is lawful to receive and admit those suggestions which are not against the glory of God and love toward the neighbour, without demanding from what spirit such a suggestion came, yet we must take heed that we busy not ourselves too much about unnecessary things according to Christ's admonition, Martha, Martha, thou art solicitous about many things but Mary hath chosen the better part which shall not be taken from her.[163] Be we ruled always by the saying of Christ. First seek the kingdom of God and the righteousness thereof and the rest (28) shall be cast unto you.[164] The rest, That is all things fitting for this little world of ours. Food and Raiment and necessary arts for our life

---

Aphorism:46:

Nothing so becometh a Man as constancy in words and deeds, And when the like rejoiceth with the like. No men are more happy than such because the holy Angels are conversant with such men, And have them in their custody. But on the other side men are turned away to nothing even as Chaff is turned with the wind, And for them we have chosen this 46th Aphorism. For as everyone hath carried himself even so he hath allured to himself the Spirits of his nature and condition But one exhorteth very truly that no man would go beyond his calling herein lest he should allure some malign Spirit unto himself from the uttermost parts of the world by

---

[162] Psalm 118:9.

[163] Luke 10:41-42.

[164] Matthew 6:33.

whom he might be deceived and drawn unto his final hurt. This precept is very manifest. For Midas when he would convert all things into Gold, Drew unto himself such a Spirit that he might be excellent in his doing but he was deceived by him and he died by famishment and hunger, Had not God in mercy corrected his foolishness. The like happened in our time to a young woman about Frankfurt at Odera, So that she snatched money from everything and devoured it. O then would to God Men would weigh with themselves this precept and not take Midas his history and the like for fables. Then surely they would be more diligent in moderating their affections and thoughts and not be vexed continually with the Spirits of the Golden Mountains of utopia. Lastly let us observe diligently that we cast such presumptions out of our minds by the word of God even while we are fresh and have not made a custom of the word divine to please our idle empty mind.

Aphorism:47:

Whosoever is faithfully conversant in his vocation he shall have the Spirits his constant fellows of his Study who will supply all success to him. For if have also any knowledge in magick they count it not grievous to show themselves to him and to talk familiarly with him, and in diverse of the same ministries whereto they are addicted in good things to the good unto salvation, In bad things to the bad all evil and hurt. Examples of Histories are not wanting in the whole world that such things have happened therein Theodolius is an example among good men before the victory of Arbogast, Among the bad Brute[165] before he was slain when as he was followed by Caesar's genius or Spirit and was punished so that he might be so served as he had done to the father of that country and his own father.

---

[165] Brutus.

Aphorism:48:

All magick is the revelation of that kind of Spirits of what sort the magick is, so the nine Muses of Hesiod calls for 9 kinds of Magick as he manifestly testifies of himself in his Theogoma Ulysses his genius called Homer in Psigogagia the spirits Hermes concerning the higher things of the mind. God himself called Moses out of the Bush. Thus the three magicians who came to Christ at Jerusalem were doubtless called unto this vocation, the Angel of the lord being their guide And Daniel was called by the Angel of the lord. It is not thus that anyone should glory. For it is not of him that willeth nor of him that runneth, But either of God that showeth mercy, or of some other spiritual fate, from hence all Magick springeth whether it be good or bad after this manner Tages the first teacher of the Roman's magick sprang out of the earth, Diana of the Ephesians showeth as it were from Heaven her worship,[166] And so Apollo and the universal religion of the Gentiles was received from the same Spirits neither are they Man's inventions as the Sadducees hold.

Aphorism:49: and the last:

Let the conclusion of this Isagoge be the same that is spoken (29) of above by us, for as much as there is one God from whom is derived all good: And again seeing there is but one sin to wit disobedience to God's will and Commandments from whence proceeds all evil. So the fear of the Lord is the beginning of wisdom[167] and is all the profit of Magick. For obedience to the will of God follows the fear of God the presence of God and his holy spirit And the ministries of the Holy Angels follow this his will and all good things out of the never drawn dry treasuries of God.

But the unprofitable and damned Magick springeth from Sathan when we lose the fear of God from our hearts and suffer him to reign among us. There presently the prince of this world the God of this age hath appointed such a one of his kingdom that he might find such a one profitable for his kingdom. Thus he taketh the Godless Magician even as a silly fly is taken in the Cobweb of A Spider, And so Sathan deceiveth them hunting them into his nets of

---

[166] Acts 19:35.

[167] Psalms 110:10.

desires until he bring them into the matter of eternal fire he elevates and carrieth them up on high that they may have the greater fall.

Bring about gentle reader thy eyes and mind unto the holy histories and also to the profane and gather all things of the Magicians according to the double Science of knowledge of good and evil, which things that they may be the better discerned we have hereafter placed the division and subdivision of Magick or Science in which whosoever will He may contemplate what is to be followed, what to be avoided. And according as everyone shall labour in that competency and firm life that is given him.

Sciences twofold:~:	**.1.** **Of** good	**.1.** **The** wisdom of God	**.1.** The knowledge of God's word and a life directed according to his word.
			.2. The knowledge of the Government of God by Angels which the Scripture calleth watchmen and to understand the mysteries of Angels.
		.2. The wisdom of man given to man	**.1.** The knowledge of natural things.
			.2. The prudence of human things.
	.2. **Of** evil	**.2.** **Bad** wisdom	**.1.** The contempt of the word of God and to live after the will of the Devil.
			.2. Ignorance of the government of God by Angels
			.3. To despise the custody of Angels or to be fellows with the devils.
			.4. Idolatry
			.5. Atheism

.2.	**The** Science of venifices .1. in nature and to use them
Evil Spirits	**Prudence** in all evil arts .2. unto the hurt of mankind. And to use them in [contempt][168] of God and to the loss and destruction of men

---

Finis:~: (30)

---

[168] There is a space where a word is missing from the text here, which I have inserted from the other texts.

Sciences two fold:

1: Of good.

The wisdome of God.
- The knowledge of Gods word and a life directed according to his word.
- The knowledge of the Gouerment of God by Angells which the Scripture calleth watchmen and to vnderstand the misteries of Angells.

The wisdome man giuen to mak.
- The knowledg of naturall things.
- The prudence of humain things.

2: Of euill.

Bad wisdome.
- The contempt of the word of God and to liue after the will of the Diuell.
- Jgnorance of the gouerment of God by Angells.
- To despise the custody of Angells or to be fellowes with the diuill.
- Jdollatry.
- Atheisme.

2: Euill Spirits.
- The Science of venifices in nature and to vse them.
- Prudence in all euill arts vnto the hurt of mankind. And to vse them in of God and to the losse and distruction of men.

Finis: ω:

19 - *The last page of the Arbatel in this MS, as shown transcribed in the preceding text.*

Moving[169] and Summoning with the prayers appropriate for the day together with the Psalmist for the day and the Litany

Call the common invocation in Agrippa for the day of the works and the Angel appropriated to the day commanding the Angel to do his office on that day &c not forgetting the Devil lies to the Crystal naming him in those proper invocation and say that 3 times and though you please in fair time and appearance yet welcome them particularly each one by himself, then the group all welcome

After 7 days performing the above said with fumigations with proper fumes[170] before you begin your work and in the middle also: and faint not.

3 days before the time call 3 times a Day and look toward the part of the world that the planet governs, the proper planet delight in when you invocate the devil

12 hours before the moon is rising or full ask for your desire and at the moment of the asked. (31)

---

[169] The following section to the end of fo.30 is in the second hand. The text is not very coherent or flowing.

[170] I.e. incense fragrances.

Signum Pentaculum Salomonis:

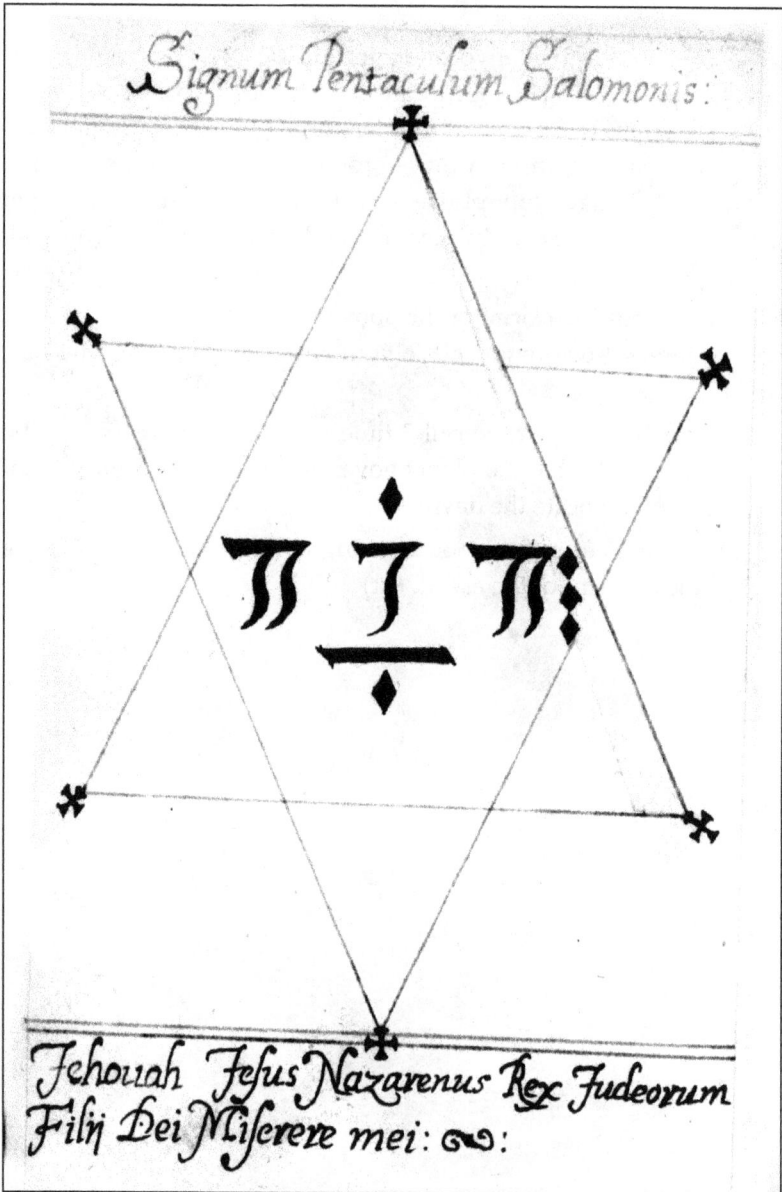

20 - The Sign of the Pentaculum of Solomon, reproduced here in the MS. Below are the words Jehovah Jesus Nazarenus Rex Judeorum Filii Dei Miserere mei:~: Note the stylised Hebrew for Tetragrammaton in the centre (IHVH)

(32)

Read this part of the first Chapter of the
Gospel by Saint John:

1.   **In the beginning** was the word And the word was with God and that word was God.

2.   The same was in the beginning with God.

3.   All things were made by it And without it was made nothing that was made.

4.   In it was life And the life was the light of men.

5.   And the light shined in the darkness And the darkness comprehended it not.

6.   There was a man sent from God whose name was John.

7.   The same came for a witness to bear witness of the light That all men through him might believe.

8.   He was not that light but he was sent to bear witness of the light.

9.   That was the true light which lighteth every man that cometh into the world.

10. He was in the world And the world was made by him And the world knew him not.

11. He came into his own And his own received him not.

12. But as many as received him To them he gave power to be the sons of God even to them that believed in his name.

13. Which are born not of blood Nor of the will of the flesh Nor of the will of man but of God.

14. And the word was made flesh and dwelt amongst us And we saw the glory thereof. As the glory of the only begotten son of God Father Full of Grace and truth.

To whom be all Honour, Glory, Praise, Power, Might, Majesty, Dominion, Rule, And Authority, world without end. **Amen.**

Then read the 91st Psalm:~:

1.   **Whoso dwelleth** under the defence of the most high shall abide under the shadow of the Almighty.

2.   I will say unto the lord Thou art my hope and my stronghold. My God in him will I trust.

3.   For He shall deliver thee from the snare of the Hunter and from the noisome Pestilence.-

4. He shall defend thee under his wings And thou shalt be safe under his feathers His faithfulness and truth shall be they Shield & Buckler.

5. Thou shalt not be afraid for any terror by Night nor for the arrow that flyeth by day.

6. For the Pestilence that walketh in the darkness Nor for the sickness that destroyeth in the noon day.

7. A thousand shall fall before thee and ten Thousand at thy right hand. But they shall not come nigh thee.

8. Yea with thine eyes thou shalt behold and see the reward of the ungodly.

9. For thou lord art my hope. Thou hast set thine House of defence very high.

10. There shall no evil happen unto thee Neither shall any Plague come nigh thy dwelling.

11. For he shall give his Angels charge over thee to keep thee in all thy ways.

12. They shall bear thee in their hands, That thou hurt not thy foot against a stone.

13. Thou shalt go upon the Lion and Adder. The young lion and the Dragon shalt thou tread under thy feet.

14. Because he hath set his love upon me Therefore shall I deliver him I shall set him up because he hath known my Name.

15. He shall call upon me And I will hear him, yea I am with him in trouble. I will deliver him and bring him to Honour.

16. With long life will I satisfy him, And show him my salutation.

Glory be to The Father, And to the Son, And to the Holy Ghost.

As it was in the beginning is now and ever shall be world without end. **Amen.**

(33)

Prayers of Benediction:~:

O most Holy and blessed God pour out here thy mercifulness and vouchsafe by the holiness of your goodness to bless consecrate and sanctify me as thou blesses Abraham Isaac and Jacob. Grant me I beseech thee Almighty God thy blessing to make me holy + God the Father bless me + God the Son bless me + God the Holy Ghost bless me + I beseech the holy and blessed Trinity three persons and one God in unity bless me O Glorious God with thy blessing everlasting +

I beseech thee O merciful lord Jesus Christ Son of the everliving God bless me with thy blessing everlasting. **Amen.**

O most holy and everliving God give me virtue and power to bless sanctify and make me holy by the same lord Jesus Christ and by the coming of the Holy Ghost proceeding from the father and the Son Thou that are three persons and one God in substance to thee I do make my vocation and prayers. Bless me with thy blessing everlasting. **Amen**

Sanctus, Sanctus, Sanctus Dominus, Deus, Sabaoth, Jesus Christ give virtue and power unto me in making the sign of the holy + I may be made holy and sanctified in every operation And by the power of the Holy Ghost which livest and reignest with the Father and the Son one God bless me in this thy work beginning and in all my works now and ever. **Amen.**

O God which art the maker and creator of all things visible and invisible Inspire me with thy blessing Even as thou didst bless all the world So bless O lord I humbly beseech thee And sanctify me thy creature in all holiness and blessed life lauding and praising thee with all thy holy and blessed Angels now and ever. **Amen**

+ Jehovah + Jehovah + Jehovah + The time was which time is. And the time to come + O Adonay + Agla + Tetragrammaton + Lux lux lux + In nomine Patris + Et filii + Et Spiritus Sanctus. + **Amen**

Most Glorious God receive my Prayers. **Amen.**

Signum Pentaculum Salomonis

21 - The Sign of the Pentaculum of Solomon, reproduced again here in the MS. Below are the words Jehovah Jesus Nazarenus Rex Judeorum Filii Dei Miserere mei:~: Note the added names of Pater (Father), Filius (Son) and Spiritus Sanctus (Holy Spirit) around the hexagram and the stylised Hebrew for Tetragrammaton in the centre (IHVH)

Read the: 80: Psalm:~: (34)

1. **Hear oh thou Shepherd of Israel** That thou leddest Joseph like a Sheep show thyself also Thou that sittest upon the Cherubims.

2. Before Ephraim Benjamin and Manasseh stir up thy strength and come and help us.

3. Turn us again O God Show the light of thy countenance and we shall be whole.

4. O Lord God of hosts how long wilt thou be angry with thy people that prayeth.

5. Thou feedest them with the bread of tears and givest them plenteousness of tears to drink.

6. Then hast thou made us a very strife unto our neighbours and our enemies laugh us to scorn.

7. Turn us again thou God of Hosts show the light of thy countenance and we shall be whole.

8. Thou hast brought a vine out of Egypt Thou hast cast out the heathen and planted it.

9. Thou madest room for it and when it had taken root it filled the land.

10. The hills were covered with the shadow of it and the boughs thereof were like the goodly Cedar trees.

11. She stretched out her branches unto the Sea And her boughs unto the river.

12. Why hast thou then broken down her hedge that all they that go by pluck of her Grapes.

13. The wild Boar of the wood doth root it up and the wild beasts of the field devour it.

14. Turn thee again thou God of Hearts look down from Heaven behold and visit this vine.

15. And the place of the vineyard that thy right hand hath planted and the branches that thou madest so strong for thy self.

16. It is burnt with fire and cut down And they shall perish at the rebuke of thy countenance.

17. Let thy hand be upon the man of thy right hand And upon the Son of man whom thou madest so strong for thine own self.

18. And so will not we go back from the[e] O let us live and we shall call upon thy name.

19. Turn us again O Lord God of Hosts show the light of thy countenance and we shall be whole.

Glory be to the Father and to the Son and to the Holy Ghost

As it was in the beginning is now And ever shall be world without end. **Amen.**

The :45: Psalm

1. **My heart is inditing**[171] **of a good matter.** I speak of the things which I have made unto the King.

2. My tongue is the pen of a ready writer.

3. Thou art fairer than the children of men full of grace are thy lips because god hath blessed thee forever.

4. Gird thee with thy Sword upon thy thigh O thou most mighty according to thy worship and renown.

5. Good luck have thou with thine honour. Ride on because of the word of truth of meekness and righteousness and thy right hand shall teach thee terrible things.

6. Thine arrows are very sharp And the people shall be subdued unto thee even in the midst among the King's enemies.

7. Thy seat O Lord endureth forever The sceptre of thy Kingdom is a right sceptre.

8. Thou hast loved righteousness and hated iniquity wherefore God even thy God hath anointed thee with the oil of gladness above thy followers.

9. All thy garments smell of Myrrh Aloes and Cassia out of the Ivory palaces whereby they have made thee glad. (35)

10. King's daughters were among thy honourable women upon thy right hand did stand the Queen in a vesture of Gold wrought about with diverse colours.

11. Hearken O daughter and consider incline thine ear, forget also thine own people and thy father's house.

---

[171] I.e. composing.

12. So shall the king have pleasure in thy beauty for he is thy lord God and worship thou him.

13. And the daughter of Tyre shall be there with a gift like as the rich also among the people shall make her supplications before thee.

14. The King's daughter is all glorious within her clothing of wrought Gold.

15. She brought unto the king in raiment of needlework the virgins that be her fellows shall bear her company and shall be brought unto thee.

16. With joy and gladness shall they be brought and shall enter into the King's palace.

17. Instead of thy fathers thou shalt have children whom thou mayest make princes in all lands.

18. I will remember thy name from one Generation unto another Therefore shall the people give thanks unto thee world without end. **Amen.**

Glory be to the Father, and to the Son, and to the Holy Ghost.

As it was in the beginning is now and ever shall be world without end. **Amen.**

A Prayer whereby to have sight of the Angels:~:

O **Omnipotent** Eternal and incomparable God creator of Heaven and Earth God of all things visible and invisible Most mighty Jehovah By whose mighty power and virtue all things are and have their effects and operations vouchsafe O most mighty Majesty for Jesus Christ his sake my saviour and redeemer In whom I trust And in whose + Incarnation + Holy nativity + Passion + Resurrection + And Glorious Ascension + I thy humble servant + Doth faithfully believe. To forgive me all my sins secret and known And regenerate my heart And replenish my soul with the grace of the Holy Ghost + That I may be made worthy of a most unworthy sinner To see thy holy Angels appearing unto me To minister and to reveal unto me The hidden secret of thy holy and blessed Science Sealed up in the Character of life + Moses thy Prophets and to our ancient fathers whose lives were holy Declaring unto them by holy Angels thy messengers the hidden mysteries of holy Science. Since the beginning of the world's creation for the honour and glory of thy most holy and blessed name, which with thy Seal shuttest up this Secret in the dark bosom of deep oblivion from the nations of the Earth.

Oh most mighty Jehovah whose seat is the highest Heaven and the earth thy footstool My loving lord God and creator, Purify my Soul and Conscience, And rectify my mind and thoughts and mundifie[172] my body Soul and spirits of all Impurities And open unto me (Though unworthy creature) This thy secret mystery And through thy mercy Give unto me an understanding heart Perceiving those things which thou teachest me. O Lord send down the Comforter from above to direct in all truth In this thy infinite treasures. Instruct me in thy holy and blessed Science The which I seek for my comfort and consolation. But not my will but thine be done in all things for the honour and glory of thy most holy and blessed name So my will be ever to fulfil thy will in all things Let therefore O most Glorious God Thy blessing and Benediction come upon me thy creature, Through Jesus Christ thy only begotten son our Lord and only saviour And the Holy Ghost our most sweet comforter. **To whom be** All Honour, Glory, Praise, Power, Might, Majesty, Dominion, Rule, and Authority Ascribed, world without end. **Amen.** (36)

---

[172] An old term meaning "Purify".

Signum Pentaculum Salomonis

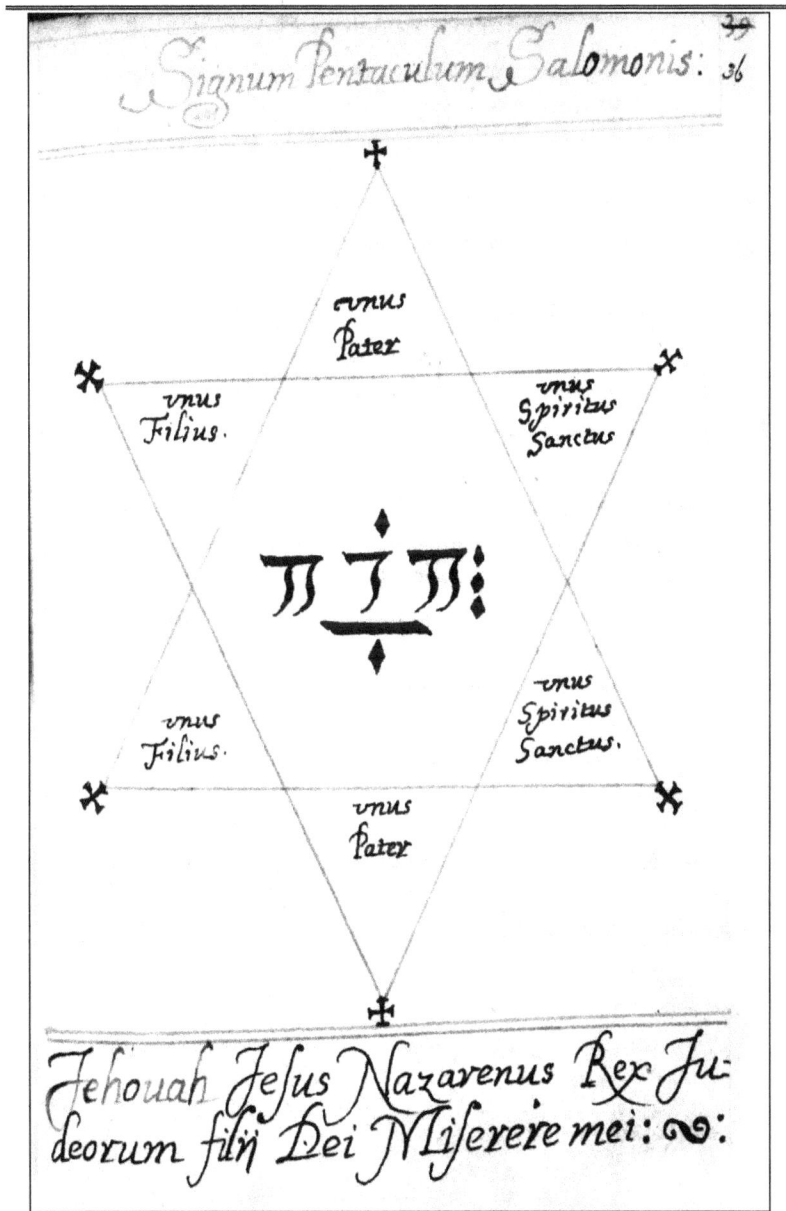

Signum Pentaculum Salomonis:

✠

unus Pater

unus Filius.

unus Spiritus Sanctus

יְהֹוָה

unus Filius.

unus Spiritus Sanctus.

unus Pater

✠

Jehouah Jesus Nazarenus Rex Judeorum filij Dei Miserere mei:~:

22 - The Sign of the Pentaculum of Solomon, the third version in the MS. Below are the words Jehovah Jesus Nazarenus Rex Judeorum Filii Dei Miserere mei:~: Note the added names of unus Pater (one Father), unus Filius (one Son) and unus Spiritus Sanctus (one Holy Spirit) around the hexagram. This is clearly a sequence with additional words in each version of the Pentaculum.

Read this part of the first Chapter of the
Gospel by Saint Luke:~:

26. **The Angel Gabriel** was sent from God unto a city in Galilee named Nazareth.

27. To a virgin affianced to a man whose name was Joseph of the house of David. And the virgin's name was Mary.

28. And the Angel went in unto her and said Hail thou that art freely beloved the lord is with thee Blessed art thou amongst women.

29. And when she saw him she was troubled at his saying and thought what manner of salutation that should be.

30. Then the Angel said unto her fear not Mary for thou hast found favour with God.

31. For Lo thou shalt conceive in thy womb and bear a son And shalt call his name, Jesus.

32. He shall be great And shall be called the son of the most high and the lord God shall give unto him the throne of his father David.

33. And he shall reign over the house of Jacob forever and of his kingdom shall be none end.

34. Then said Mary unto the Angel how shall this be seeing I know not man.

35. And the Angel answered and said unto her. The Holy Ghost shall come upon thee and the power of the most high shall overshadow thee Therefore also that holy thing which shall be born of thee shall be called the Son of God.

38. Then Mary said Behold the handmaid of the lord Be it unto me according to thy word.

46. My soul doth magnify the lord and my spirit hath rejoiced in God my saviour.

47. For he hath regarded the lowliness of his Handmaiden.

48. For behold from henceforth all Generations shall call me blessed.

49. For he that is mighty hath magnified me And holy is his name. (37)

50. And his mercy is on them that fear him throughout all Generations.

51.   He hath showed strength with his arm He hath scattered the proud in the Imagination of their Hearts.

52.   He hath put down the mighty from their seat and hath exalted the humble and meek.

53.   He hath filled the hungry with good things And the rich he hath sent empty away.

54.   He remembering his mercy hath helped his servant Israel as he promised to our forefathers Abraham and his seed forever.

Glory be to The Father, And to the Son, And to the Holy Ghost.

As it was in the beginning is now and ever shall be world without end. **Amen.**

The :103: Psalm

1.   **Praise the Lord** O my soul and all that is within me Raise his holy name.

2.   Praise the lord O my soul and forget not his benefits.

3.   Which forgiveth all thy sins And healeth all thine infirmities.

4.   Which saveth thy life from destruction and crowneth thee with mercy and loving kindness.

5.   Which satisfieth thy mouth with good things making thee young and[173] lusty as an Eagle.

6.   The lord executeth righteousness and Judgement for all them that are oppressed with wrong.

7.   He showed his ways unto Moses his works unto the Children of Israel.

8.   The lord is full of compassion and mercy long suffering and of great goodness.

9.   He will not always be chiding Neither keepeth he his anger for ever.

10.   He hath not dealt with us after our sins Nor rewarded us according to our wickedness.

11.   For look how high the Heaven is in comparison of the Earth. So great is his mercy also toward them that fear him.

---

[173] 'And' is repeated here.

12. Look how wide also the East is from the west. So far hath he set out sins from us.

13. Yea look as a father pitieth his own children Even so is the lord merciful to them that fear him.

14. For he knoweth whereof we be made He remembreth that we are but dust.

15. The days of man are but as Grass for he flourisheth as flowers of the field.

16. For as soon as the wind goeth over It is gone The place thereof shall know it no more.

17. But the merciful goodness of the lord endureth for ever and ever upon them that fear him And his righteousness upon children's children.

18. Even upon such as keep his covenant And think upon his commandments to do them.

19. The lord hath prepared his seat in Heaven And his Kingdom ruleth over all.

20. O praise the lord ye Angels of his that excel in strength ye that fulfil his commandments And hearken unto the voice of his word.

21. O praise the lord all ye his Hosts ye servants of his that do his pleasure.

22. O speak good of the lord all ye works of his in all places of his dominion. Praise thou the lord O my soul.

Glory be to The Father and to the Son And to the Holy Ghost.

As it was in the beginning is now and ever shall be world without end. **Amen.**

Te deum laudamus:~:[174]

We praise thee O God we knowledge thee to be the Lord.

All the Earth doth worship thee the father everlasting.

To thee all Angels cry aloud The heavens and all the powers therein.

---

[174] We praise thee O God (latin), an early Christian hymn of praise from the 4th century which was adopted by the Roman Catholic church.

To thee Cherubim and Seraphim continually do cry.

Holy Holy Holy Lord God of Sabaoth.

Heaven and Earth are full of the majesty of thy glory.

The Glorious company of the Apostles praises thee.

The goodly fellowship of the Prophets praises thee. (38)

The noble Army of Martyrs Praise thee.

The holy Church throughout all the world doth knowledge thee.

The father of an infinite Majesty.

The Honourable true and only Son.

Also the Holy Ghost the Comforter.

Thou art the King of Glory O Christ

Thou art the everlasting Son of the father.

When thou tookest upon thee to deliver man Thou didst not abhor the virgin's womb.

When thou hadst overcome the sharpness of death Thou didst open the Kingdom of Heaven to all believers.

Thou sittest on the right hand of God In the Glory of the father.

We believe that thou shall come to be our Judge.

We therefore pray thee help thy servants whom thou hast redeemed with thy precious blood.

Make them to be numbered with thy saints in glory everlasting.

O Lord Save thy People And bless thine Heritage.

Govern them and lift them up forever.

Day by day we magnify thee

And we worship thy name ever world without end.

Vouchsafe O Lord to keep us this day without sin

O Lord have mercy upon us Have mercy upon us.

O Lord let thy mercy light upon us as our trust is in thee.

O Lord in thee have we trusted let us never be confounded.

Glory be to The Father And to the Son And to the Holy Ghost.

As it was in the beginning Is now and ever shall be world without end. **Amen.**

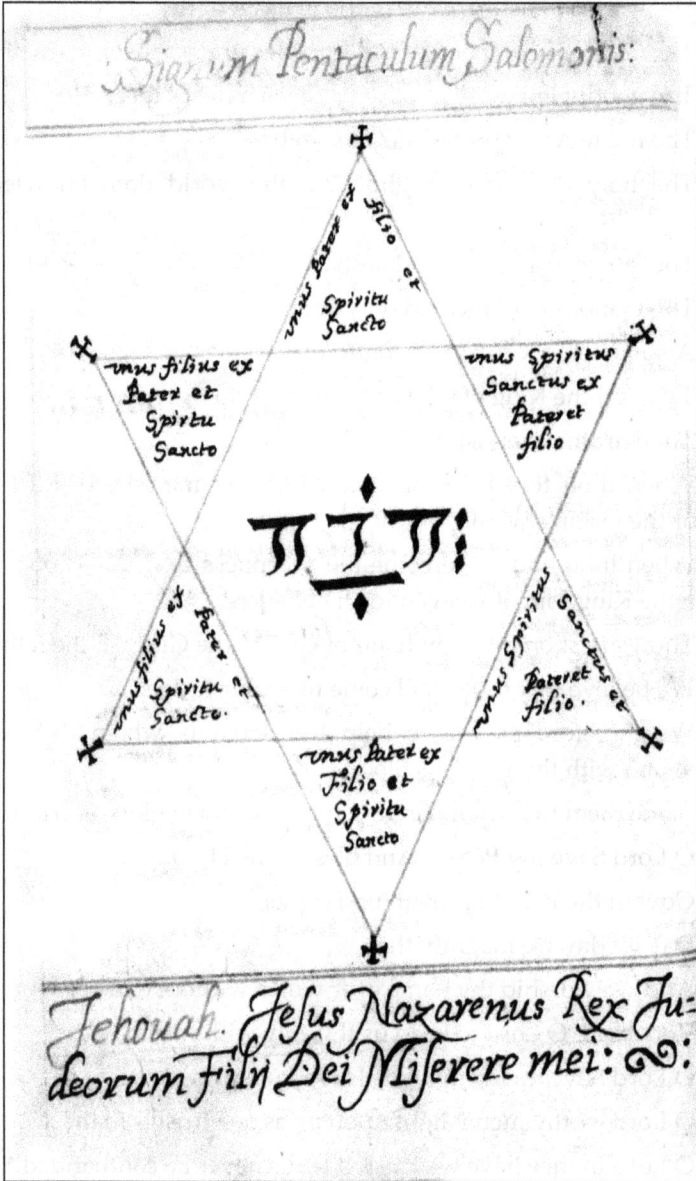

23 - *The Sign of the Pentaculum of Solomon. Below are the words Jehovah Jesus Nazarenus Rex Judeorum Filii Dei Miserere mei:~: The fourth in the series of images in the MS, with each edge triangle now containing a permutation of the Latin unus with Pater & Filio/us & Spiritu/s Sanctu/s*

(39)

To call three good Angels into a Crystal Stone or looking Glass to thine own sight do as followeth

First bless thyself, Saying In the name of the Father + and of the Son + And of the Holy Ghost. + **Amen.** ~

Then devoutly say this prayer following on thy knees.

Let me be lightened O Lord God Almighty which said let light be made and it was done. Oh Holy and most Holy Lord God + The Father + The Son + And the Holy Ghost + The Spirit living I **A** do beseech thee to let there be so much light Only and Only sufficient light that I **A** may see and not be set O holy Lord God give unto me thy unworthy servant power to see Three of thy good Angels in this Crystal Stone (or Glass) Sweet Jesu give me wisdom and Grace to see – Almighty Father and everliving king of all Glory which didst send the Holy Ghost upon the Apostles, vouchsafe to send thy holy Spirit upon me And with thy holy hand bless me Open my senses that I may see thy holy Angels. Only and only blessed which hast created me to thine own Image and likeness And redeemed me with the precious blood of thy dear Son Give me grace and power to see Three of thy good Angels in this Stone which may show unto me the truth of all such questions as I shall demand. Grant this O heavenly father for Jesus Christ his sake To whom with the Holy Ghost be all honour and Glory now and forever more. **Amen.**

Then say as followeth. O you good Angels of God Only and Only come hastily and tarry not make your personal appearance visibly to my sight in this Crystal Stone. In the name of our Lord Jesus Christ wheresoever you be In Heaven In Earth in the firmament Or else wheresoever. Come hither in fair Angel's form and shape Enter into this Crystal so bright and clear That I may perceive and see you. Come + In the name of the Father + The Son + And the Holy Ghost + and tarry not. Come. Come. Come.

This must be repeated 3 times **If** they appear not at the first or 2.

When they are appeared, Say, O you good Angels of God welcome are you In the worship of the blessed Trinity praying and desiring you to show me the truth of all such questions as I shall demand of you And nothing but the truth as you will answer it at the day of doom before your God and mine.

Then make your demands And when you have had what you desire, Say, You good Angels we thank you And licence you to depart for this time Being prest[175] and ready to come again whensoever I shall call you. Go in peace + In the name of the Father + And of the Son + And of the Holy Ghost + Amen. ~:

You may call the Angels to yourself according to the method of the next Experiment altering very little As you may perceive by the Latin Prayer following.[176]

O Domine Jesu Christe Rex Glorie per virtutem illorum qui hoc nomen **Hermelie**[177] invocant Et per potestam et miserecordeam tuam Domine mitte mihi indignum familum tuum Tres Angelos bonos veros iustos optimos et excelentissimos Angelos tuos veretatis Ex parte tua dextera in mediumistius speculi advisum mihi indignum familum tuum verum iudicum apariant mihi et verum iuditium faciant mihi de re nobis dubeo et in certa absqe aliquo dolo vel frauda: **Amen:~:**[178]

All experiments of this nature That are to call Angels into a Stone or Glass If they be to call them to thyself Thou mayest call them to a Child only changing the words as you see before. So likewise the contrary &c. (40)

How to call Three Heavenly Angels into A Crystal Stone or Looking Glass to the visible sight of A Child:~:

First Say this Prayer. O Lord God Almighty most merciful father and King of Heaven which hast created all things In Heaven, Earth, Hell and elsewhere which wast before all worlds and art Permanent And after the world continues forever, O Holy Father I beseech thee for Jesus Christ his sake thy dear and only Son <u>our Lord</u> To send unto me Three of thy good Angels from thy right

---

[175] An old word meaning 'prompt' in this context.

[176] This is the prayer said to have been copied by John a Windor from one of Dr John Dee's books. See Sloane MS 3846 fo.113v-114.

[177] Probably a corruption of Hermes, the Greek god associated with magic.

[178] "O Lord Jesus Christ, King, Glorious through the excellence of those who invoke this name Hermelie. And by your power and compassion, Lord, send me, thy unworthy servant, three Angels good, true, legitimate, your best and most excellent Angels in truth, from the division on your right to appear in the middle of this mirror unto me, thy unworthy servant. May they uncover true judgement for me regarding things of ours that I doubt and anything that may in certainty cause grief or loss. Amen."

hand of Glory. True sayers and speakers visible to appear in this Crystal Stone (or Glass) to the visible sight of this Child Maid and virgin And to show us the truth of all such questions as we shall demand. Grant this O Lord God Almighty which livest and Reignest ever one God world without end. **Amen.**

Then make a Cross on the forehead of the Child with the Thumb of thy right Hand **Saying** (pater noster: credo: ave)[179]

In nomine Patris et filii et Spiritus Sanctus **Amen**

Then with a new Pen write on the midst[180] of the Stone or Glass with Oil Olive this name. **Hermelys.**

Then set the Child between thy legs Thou sitting in a Chair And let him say after thee, **The** Lord's Prayer **The** Belief **And** These names following + On + El(l) + Eloy + Eley + Messias + Sother + Emanuell + Sabaoth + In the name of the Father + And of the Son + And of the Holy Ghost + Amen. ~. **Then say to thyself this Prayer following.~.** O Lord Jesus Christ King of Glory by virtue of those whom they call Hermely and by thy power and mercy Send unto us Three of thy good Angels from thy right hand of Glory Into the midst of this Crystal Stone (or Glass) To the visible Sight of this Child maid and virgin Let them make true answers True Judgement and true appearance Revealing unto us all things doubtful and uncertain without all falsehood fraud or deceit Grant this Sweet Jesus I most humbly pray and beseech thee **Amen**

This last Prayer must be repeated three times If the Angels appear not at the first or second time **Then shall you see** Three bright Angels with Crowns of Gold on their Heads appear to the Child who will answer And show thee by the Child anything thou shalt require. **But when they are appeared say as followeth.~**

You Angels of God welcome are ye in the worship of the blessed and Glorious Trinity praying and desiring that you will show unto us the truth of all such questions and things as we shall this day ask or demand of you Let them be answered faithfully justly and truly without all fraud guile deceit or delay As you shall

---

[179] These words are added here in a different hand, the second one found through the MS.

[180] I.e. middle.

answer the contrary at the dreadful day of Doom before your God and mine you Angels of God let us have the truth And nothing but the truth In the name of Jesus.

Then make your demands as shall be shown you hereafter.

But If you mistrust them to be false Angels say as followeth

If you be lying false and untrue Angels which are come to delude and mock us The Servants of the everliving God, Cursed be you before the Majesty of God, And the Malediction and curse of God the Father God the Son And God the Holy Ghost be upon you And every one of you To blaspheme Curse and excommunicate you and every one of you Into everlasting pains of Hellfire presently and immediately unless you depart and trouble us no more + fiat + fiat + fiat + So be it + Amen + In nomine Patris + et filii + et Spiritus Sanctus + Amen ~:

When they are departed As if they be false Angels they will then say the former prayer again Three times if need be.

If they be true Angels They will not depart. (41)

These Angels being once appeared will not depart the Glass or Stone until the Sun be set **Except** you licence them **Therefore** If you call them at the Sun Rising they will all that day be ready to answer your demands until the Sun setting of the same day.

The prayer is usually Said in Latin As it now followeth[181]

O Domine Jesu Christe Rex Glorie per vertutem illorum qui hoc nomen **Hermelie** invocant Et per potestam et miserecordeam tuam Domine Mitte nobis tres Angelos bonos veros iustos optimos et excelentissimos Angelos tuos veretatis Ex parte tua dextera mediumistius Speculi advisum istius Pueri virginis verum iudicum apareant, et verum iuditium faciant isto puero virgini de re nobis dubeo et in certa absque alique dolo vell frauda: + **Amen:~:**[182]

---

[181] This is the same prayer as seen several paragraphs previously.

[182] "O Lord Jesus Christ, King, Glorious through the excellence of those who invoke this name Hermelie. And by your power and compassion, Lord, send me three Angels good, true, legitimate, your best and most excellent Angels in truth, from the division on your right to appear in the middle of this mirror unto me, by this son of a virgin. May they uncover true judgement by this son of a virgin, regarding things of ours that I doubt and anything that may in certainty cause grief or loss. Amen."

You may work the former Experiment To call the Angels to yourself by this Experiment Only altering the Plural number to the Singular As you may perceive by the Latin prayers Both which Prayers only differ in that **If thou have the gift to have sight thyself it is a Blessing That God giveth to very few But to those that haveth it in their infancy And those often time lose it again**[183] But Prayer and a good belief prevaileth much For faith is the Key to this and all other works And without it nothing can be effected.

The Child should not be above 12 years of Age when you enter him or her[184] For you may work as well with a Maid child as with a boy.

When you have called either Angel or spirit Except you presently send them about some speedy business you must license them to depart As your Spirit of Prophecy and such like when you call for them to have long conference with them.

How you shall make your demands to the Three Angels And first for a Friend:~:~:

You Angels of God There is a friend of mine called AB of C in the Country of D that I have not seen nor heard of a long time Tell us ye Angels of God how he doth whether he be in health or not Or whether he be dead or alive Then they will tell you Then you may say you Angels of God show us the said AB what he is doing whether he be in House or field or in what place he is and what he is now doing Show us the truth in the name of Jesus. Then they will show you but they will name no place Except you name it first Therefore make your demands thus you Angels of God tell us truly In the name of the holy and blessed Trinity how far off is the place where this AB is Is it 5, 6, 7, 8, 10, 20, &c miles off Tell us in the name of God Then they will tell you Then say is it East, west, North or South from this place Then they will tell you Then say is it such a place They will answer it is or it is not If they say it is not name some other place &c till you have named it and they have told you it is the place. They will show the Child The Town House Sign if it have any, the very room and what furniture Pictures &c is in the room And what else you will demand.

---

[183] This section seems to be aimed at justifying the use of young children as the skryers, a common practice since the times of ancient Egypt.

[184] Into a circle.

How you shall make your demands for Theft to the Three Angels

You Angels of God Show unto us the truth of this question In the name of the Holy Blessed and Glorious Trinity. AB of C In the country of D Had his house broken up and lost such and such things Or lost such and such things from such a place upon such a day &c. You Angels of God show us the Thief or Thieves that stole these Goods. Then they will show the Thief or Thieves That the Child shall tell you of what Complexion what Stature, what apparel, And what blemish any of them have &c. If you will know their dwelling you must examine as before, whether East, W. N, or South &c. Likewise you may demand what where and how they have bestowed the Goods &c. (42)

For Treasure hidden:~:

You must have A Turf or a piece of the Earth where you mistrust Treasure to be hidden. Having the Turf or piece of earth in your Hand, **Say**

You Angels of God Tell us truly in the name of the Holy Blessed and Glorious Trinity whether In the Ground (or Room) from whence this Turf (or piece of earth) was taken There be any treasure hidden or not Tell us truly in the name of Jesus. If they say there is, Then say **you Angels of God** Tell us truly what it is whether it be Coin Plate Jewels Books Household stuff or what it is They having told you say you Angels of God tell us truly whether it lie just under where this Turf was taken up or how far from that place a foot, 2, 3, 4, 5, 10, 20 foot or how far They having told you Say you Angels of God Show us the place and Open the Ground and show us in what fashion it lyeth and what it is All which they will show. Also how deep it lyeth &c.

In this manner you must work for Coals, Lead, Tin, Iron, Copper mines &c. They will tell you how deep and how the colours of Earth will alter in every foot, 2 or 3, &c. For these and such like this will suffice.

For Cattle that are Stolen or Strayed away:

You Angels of God upon such a day naming the day, AB of C in the County of D lost such and such cattle naming them forth of a Ground called E within the foresaid parish of C from whence they were Stolen or are strayed If you cannot name the day certain when they were lost Name the day when they were last seen And the day they were missed and proceed as before. **Tell us you Angels of God.** In the name of the Holy Blessed and Glorious Trinity what are become of these cattle are they Stolen or Strayed. They will tell you Then say how far off are they one mile, 2, 3, 5, 10, or 20 miles Or how many miles off are they They having told you Say Is it East, W, N, or South they will tell you Then say is it such a place &c As is before sufficiently taught Then Say you Angels of God Show us the Party or Parties that hath Stolen these Cattle (If they be Stolen) If they be not Stolen Call to see the place where they are &c, But how to make them return home again shall be shown hereafter.

For Sickness:~:

You Angels of God There is a Man called by the name of AB dwelling in the Town of C in the Parrish of D dwelling in Such a street in the said town of C being of such a Trade or Profession. (Or There is a woman called by the name of EB, the wife of AB dwelling in the Parrish of C in the County of D, being of such a Trade or Profession.)

This AB Is dangerously sick he complains of extreme pain in his Side, his Back, his Belly, &c (Or he was taken lame in his Legs, Arms, or in such and such members.) **Tell us you Angels of God** whether this AB shall live or die. If they say he shall Die Ask how long it will be &c. If they say he (or she) shall recover Ask whether you shall do it and whether it must be done by Physick or not If they say by Physick First ask what disease it is naming what disease you think it is Till you have found it Then whether such a Medicine will recover him or not If they say it will not name some other That you know to be fit for the disease &c Till you have found what will do it then ask how long it shall be before he shall be recovered &c

If they say he may be recovered without Physick Say you Angels of God help us to such a principal Angel or Spirits as shall recover this AB and tell me you Angels of God In how long time he will do it Then they will tell you And the Angel or Spirit will appear to the Child If it be an Angel that appeareth say as followeth **Thou Angel of God** welcome art thou In the worship of the holy Lord of Heaven And the blessed and Glorious Trinity Praying and desiring thee That thou wilt recover and perfectly make whole AB of C, In the County of D, of such a profession who is grieviously tormented, Pained or Grieved, &c In such and such a part of his body And hath been so this long &c Thou Angel of God do this that I have said faithfully Justly and truly without all fraud guile deceit or delay by such a time (Naming the time the Angels before told you) As you shall answer to the contrary at the dreadful day of Doom before your God and mine. **Then say** Thou good Angel of God wilt thou do this thing for me faithfully Justly and truly. He will (43) Then say Thou Angel of God In token that thou wilt do this thing for me Cross thy Hands and kiss them and Swear it by the mighty power of the great God of Heaven. That being done Say **Thou good Angel of God,** At this time I do licence thee to depart **In the name** of the Father, And of the Son And of the Holy Ghost so be it **Amen.** If it be a Spirit that Appear Thou must bind him as followeth.

How you shall bind a Spirit for diverse Purposes As first for this last Experiment for Sickness or Lameness.

The first part of the Bond:~:

Thou Spirit here appeared Open thine Ears and hear and be obedient and do my will faithfully Justly and truly without all fraud Guile deceit or delay upon pain and peril of they present and everlasting damnation. I the servant of the everliving God the maker and Creator of all things visible and invisible, I do bind thee charge thee and command thee Thou Spirit By the mighty power of God the Father, God the Son, And God the Holy Ghost Being three persons in Trinity And but one God in unity, which thou knowest is the power of all powers And the sum of all things By all that this our God and Heavenly father is able to do which thou knowest is all in all nothing impossible unto him And by thy head and ruler and by all that thou art subject unto I bind thee charge thee and command thee Thou Spirit upon pain and peril of thy present and everlasting damnation.

For Sickness or Lameness:~:

That thou doest without all fraud guile deceit or delay do all that lyeth in thy power to the uttermost To recover the health of AB of C, In the County of D &c who is grieviously pained (naming his grief) Thou shalt I say recover perfectly the health of AB without all fraud guile deceit or delay by such A time upon pain and peril of thy present and everlasting damnation.

The latter part of the Bond:

I do bind thee hereunto Thou Spirit that this be faithfully Justly and truly done and performed By Heaven by Earth by Hell by the Sea and by all the virtues and powers therein contained And by the mighty Infinite and incomprehensible power whereby God the Father did make and create Heaven Earth Hell Sea thee me and all Creatures And I beseech the living God the maker and creator of all things visible and Invisible That thou mayest be confounded deprived degraded dedignified and cast out from the state office and dignity that thou now standest in Into everlasting pains of Hellfire presently and immediately unless thou doest fulfil my commandment in all respects as I have said. So be it. **Fiat fiat fiat +** In Nomine Patris + Et filii + Et Spiritus Sanctus +

How you shall call for a Spirit of Prophecy

The Three Angels being Invocated Say **You Angels of God** I do charge you In the name of the Holy Blessed and Glorious Trinity that you fetch me hither a principal Spirit of Prophecy, That may faithfully justly and truly tell me of all things that is past And of all things that is done at this present And of all things that are to come whatsoever I shall demand of him Let him be as mighty an Angel or Spirit of Prophecy as any of the Prophets had in former times.

Being appeared If it be an Angel give him his welcome and invocate him as before. **If it be a Spirit say the first part of the bond as before** Thou Spirit of Prophecy here appeared open thine Ears and hear &c. **Reading the first part of the Bond. Then say** That thou be ready prest faithfully justly and truly to tell me all such things as I shall ask or demand of you Either of things Past Things present or Things to come without all fraud guile deceit or delay upon pain and peril of thy present and everlasting damnation **Then read the latter part of the bond as before** I do bind thee hereunto thou Spirit of Prophecy &c **Concluding with** So be it. **Fiat, fiat, fiat.** Amen. + In nomine Patris + Et Filii + Et Spiritus Sanctus + amen + (44)

To cause Cattle to return to the Place from whence they were Strayed or Stolen.

You having made your demands to the Angels as before said, Say **you Angels of God** bring us such a principal Spirit As may cause these Cattle to return to the place from whence they were strayed Stolen or went away And tell us in what time he shall do it They having told you and brought the Spirit into the Glass bind him, viz **Thou Spirit here appeared &c** Reading out the first part of the Bond Then say, **That thou dost presently** look out such and such Cattle being the Goods of AB of C in the County of D, That were Stolen Strayed or went away out of a Ground or Common &c called E, On such a day or night Or they were seen such a day And were missed such a day between which two days they were gone forth of the foresaid Ground called E. Thou shalt seek out these Cattle wheresoever they Be upon the face of the whole Earth Thou shalt not suffer Hedge Ditch nor no enclosure whatsoever to stay these Cattle until thou hast brought them unto the place from whence they were Stolen Strayed or went away Thou shalt do all this that I have said by such a time **Then read the latter part of the Bond.** I do bind thee hereunto thou Spirit &c.

To cause a Thief to bring stolen Goods again:

Having made your demands to the Angels And the Spirit appeared and the first part of the Bond pronounced Say as followeth.

That thou dost presently go to the Thief that hath stolen such and such things being the Goods of AB in C in the County of D, And were stolen from such a part of his House being in the same Town of C, On such a day. Thou shalt I say go presently and Immediately unto the Thief that hath stolen these Goods And thou shalt so haunt him So vex him And so torment him with such Ugly Odious fearful and most dreadful sights and apparitions As if Twenty Devils in the likeness of Rampaging Lions and Roaring Bears were always haunting and following him as if they were carrying him away In such Horrible fearful and Dreadful Sights Hauntings and apparitions That no creature is able to endure or behold Then shalt so vex him both in body and mind not suffering him to take any rest, Eating Drinking Sleeping waking Playing working Or whatsoever until such time thou Cause him to bring the Stolen goods again unto the place from whence they were stolen. Or to such a place &c Thou shalt force this thief to do so by such a time. **Then say the latter part of the Bond** I do bind thee hereunto thou Spirit &c.

To cause one that is run away to return:

The Angels Invocated, your demands Answered The Spirit appeared And the first part of the Bond repeated say as followeth.

That thou dost presently and immediately look out AB being the Son of CB of D in the County of E, And was servant to FG of H in the County of J of Such a Trade, Or of such a Profession who ran away from his Master upon such a day And hath carried away such and such things with him, Or went away from his wife on such a day &c, Or hath done such an exploit and is fled &c. **Thou shalt** seek out the said AB wheresoever he shall be upon the face of the whole Earth Thou shalt so haunt him vex him and torment him with such Ugly Odious fearful and dreadful sights and apparitions As if Twenty Devils in the likeness of Romping Lions or Roaring Bears were always haunting and following him as if they were carrying him away with such horrible fearful and dreadful hauntings and apparitions that no creature is able to endure or behold Then shalt so vex him both in body and mind not suffering him to take any ease rest or quiet day nor Night Eating Drinking Sleeping waking Playing working Or whatsoever until such time that thou cause him to return to the place he went away from And to bring those things with him again that he carried with him &c.

Thou shalt do all this that I have said faithfully Justly and truly without all fraud guile deceit or delay So that this thing may be effected and performed by such a time **Then say the latter part of the Bond**

By this that is already said may easily be perceived how to make demands for any Experiment witchcraft excepted which now shall follow. (45)

How you shall work for witchcraft:~:

If it be for one particular person Say **You Angels of God** There is a Man or woman called AB of C In the County of D, That upon such a day was suddenly taken In such and such manner. (Naming the time and the manner of the party's sickness And the place it took him in if it may be known) Tell us you Angels of God what was the cause of this man's Sickness or infirmity, was it witchcraft Y[es] or no. If they say it was witchcraft Then say **you Angels of God** In the name of the Holy Blessed and Glorious Trinity I charge you to call us the witch or witches with their assistants by what name or title soever they are called –which doth molest and trouble AB of C &c Call them I say into this Glass **They** being appeared say as followeth If there be but one witch and one Spirit.

O thou cursed and damned witch And thou Spirit of witchcraft and sorcery assistant to this hellish and cursed Creature by what name or title soever thou art called which dost hale pull terrify and torment the body carcass and limbs of AB of C in the County of D &c Open your ears and hear and be obedient and do my will faithfully justly and truly without all fraud guile deceit or delay upon pain and peril of your present and everlasting damnations. I the servant of the everliving God the maker and creator of all things visible and invisible, I do bind you Charge you and command you And each of you severally and jointly by the mighty Power of God the Father, God the Son, And God the Holy Ghost being three persons in Trinity and but one God in unity which you do know is the power of all powers and the sum of all things By all that this our God and Heavenly father is able to do which you know is all in all And nothing impossible unto him And by your heads and Rulers and by all that you are subject unto I do bind you charge you and command you and either of you upon pain and peril of your present and everlasting damnations That you nor neither of you neither that any other wicked witch Spirit or Fairie for you by you or by your means do at any time hereafter to the end of the world meddle or make any more or any farther at all in any kind of respect with AB of C in the County of D, but that you let this poor Christian man AB be in peace quiet and rest without any vexations molestations hurts Griefs Gripings takings hailings pullings Headache Stomachache Bellyache Backache Boneache Limbache Tremblings quivering Shakings Heatings Burnings Prickings Shootings Ragings purges pains Griefs Lamings Swellings Pinings Confusings Killings Tortures Torments Stitches Temptations vexations molestations hurts or damages in any sort or wise howsoever. I do bind you charge you and command you and either of you severally and jointly hereunto by Heaven by Earth by Hell by the Sea and by all the virtues and powers therein contained And furthermore I bind you severally and Jointly by the mighty infinite and incomprehensible power whereby God the Father did make and create Heaven Earth Hell Sea you me and all creatures That thou dost restore the health unto AB which you gave not That is to say That every part and parcel of the body head and stomach of AB whatsoever you or either of you have impaired the healthful state of by any kind of ways or means whatsoever may be made presently perfectly whole and well in all kind of respects, By such a time. And I beseech the living God the maker and Creator of all things visible and Invisible that you and either of you may be confounded deprived disgraced dedignified and cast out from the state office and dignity that you now stand in Into everlasting pain of Hellfire presently and immediately unless you do fulfil my commandment In all respects as I have said. So be it

Fiat fiat fiat Amen + In nomine Patris + &c

But if it be for a family and Cattle where there are more witches than one and many Spirit then work as followeth and say, **You Angels of God** There is a man Called by the name of AB of C in the County of D and also E wife to the foresaid AB and F the Son of AB &c, Also such and such of his servants &c Also his Cattle dieth **Naming** the manner of their sickness **As also** the like of their Cattle &c and say **you Angels of God** Tell us in the name of (46) The Holy Blessed and Glorious Trinity what is the Cause of these harms that hath happened to this AB and his family and his Cattle Is it witchcraft ye or no If they say witchcraft, you may ask if you will how many of the witches And for what cause &c Then call as is before taught for the witches and their assistants. If you please you make speak to her the prime witch that was the setter on of the rest to stand by herself &c All being answered And the witches with their assistants appeared, Say **O you cursed and Damned witches** And you Spirits of witchcraft and sorcery Assistants to these Hellish and cursed creatures And you fairie spirits Elves or Pygmies Or by what other Style, name, Title or Addition soever you are called which do hale pull terrify and torment The body Carcass and limbs of AB of C &c And also of E his wife &c **Open your Ears** and hear and be obedient and do my will faithfully justly and truly without all fraud guile deceit or delay upon pain and peril of your present and everlasting damnations. I the servant of the everliving God the maker and creator of all things visible and Invisible I do bind you charge you and command you and every one of you severally and jointly by the mighty power of God the Father God the Son and God the Holy Ghost being Three persons in Trinity And but one God in unity which you do know is the power of all powers and the sum of all things. By all that this our God and Heavenly father is able to do which you do know is all in all and that there is no thing impossible unto him And by your Heads and rulers And all that you are subject unto I do bind you charge you and command you And everyone of you severally and jointly upon pain and peril of your present and everlasting damnation That you nor none of you neither that any other wicked witch Spirit or Fairie for you by you or either of you or by your means do at any time hereafter to the end of the world Meddle or make any more or any further at all In any kind of respect with AB of C &c either with his wife his Children his Servants his Goods his Cattle That is to say with any of his Housebeasts his Oxen His Kine his Bullocks his Sheep his Lambs or any thing unto him appertaining throughout the whole lot of his inheritance but that you let them be in peace quiet and rest without any vexations molestations hurts Griefs Gripings takings hailings pullings Headaches Stomachaches Bellyaches Backaches boneaches limbaches Tremblings quivering Shakings heatings burnings prickings shootings ragings pangs pains griefs Lamings swellings pinings confusing killings tortures torments Stitches Temptations vexations hurts or damages In any sort or wise howsoever **I do bind you** charge you and command you and every one of you Severally and jointly hereunto by Heaven by Earth by Hell by the Sea by all the virtues and powers therein contained **and furthermore I bind you** and every one of you Severally and Jointly by the mighty infinite and incomprehensible power whereby God the Father did make and create Heaven Earth Hell Sea me and all creatures **That** you do restore the health unto the said AB, his wife children his Servants his Goods his Cattle That you gain not So that the said AB, his wife his Children his Servants his Goods his Cattle whatsoever you or any of you have impaired the healthful state of may be made presently and perfectly whole and well in all kind of respects, By such a time, **And I beseech the everliving God** The maker and creator of all things visible and invisible that you and every one of you may be confounded deprived degraded de-dignified and cast out from the State office and dignity that you now stand in Into everlasting pains of Hellfire presently and immediately unless you do fulfil my commandments In all respects as I have said. So be it. **Amen. Fiat fiat fiat** + In nomine Patris + et filii + et Spiritus Sanctus + Amen (47)

How you shall work to have sight and conference with one Good Angel

Say as followeth. Our help is in the lord and in his holy name O lord hear our prayers. The lord is with us **Amen**. So be it. +

We will not fear nor be sorrowful because god is our father **Let us** fear the Lord our God and reverence him only + To whom be all honour virtue power and Glory both now and evermore **Amen** + For + **Whosoever** calleth upon the name of the Lord shall be saved. +. So be it **& then say** the Lord's Prayer **And** the Creed. **Then as followeth ~**

I call upon thee and Invocate thee O Omnipotent God which art King of all things Eternal Governor of all the world uncorrupt unspotted undefiled Invisible wonderful most faultless inreprehensible Almighty ruler Great and holy + Adonay + Eloy + Sabaoth + God of Gods and father of all Glories and most renowned virtues The truth itself High King father of our Lord and Saviour Jesus Christ Give thy benediction and blessing unto me thy humble servant **AG** And to all things that I take in hand to bring to pass at this time Through thy most Holy and blessed name + Grant this O Heavenly father for Jesus Christ his sake thy only Son And our only saviour To whom with the Holy Ghost be all Honour Glory praise power might majesty Rule Dominion and Authority world without end. **Amen. Then say**

Look upon me thy humble servant I beseech thee O my Lord God and Saviour Jesus Christ And have mercy upon me thy humble servant I humbly beseech thee. Thou art my helper and my refuge O Lord + Jesus + Christ + In thee only have I trusted and in no other neither will at any time hereafter trust in any other besides thee. Help me therefore O most mighty God which art + Alpha + et ω + The first and the last whose virtue and aid I most humbly desire and heartily require Have mercy upon me O my God have mercy upon me and bless me with thy blessing everlasting. **Amen.**

+ In nomine Patris + Et filii + Et Spiritus Sanctus +Amen

Most Glorious God receive my Prayer. Amen.

O Omnipotent and unresistable Jehovah who by the death of thy natural Son Our blessed Saviour Jesus Christ didst break the head of the Serpent and destroy the power of the Devil I humbly pray thy divine majesty to purge and free this place and Crystal stone (or Glass) from all infernal power To inhibit and discharge all apostate and descending Spirits from ever daring to approach near my person Or this place or presuming to appear in this Crystal stone (or Glass) To me **AB** thine unworthy servant for whom thy most blessed Son shed his most precious blood. To whom with thee and the Holy Ghost I yield all honour Laud praise Glory power might Majesty dominion rule and authority now and forever more world without end **Amen**

The :51:Psalm

1. **Have mercy upon me O God** after thy great goodness According unto the multitude of thy mercies do away mine offences.

2. Wash me thoroughly from my wickedness and cleanse me from my sin.

3. For I knowledge my faults and my sin is ever before me.

4. Against thee only have I sinned and done this evil in thy sight. That thou mightiest be justified in thy saying And clear when thou art judged.

5. Behold I was shapen in wickedness and in sin hath my mother conceived me.

6. But lo thou requires truth in the inward parts And shalt make me to understand wisdom secretly.

7. Thou shalt purge me with Hyssop and I shall be clean Thou shalt wash me and I shall be whiter than snow.

8. Thou shalt make me hear of joy and gladness That the bones which thou hast broken may rejoice.

9. Turn thy face from my sins and put out all my misdeeds.

10. Make me a clean heart O God and renew a right Spirit within me.

11. Cast me not away from thy presence And take not thy holy spirit from me.

12. O give me the comfort of thy help again and stablish me with thy free spirit.

13. Then shall I teach thy ways unto the wicked. And sinners shall be converted unto thee.

14. Deliver me from blood guiltiness O God thou that art the God of my health And my tongue shall sing of thy righteousness (48)

15. Thou shalt open my lips o lord and my mouth shall show thy praise.

16. For thou desirest no sacrifice else would I give it thee but thou delightest not in burnt offerings.

17. The sacrifice of God is a troubled spirit a broken and a contrite heart O God shalt thou not refuse.

18. O be favourable and gracious unto Sion Build thou the walls of Jerusalem.

19. Then shalt thou be pleased with the sacrifice of righteousness; with the burnt offerings and oblations. Then shall they offer young bullocks up on thine altar. **Glory be to the father &c**

The :46:Psalm

1. **God is our hope** and strength a very present help in trouble.

2. Therefore will not we fear though the Earth be moved and though the hills be carried into the mids[185] of the Sea.

3. Though the waters thereof Rage and swell and though the mountains shake at the tempest of the same.

4. The rivers of the flood thereof shall make glad the city of God The holy place of the tabernacle of the most highest.

5. God is in the middest of her Therefore shall he not be removed. God shall help her and that right early.

6. The heathen make much ado and the kingdoms are moved But God hath showed his voice and the Earth shall melt away.

7. The Lord of Hosts is with us The God of Jacob is our refuge.

8. O come hither and behold the works of the lord what destruction he hath brought upon the Earth.

9. He maketh wars to cease in all the world he breaketh the bow and snappeth the spear in sunder, and burneth the chariots in the fire.

10. Be still then and know that I am God I will be exalted among the heathen and I will be exalted in the earth.

---

[185] Heart or centre.

11.   The Lord of Hosts is with us The God of Jacob is our refuge.
        Glory be ~

The :91:Psalm:~:

1.   **Whoso dwelleth** under the defence of the most high shall
        abide &c

You shall find this Psalm written in Page :35:[186]

---

1.   **The lord is my Shepherd** Therefore can I lack nothing.

2.   He shall feed me in a green pasture And lead me forth
        besides the waters of comfort.

3.   He shall convert my soul and bring me forth in the paths of
        righteousness for his name's sake.

4.   Yea though I walk through the valley of the shadow of death
        I will fear no evil for thou art with me Thy rod and thy staff
        comfort me.

5.   Thou shalt prepare a table before me against them that
        trouble me Thou hast anointed my head with oil And my
        cup shall be full.

6.   But thy loving kindness and mercy shall follow me all the
        days of my life And I will dwell in the house of the lord
        forever.

Glory be to the father and to the Son and to the Holy Ghost. As
it was in the beginning is now and ever shall be world without end
Amen.

Then read this prayer following Three times with great
devotion If the angel appear not at the first or second repetition.

O thou most glorious Sacred and indivisible Trinity God the
father God the Son and God the holy Ghost upon the bended Knees
of my soul and body I do most humbly and heartily implore thy
Sacred Majesty at this present If it be thy holy will to give and grant
unto me thy humble Servant **AB** The immediate visual vocal and
audible presence and ministry of one of thy blessed persevering
holy Angels In such an amiable peacable constant and
unchangeable form and manner as thy heavenly mercy and

---

[186] This refers to the original numbering of the MS, i.e. fo.35, which was
renumbered to fo.32.

wisdom towards me knoweth my frail nature most capable of without any hurt or astonishment offered or done to my mind or body to minister unto me to show and reveal unto me thy unworthy servant all such questions and things as I thy humble servant shall demand of him And I most humbly beseech (49) thy Sacred Majesty to prepare and enable the faculties of my soul and body with sufficient Grace and power from thee to receive and use aright this thy so great a blessing for which I am an humble servant unto thee Grant this O heavenly father for Jesus Christ his sake thy dear and only Son And our Lord and only Saviour unto whom with the Holy Ghost I yield all honour laud praise Glory power might Majesty dominion rule and authority both now and evermore. **Amen.**

When he is appeared If his appearance be not perfect **Say**

If thou be that visible vocal and audible Angel which I have prayed for Show thyself apparently to the visible sight of me **AB** The servant of the everliving God without all fraud guile deceit or delay as thou shalt answer to the contrary at the dreadful day of doom.

Being perfectly appeared demand his name the which being obtained Say **Art thou C** (naming his name) that blessed persevering holy Angel for whom I have prayed unto the Great God of Heaven and Earth. **If he answer** He is

Then say Blessed and welcome art thou **C** Thou comest to me in the name of the Lord. **Then say this Prayer following.**

O Omnipotent and unsearchable Jehovah Lord and disposer of all holy Angels I give thy sacred Majesty most humble and hearty thanks for thy great mercy and Special favour towards me thy unworthy servant In licensing and commending this thy blessed Angel **C** to appear to the sight of me thy humble servant **AB** In the form and in the manner and unto the end petitioned I most humbly beseech thy divine Majesty further to licence and command this thy said holy Angel So fully and perfectly to dilate and manifest himself To me thy humble Servant as out of thy mercy and wisdom thou art pleased shall at all times suffice for this blessed work which in thy name and fear I have begun and desire to continue

Then say to the Angel Thou holy and blessed Angel In the name of Jesus Christ by virtue whereof thou appearest I desire thee to give me plain and true answers of my questions doubts and demands to the plain understanding of me **AB** the servant of the ever living God. **Then say this prayer**

+ O thou most Glorious infinite and Heavenly Lord God what is man that thou regardest him Or the Son of man that thou visitest him Man is as a thing of nothing his time passeth away like a Shadow In particular I confess myself to be but dust and ashes a worm and no man the very matter and subject of thine eternal wrath and indignation yet thou feedest me with thy good things and givest me mercy instead of Judgement to drink Thou dost accumulate and multiply thy benefits upon me And in particular is thy special favour of the immediate visible vocal and audible presence and ministry of thy blessed Angel **C** A favour which thou hast denied to the sons of men For those benefits and this what I shall say and render unto my lord but that Thou art my God and I will praise thee Thou art my God and I will exalt thee. I will take the cup of Salvation and call upon the name of the lord. I will pay my vows unto the lord in the presence of all his people The which that I may do I humbly crave thy assisting grace O heavenly father for thy Christ's sake to whom with thee and thy sacred spirit I give all honour and glory power praise majesty and dominion now and forever. **Amen.**

Then make your demands to the Angel Having what you desire give the Angel license to depart **Saying**

Thou good Angel C I thank thee And for this time I license thee to depart to the place appointed thee of God. Go in peace + In the name of the Father + And of the Son + And of the Holy Ghost + Amen + **Finis** (50)

How you shall call for a good Angel:

When you will call for any of the Angels of the days of the week or any other good Angel that you know his name The three Angels being invocated and appeared. **Say this prayer viz**

O Sweet God and Heavenly Father maker and Creator of all things visible and invisible I thy unworthy servant **AB** do beseech thee of thy fatherly goodness and mercy That thou wilt vouchsafe to give leave and licence to thy holy and blessed Angel **Gabriel** (or any other Angel you will name) to make his appearance in the midst of this Glass (or crystal Stone) to the visible sight of me thy unworthy servant **AB** (of this child maid and virgin) now when I shall call him with commission from thee to answer me faithfully justly and truly unto all such questions as I shall demand And to do all such things as for me I shall desire of him to do Grant this O heavenly father for Jesus Christ his sake our only mediator and Advocate. **Amen:**

Then call the Angel as followeth + Gabriel + **Gabriel +** Gabriel + **come** hastily and tarry not **+** In the name of the Father **+** And of the Son + And of the Holy Ghost + So be it + Amen +

Being appeared say Gabriel welcome art thou in the worship of the holy lord of Heaven And the blessed and Glorious Trinity Praying and desiring thee that thou wilt answer me faithfully justly and truly unto all such questions as I shall demand of thee And to do all such things for me as I shall desire of thee to do without all fraud guile deceit or delay as thou shalt answer to the contrary at the dreadful day of doom. **Gabriel wilt thou do all that I have said** he will say he will **then say** Gabriel in token that thou wilt do it cross thy hand and kiss them **That being done** make your demands, **that done** licence him to depart.

How to call Three Heavenly Angels into a Crystal Stone or Skrying Glass To the visible Sight of a Child &c

In primis recipe Lapidem Christalen vell Berelam.[187] The Clearer the better. Lay it on the Altar on the same side that the Gospel is read on. And let the Priest say a Mass on the same side of

---

[187] "**First**, take back the Crystal or Beryl Stone."

the Altar. And when the Mass is said Stand as nigh[188] the Altar as you may. Then say this consecration following.

Conjuro te lapidem Christalum vell Berelam per virtutem omnipotentis dei per Sanctum Sacramentum quod celebratum est iusta te per istum Emannuelem qui lectur est super te et per ista nomina + Adonay + Adoy + Emanuell + Onele + et + Onele + Tetragrammaton + Anela + Et per omnia dei nomina in effabilia per virtutem + Regis Salomonis + qui inclusit spirite in vase virtio ut qua in te scripta + In nomine Patris + et filii + et Spirits sancti + nullus spirits vell Angelus inclusus non habeat potestatem eundo me iusti negore nisi falendi aliquot modo fit virtus. Sed deducet et nobis demonstrabit et quibus in que iuste gratus fuit per eum qui venturus est iudicare vinos et mortnos et seculum per ignem.[189]

Tu ne recipe puriam quiem infra etatem Christian amoriam Et non ultra[190]

Then you shall write on the Stone or Glass with olive oil these names Onele vell Onele. For Onele will show the deed how it was done And Onele what thou shalt ask of him.

Then the Master shall say softly to himself over the Stone or Glass 3 times as followeth.

+ Eloy + Eli + Eli + Lamasabathani + Adonay + Tetragrammaton + Alpha + et + ω + principium + et + futurum + In nomine Patris + et filii + et Spiritus Sancti + Amen + fiat + fiat + fiat + tibi lux + et in Nomine Domine noster Jesu Christi omnipotenti qui dixit + fiat lux + et facta erat lux + (51) fiat tibi lux ad videndum Onele vell Onele Angelum et lumine suffitientum erdas quantum Andivisti istius

---

[188] I.e. as close.

[189] "**I summon thee**, Crystal or Beryl **stone**, by the power of the all-powerful God, by the Holy Sacrament that is celebrated for thee, the just, by that Emanuel that is chosen above thee, and by these names + Adonay + Adoy + Emanuell + Onele + and + Onele + Tetragrammaton + Anela + and by all the ineffable names of God, by the power of + King Solomon + who incarcerated a spirit in a vase by virtue of that which I inscribe on thee + In the name of the Father + and the son + and the holy Ghost + no incarcerated spirit or angel shall have the power of going while I deny them all such power or cheat them of it. But he leads and shows us now those in whom there was acceptable legitimacy through him that shall come and judge the living and the dead and the ages through fire."

[190] "**Thou shalt not retake** now rest from the beloved age of Christianity nor anything else."

penam A ut non sit impeditus per te lucem qui in omnia sibi demonstratum ab Angilo nobis absque impedimento vexacitu valet declarum omnipotens sempiterne Deus qui spiritus sanctus super Angelos et Apostolos tuos misisti eundem spiritum super hunc peerum A mittere digneris ipin ore tuo benedicte (X) et illumine sensum eius ad videndum et audiendum Onele vell Onele exorciso te A puerum per dium vium per deum verum per deum Sanctum quite puerum A Ad felicitudinem suam creaturam dignatus est precioso sanguine suo redimisti exorciso te etiam per baptisimum quodie minibus sacerdotis recipisti et per Christi, natus unuxtionum et per virginitatem tuam ut non sit impeditus timorem, nise aligno modo quia veritatem de quibus cuuque tibi ab Angelo per signa monstrata ant verbo declarata absque fallasia nobis demonstres ad innatem domine nostrum Jesum Christi cui est honor in secula seculorum.[191]

Then let the Child say after the Master word by word as followeth

---

[191] "+ Eloy + Eli + Eli + Lamasabathani + Adonay + Tetragrammaton + Alpha + and + omega + the beginning + and + the future + In the name of the father + and the son + and the Holy Spirit + Amen + let there be + let there be + let there be + light unto thee + and in the Name of our Lord Jesus Christ the all-powerful who said + let there be light + and it was done there was light + let there be light unto thee in order to see Onele or the Angel Onele and the light suffusing the earth as far and wide as that [sound] which you produced is heard so that unto the light there may not be anything through thee obstructing the light, which is strong enough even when jolted or shaken as is demonstrated from the angels to us all the way through the impediment, while it is made evident that thou art the all-powerful ever-lasting God that has sent a spirit to go above the Angels and Apostles and to perish above those [unless] you shall deem him worthy to send your benediction from within your mouth (X) and illumine them so that they must live and hear Onele or Onele, I exorcise thee, boy, by the divine way, by the true god, by the Holy god, o able boy. He who is his creature is deemed worthy of happiness, redeemed through his precious blood, I exorcise thee again by the baptism you have regained one day from the vermillion-clad priest, by Christ, born from woman alone and by thy virginity so that thou mayest not be impeded by fear, nor inclined any other way than the truth from which and by which signs from the angels shall be shown before words declared from deceitfulness, [so that] thou showest us, lord, to that which is innate unto our Jesus Christ upon whom is honour in the century of centuries."

O Domine Jesu Christi mitte nobis tres bonas Angelos ex parte tua in istiam Lapidem Christalem vell Berealem qui dicent et demonstrent nobis veritatem atqe dies de quibus interogationibus sietribus vicibus ut supra domine Angele princepio tibi et interogabo veretatem et appere mihi signa illorum bonorum et omnis principium atque sive + In nomine Patris + et filii + et Spiritus Sancti + Amen + et virginitatem meam qua tenus demonstres nobis de quibus nos interogabimus veritatem et per ista nomina + Heloy + Sabaoth + Adonay + Tetragrammaton + Alpha + et + Omega + Principium + et + finis +[192]

Say this 3 times And when the Child perceiveth anything in the Stone He must say after the Master

Sacra[193] **Angel** I hold thee and charge thee by the virtue and power of Almighty God The Father Son And Holy Ghost As thou and I shall give and yield account at the dreadful day of Judgement before thy Lord and mine Thou Angel Onele or Onele Tell me or Show me faithfully and truly without any fraud or dissimulation what Man or woman hath Stolen or born away out of the House of B On such a day of the month or night. In such an House of the same day or night such and such Goods &c, That were stolen I charge thee by all the virtues and powers of God as aforesaid That thou tell me and show me the very truth, How it was done and by whom And where it is now without any fraud guile or dissimulation. **And so for any other thing.**

The Master must have the Pentagulum following in his hand drawn in virgin Parchment.

When you have your desire say as followest

---

[192] "**O Lord Jesus Christ** send to us three good Angels out of your division into this Crystal or Beryl Stone whereby they speak and show us the truth and on that day on which there are questionings thrice in alternation so that I may begin to speak to thee and question above the truth the Lord of Angels, and wilt thou fashion me signs of those good things and the beginning of it all or also + In the name of the Father + and the son + and the Holy Ghost + Amen + and whereby do you hold my virginity and show us the truth which we examine and by these names + Heloy + Sabaoth + Adonay + Tetragrammaton + Alpha + and + Omega + Beginning + and + end +"

[193] The abbreviation S^r is used, which is a contraction of Sacra, meaning holy.

The Angels of God I charge you and command you by the virtues and power of God and the Holy Trinity that you depart out of the Stone or Glass into the place that God hath appointed for you And ordained you to And that whensoever I do call for you That you do come without any tarrying or delay And without any hurt of Man woman or Child Or of any other creature of God Go in peace Peace be between thee and me And between us and you + In nomine Patris + et filii + et Spiritus sancti + Amen + fiat + fiat + fiat +

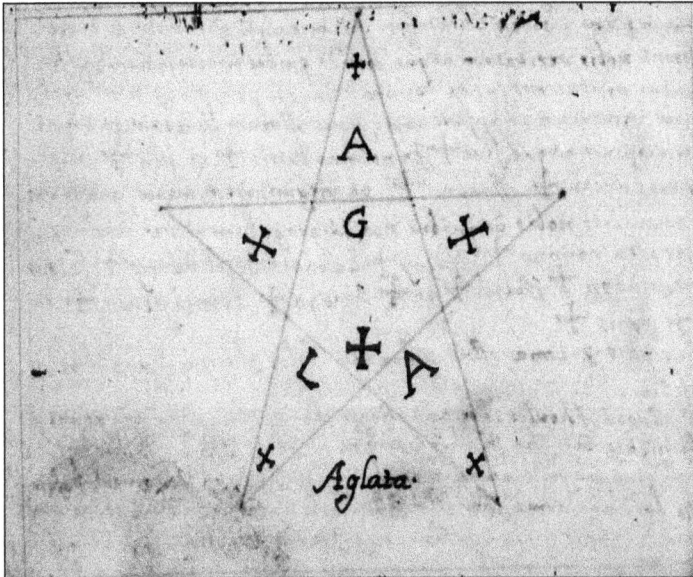

24 – *Pentagram used in previous charm How You Shall Call for a Good Angel, with the divine name Agla contained within, and Aglara written below*

(52)

How to Call the Angels into A Glass of Water

You must have a urinal[194] Or a Crystal Beer or wine Glass very clean washed Then filled iii [3] quarters full of Spring water Then cover it with a paper wherein must be drawn these lines and characters as you see in the figure following. Then having said your prayers devoutly to God for good success in what you undertake. If it be a urinal hold it betwixt your Hands so that your fingers hinder not the light. If it be a Glass you may let it stand on his foot. Then call as followeth. ~

+ Babell + Gabriel + Rochell + Sara + Isaac + Joseph + and + Jacob + I charge you by these holy names of God + Elo + Elo + Goby + Goby + Emanuell + Emanuell + Tetragrammaton + Tetragrammaton + As you shall answer before Jesus Christ at the great and dreadful day of Judgement for to show me all that I shall ask or demand faithfully and truly within this Glass without any delusion or dissimulation I charge you and command you and bind you that you come into this Glass & bring all that do belong unto you for to show me anything that I shall ask or desire that I may plainly behold it with my mortal Eyes.[195]

(53)

---

[194] In this context a bottle.

[195] A similar technique is found in Sloane MS 3824, a contemporary MS. See The Book of Treasure Spirits, Rankine, 2009:156.

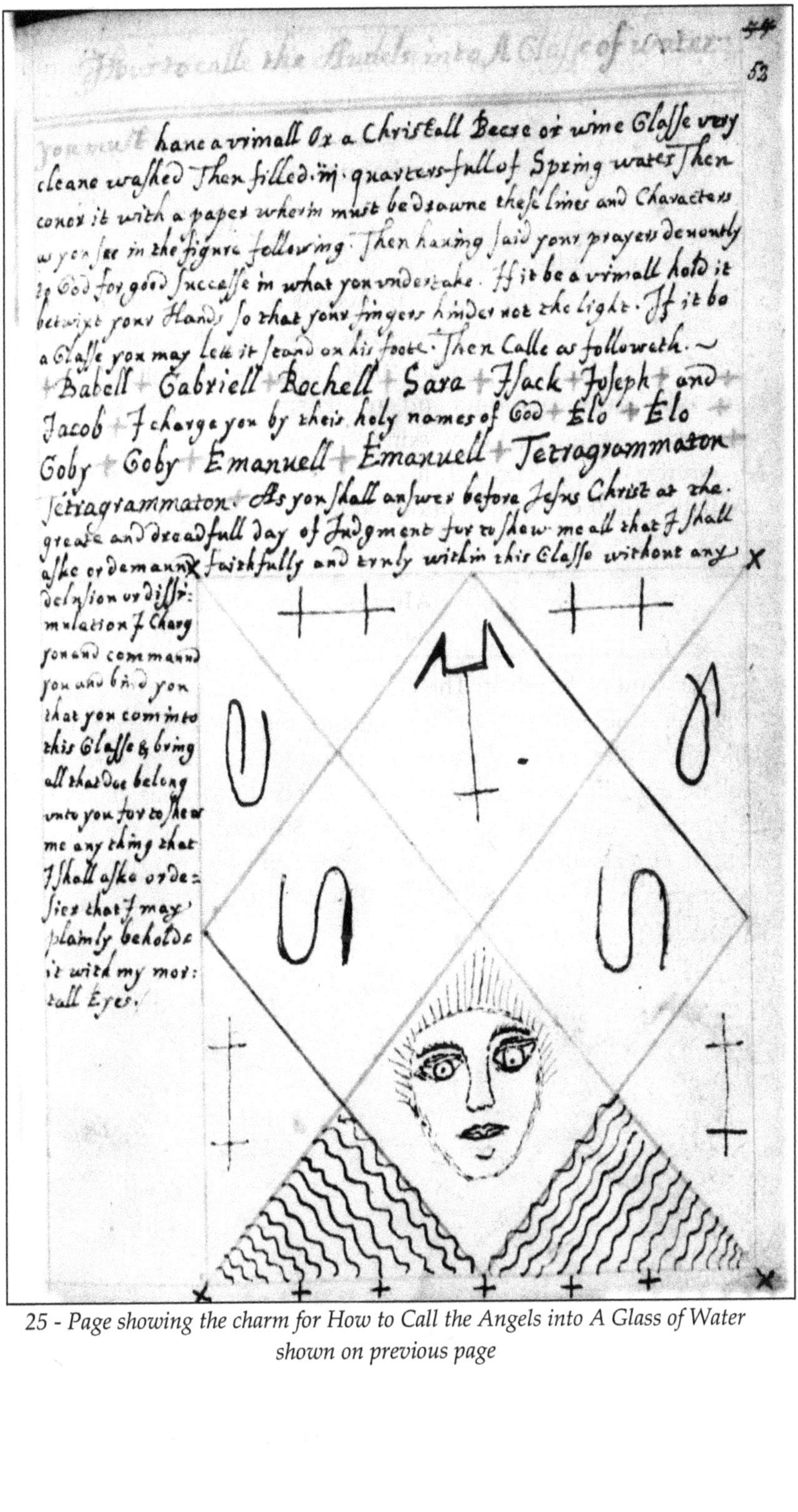

How to call the Angells into A Glasse of Water

you must hane a vriuall Or a Christall Beere or wine Glasse very
cleane washed Then filled in quarters full of Spring water Then
couer it with a paper wherin must be drawne these lines and Characters
w you see in the figure following. Then hauing said your prayers deuoutly
to God for good Successe in what you vndertake. If it be a vriuall hold it
betwixt your Hands So that your fingers hinder not the light. If it be
a Glasse you may lett it stand on his foote. Then Calle as followeth. ~
+ Babell + Gabriell + Rochell + Sara + Hack + Joseph + and +
Jacob + I charge you by their holy names of God + Elo + Elo +
Goby + Goby + Emanuell + Emanuell + Tetragrammaton +
Tetragrammaton. As you shall answer before Jesus Christ at the.
greate and dreadfull day of Judgment for to shew me all that I shall
aske or demaunt faithfully and truly within this Glasse without any
delusion or dissi:
mulation I Charg
you and command
you and bind you
that you com into
this Glasse & bring
all that doe belong
vnto you for to shew
me any thing that
I shall aske or de=
sires that I may
plainly behold
it with my mor:
tall Eyes.

25 - *Page showing the charm for How to Call the Angels into A Glass of Water shown on previous page*

God the Searcher and revealer of all things to whom nothing lies hid we humbly entreat thy Majesty that thou wouldst vouchsafe to Commit to us the Thief that have done this theft That with shame of the fact confessing it to us he may desire to come to worthy repentance by Jesus Christ our Lord.

Almighty and everlasting God the revealer of all hidden and things manifest And to whom no secrets are hid we humbly pray thee by the invocation of thy holy ones Thou wouldst command thy clean Spirits + Sabaoth + Uriell+ and + Raguell[196] + that they should obey my words and command in this small work That the Thief manifestly coming and confessing this sin, we may give thanks to thee in thy Church Through Jesus Christ thy Son which liveth and reigneth with thee world without end. (54)

A Prayer Preservative Always to be carried about Man or woman

The God of Abraham The God of Isaac The God of Jacob be my defender from all my enemies visible and invisible The mighty Jehovah make me victorious As thou didst David over great Goliath For the good faith he had in thee O Messias defend me from slanderous tongues As thou didst Susanna from the Elders[197] behold the headless **T** Cross Fly from it all evil Spirits who the Stock of David And the Tribe of Judah hath overcome. Amen Amen. (55)

---

[196] Raguel is one of the seven archangels listed in the Book of Enoch.

[197] Susanna the wife of Joachim, saved by Daniel's wisdom in Daniel 13.

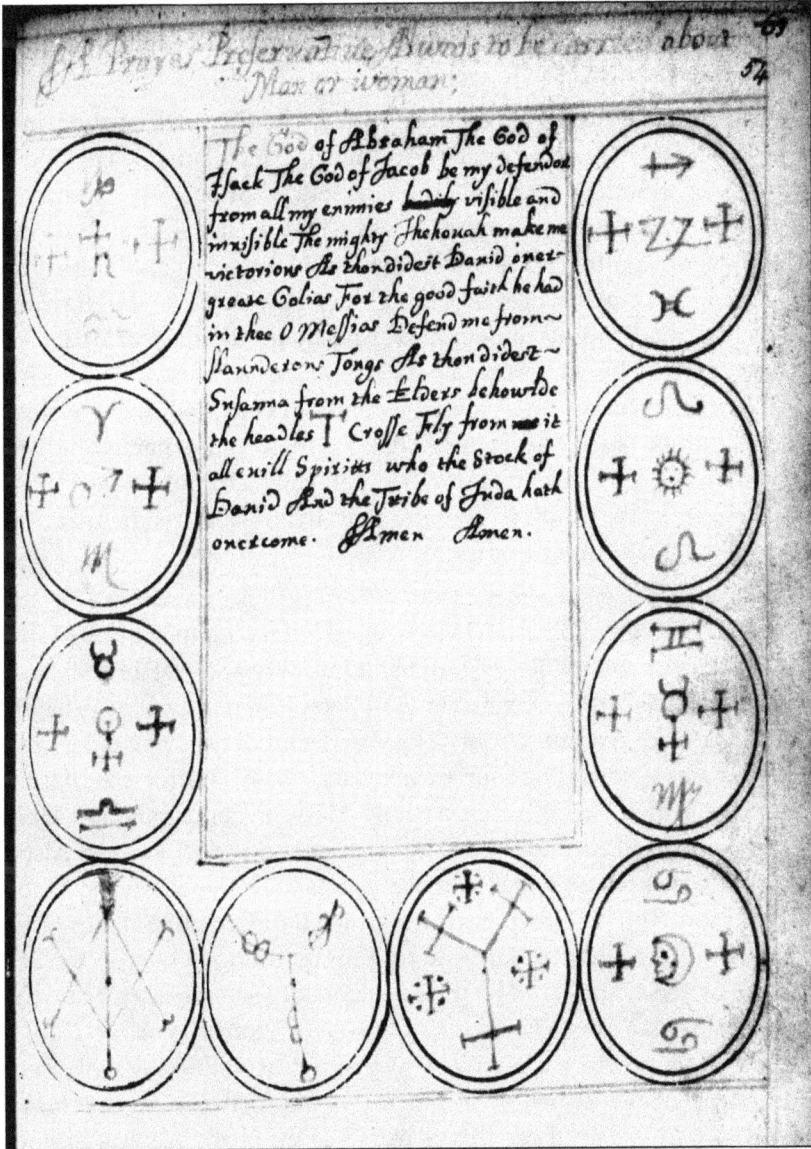

26 – *Prayer charm combining planetary and astrological symbols - see previous page A Prayer Preservative Always to be carried about Man or woman.*

For Theft

Write the names of all the Suspected in Paper severally and put every name written in a piece of Clay And put them into a basin of fair water saying as followeth.

I Conjure thee thou Earth and Clay + By the Father + the Son + and the Holy Ghost + Amen + And by all the Holy names of God + Messias + Sother + Emanuell + Sabaoth + Adonay + Panthon + Craton + Anefeton + Theos + Otheas + Eley + Eloy + And by all the virtues of God by Heaven and Earth and by the Sea and all that be in them And by our blessed virgin Mary The Mother of our Saviour Jesus Christ And by his humility And by all the holy company of Heaven And by all that God created In Heaven In Earth and in the Sea or other places And by all the names of God And by the virtues and merits of all the Saints, That amongst those names hidden within the Clay his name or her name which hath stolen those things may be known by him that liveth and reigneth world without end + Amen +

Again I Conjure thee water wherein those names are by the true and living God And by the virgin Mary mother of our Lord Jesus Christ and by her virginity and humility and by Saint Michael and Gabriel Raphael Cherubim and Seraphim and by all the Saints Angels and Archangels by Thrones Dominions Principates and Potestates And by the four Evangelists + Saint Matthew + Mark + Luke + and John + And by all holy Martyrs Confessors and Holy virgins of God And by all powers virtues and Joys of Heaven Also I conjure thee water wherein those names are by the Sun the Moon and Stars And by John Baptist the which Baptised our Saviour Jesus Christ In the flood Jordan And by him that did walk upon the Sea And by the virgins And by the Sepulchre of Jesus Christ And by the dreadful day of Judgement And by the great name of God + Tetragrammaton + That we may have true knowledge of these things that we desire And that the name of the Man or woman which hath stolen those things may rise up of the water. Per eum qui venturus est Judecare speculum per ignem amen[198]

Then say these Psalms following viz

Psalm :58: Psalm :43: Psalm :77:

Concluding every Psalm with Glory be to the father &c

Also say Athanasius Creed &c

---

[198] "By him who is to come and judge through the age of fire. Amen."

Also Te Deum Laudamus &c

Also In Principio &c

Also the Lord' Prayer and The Creed. Say all this iii [3] times and no doubt but it will be done. (56)

For Theft

For know that there are 4 Spirits in the Air which have power given them to hurt the Earth and the Sea, under which kings there are 4 Spirits that have power to show a Thief and the Theft The characters of every of which Spirits followeth.[199]

The first Obeys the King of the South His name is: Teltrion: His character is made thus

The Second Spirit serves the King of the East His name is Spiron: His characters are:

The Third is at the command of the King of the West His name is Boytheon His characters are

The fourth obeyeth the Northern King and is called Mayrion or Marion His character is

If you will experiment you must work in the day of ☾ or ☿ before the ☉ rising. And first make your Confession to God the Father.

---

[199] These are the Demon Bishops, also mentioned in Folger Vb(26) and Sloane MS 3824 fo 16-21b. See The Book of Treasure Spirits, Rankine, 2009:55-67.

And let these names of the foresaid Spirits be written in 4 Papers Or Scrolls and the Characters by the names of the Spirits One before another as is showed before Then write in the middle round Circle the name Sathan whom the Spirits do obey And the name of the thing or things stolen And the name of him or them to whom the same belong. Then say this Conjuration following.[200]

O vos Spiritus Teltrion Spiron Boytheon Mayrion vel Mahiron quorum nomina & signa hic sunt scripta vos conjuro & exorciso per Deum unum, per Deum verum, per Deum sanctum, per Patrem per filius & spiritum sanctum, & per sumam & individuam Trinitatem & per principem nostrum Dominum Alpha & Omega & per nomina omnia Dominus nostri Jesu Christi per patriarchas & prophetas & per excellentissimus nomen Deum Tetragrammaton & per passionem Domini nostri Jesu Christi & per admirabilem asensionem Domini nostri Jesu Christi ubicunas sic is in terra in aqua in aere vel in igne ut conveniatis in quo ille vel illa latro illi vel illa latrines sunt qui (hic nominabis res furatas) cepit vel ceperunt asportavit vel asportavamot de (hic nominabis locum ex quo amisae fuerunt) in alium locum & illas faciatis referre predictas res, in talem locum tali die & tali hora (hic nominabis locum diem & horam) alitur vos codemno per resurrectionnem Domini nostri Jesu Christi per Mariam matrem eius & per Sanctem Johem Baptista religari Catanis duris atque duri tormento, nisi illum vel illam, illos vel illas adducatis eum re furata, vel rebus furatis, in talem locum, tali die & hora, (fui nominabis locu diem & horam) Adhuc vos omnes Conjuro & exorciso, per sap beatissimus & excellentissimam virginem Mariam, per omnes Angelos & Archangelos, Thronas & dominations, per omnes Patriarchas & prophetas per quator Evangelistas, & per duodecem Apostolas & per omnes Martires confessors & virgins & per quator reges vestros, quod thimque sit in terra magna x aiere x vell in igne (ut supra).[201]

---

[200] The conjuration has a high degree of commonality with the conjurations in Sloane MS 3824.

[201] "**O thou Spirit** Teltrion Spiron Boytheon Mayrion or Mahiron of whom the names & signs are written here, thee I conjure & exorcise by the one God, by the true God, by the holy God, by the Father, by the son & by the holy spirit, & by the highest & indivisible Trinity & by our foremost Lord Alpha & Omega & by all the names of our Lord Jesus Christ , by the patriarchs & prophets & by the most excellent name of God Tetragrammaton & by the passion of our Lord Jesus Christ & by the wonderful ascension of our Lord Jesus Christ wherever his cradle is on the

You must experiment when ☾ is increasing either the 4. 6. 8. 10. 12. 14. &c of her age Till she is 19 days old she is fit First you must say your Conjuration Adversus[202] Orientem secondly Adversus Austrum thirdly Adversus Occidentem[203] fourthly Adversus Septentrionem[204] And in every part it is to be said 3 times.

I have seen this Experiment In another manner As followeth

The plate must be made of new virgin wax A hand breadth at the least. **The names and characters** as here you see

---

land, in the water, in the air or in the fire so that you meet with him or those who is a robber or are robbers who stole or carried away (here name an object stolen) from (here name the location from whence it was stolen) to another location & make them take back the previously mentioned thing, in such a location on such a day and at such an hour (here name a location, day and time) or else I condemn you by the resurrection of our Lord Jesus Christ, by his mother Mary & by the Holy John the Baptist to be tied up in strong chains and harsh torments if not one or the other brings back the thing that was stolen or the things that were stolen to such a place on such a day & hour (I have named the place, day & hour). For this [sic.] I conjure thee and exorcise thee, by the most wise, most blessed and most excellent virgin Mary, by all Angels & Archangels, Thrones & dominions, by all the Patriarchs & Prophets, by the four Evangelists & by the twelve Apostles & by all the Martyrs and Confessors & virgins & by your four kings, which [?] are in the great earth x air x or in fire (as above)."

[202] "Towards".

[203] The text repeats "Orientem" here, but that is clearly a copyist's mistake.

[204] The conjurations move round the circle from the East (Orient) to South (Auster), to West (Occidentem) and North (Septentrionem).

27 - *Plate for recovering stolen property, as mentioned in the text immediately preceding. Note the name of Sathan in the centre, and his four subservient demon bishops around the edges. The circle contains the following instructions on how to use it: "This is the place of the thing or things stolen with the name and surname of the party that stole it."*

The former Experiment

For Theft or a Fugitive Rise before ☉ rising on the day of ☽ or of ☿ In thy secret House Take of virgin wax about the **bigness** of thy hand and make therein the figure as before with the names of the things stolen and his name &c And then say with bended knees towards the East this Psalm **Have mercy upon me O God. Psalm.**[205]

---

[205] This is Psalm 51, previously recorded in the book.

Then the Pater Noster, Ave Maria, and the Credo in deum &c. Then say **Be thou to us O Lord** a Tower of strength against the face of mine enemies O Lord hear my prayer and let my cry come unto thee. Let us pray.

O Lord Jesus Christ the Son of the everliving God which hath formed me after thy image and likeness And for me hath suffered under Pontius Pilate & by the bitterness of thy Soul keep me **AB** Keep me safe thy unworthy sinful servant That doth not despair but hope in thee That I be not overcome with adversities or deceit who livest and reignest God forever and ever Amen + In the name of the Father + And of the Son + And of the Holy Ghost + **O holy Trinity** and inestimable unity I call upon thee and adore thee I desire thee to preserve receive and defend my body and Soul now and forever Amen.

I beseech thee by the virtue of thy Holy Cross And by the virtue of thy passion I beseech thee O lord Jesus Christ the Son of the everliving God And by the merits and prayers of the blessed virgin Mary And by the merits and Intercessions of all thy he Saints and She Saints that thou give and grant me thy grace and power over these Spirits + Theltryon + Sperion + Betherion + And Maherion + That thou suffer me by the virtue and goodness of all Men Saints and women Saints That thou give and grant me thy grace and Goodness over these Spirits That when I shall call upon them and exorcise them presently and without delay they may come out of every part and may accomplish my will and Commandment in all things And may not condemn or set light by me nor my words but may always hearken and obey to Reason of the virtues and exorcisms that shall come from my Mouth And that they may neither hurt nor offend me nor make me afraid But rather may be obedient to me in all my affairs and businesses And may be trusty to me in their works and in that which they shall do and perform them faithfully And being bound by thy power that they may perform and accomplish it by the commandment of these divine things and of the Consecrator to the honour of thy name who is blessed for ever and ever. Amen.

+ Theltrion + Sperion + Betherion + and Matherion + whose names and signs are here **I Conjure and Exorcise you** by all the virtues and by all your powers and by the divine virtue and by that obedience which you ought to acknowledge & observe towards God that you be obedient and ready to do all that I shall command you now & forever Amen.

I Conjure you and exorcise you Spirits + Theltrion + Sperion + Betherion + and Matherion + whose names and Signs are here by the living God and the holy God and the true God by the great and indivisible Trinity and by these names of God + Alpha and + Omega + And by all the names of our Lord Jesus Christ which the Patriarchs and Prophets have called upon or invocated And by the most excellent name of our lord God + Tetragrammaton + And by the passion of our Lord Jesus Christ and by his wonderful ascension That wheresoever you be In the Earth In the Sea In the fire In the water Or in the Air you meet together in one place in which the Thief either he or she or they are or may be who have stolen such and such things being the goods of AB of C in the County of D, They having stolen them or carried them away from such a place into another That you cause he or she him or her men or women that have such things to bring it back again and restore the same things Into the same place from whence they were stolen On such a day and in such an hour of the day without fail And that you suffer him or her or them not to go or depart from the same place but that you cause them there to stand until they shall have licence from me or from any other in my name And if you shall not do this + Theltrion + Sperion + Betherion + Matherion + I condemn you by the resurrection of our lord Jesus Christ And by the holy virgin Mary his Mother And by holy John Baptist And by these holy names which are not lawful to nominate but in time of great neglect + On + Usion + Adonay + Panteon + On + Ell + Eloy + Athanatos + Tetragrammaton + Alpha + ω + Emanuell + and Eracon + And by all the sanctity and power of their names I command you to be bound with chains of fire and to be grieviously tormented Except you bring back again him or her & with the things stolen to such a place In such a day and such an hour of the same day **I Conjure you** Spirits + Theltrion + Sperion + Betherion + Matherion + by the wonderful mighty power of God the Father and by virtue of all the names of that most high And by the blood of our Lord Jesus Christ and by his Sweat and by his tears and by his voice and by the nails with which his hands and feet were bored through and by the Spear wherewith his side was pierced through and by the blood and water which issued out of his wounds **I Conjure you** O you Spirits + Theltrion + Sperion + Betherion + Matherion + By the 7 Sacraments of the Church and the casting out of devils and by all terrible things in Heaven and in Earth that wheresoever you be In earth in the Air or else where you meet together in one place In which he or she is which have stolen &c until they shall be set free

148

by me or by whom I shall appoint. If you shall not do that that is aforesaid, Then (58) **I Conjure you** and adjure you O Spirits + Theltrion + Sperion + Betherion + Matherion + not by my weakness but by the virtue and power of the Holy Spirit that ye obey me and tremble ye at the performance of my commandments. Be ye afraid at the body of man. Let the Image of Christ whereby he hath created and redeemed <u>and Sanctified,</u> He Saints and She Saints command you O holy Trinity O Jesus Christ the Son of the everliving God In whom you shall find nothing of your works for he hath spoiled you of them and hath pulled down your Kingdom Therefore I Conjure you + Theltrion + Sperion + Betherion + Matherion + By the virtue of our lord and Saviour Jesus Christ and by his most holy names + Snaytheon + and by the pure name + Stimulamaton[206] + and by the most holy name + Tetragrammaton + which is an honourable and available name to Christians and terrible to the Devils And by the glorious and most blessed virgin Mary And by all the Apostles Patriarchs and Prophets and their virtues And by your 4 Kings whom you ought to obey That is what place soever you be in, Either in earth in fire &c until I shall give them liberty &c

And if you shall not do this I Conjure you by the resurrection of our lord Jesus Christ and by the virgin Mary And by holy John the Baptist and by all those holy names of God which a man may not name save in the time of great necessity or need + On + Usion + Adonay + On + Ell + Eloy + Athanitas + Taynagyteon + Tetragrammaton + Alph + et Omega + Emanuell + Eracon + Sacerdos + Ysus + And by all the power and might of them I command and charge you to be bound again with chains of fire and to be severely tormented until you shall bring back again him or her he or she with the thing or things stolen of such a man at such a day and at such an hour as is above said + fiat + fiat + fiat + Amen +

Thou must say this Conjuration 3 times in one day. In the morning, at Noon And at ☉ set. Once towards the East. 2. towards the West 3. towards the South. 4. toward the North. After the same manner do at noon. Likewise at ☉ setting. This being done and performed thou shalt bury the plate of wax before spoken of in the Earth And in that day wherein thou sealest it the Thief shall come

---

[206] This divine name is found in the Hallowing of the Book in Sloane MS 3826 (1564 or earlier) and in the Pseudomonarchia Daemonum of Johann Weyer (1563.)

again with the things stolen undoubtedly. Thou shalt make this Experiment ☽ increasing

The figure for this Experiment is at the beginning

For the accomplishment of the pleasure of the flesh:~:

In the day of ♀ and in the hour thereof make a Circle stretching forth thy wand And thy face toward the South. Say

I Conjure you Spirits Ragarad, Sathan, Iscarath, by the great God the father + by the great God the Son + And by the great God the holy Ghost + And by the most blessed virgin Mary By all the warfare of Heaven by the dreadful day of judgement I Conjure you Spirits ♀ by this sign of Venus which here is So by the flowing of blood from the side of Christ Jesus And by the rent of the veil of the Temple at the passion of our Lord Jesus Christ And by the virginity and fruitfulness of blessed Mary the mother of God And by all the names of Jesus Christ And by that unutterable name of + Tetragrammaton + which is Graven or carved upon my rod And is on my Ring That you make haste to go to the woman or maid AB And that you make her so to burn in my love that neither sleeping nor waking &c She may be at rest until I obtain what I desire of her and do perform my will with her God permitting who liveth and reigneth for ever Amen Or in this wise.

So far forth as in you lies speedily bring hither such a woman The daughter of AB and CB without vain fixion or counterfeiting of Diabolical Transformation without delay or deceit or gainsaying yea convey her hither to me truly cause her to enter into this Chamber truly without hurt or annoyance even unto her body Through our lord Jesus Christ the Son of God who liveth and reigneth for ever and ever Amen.

But if the Spirit will not appear repeat it thrice And he will come

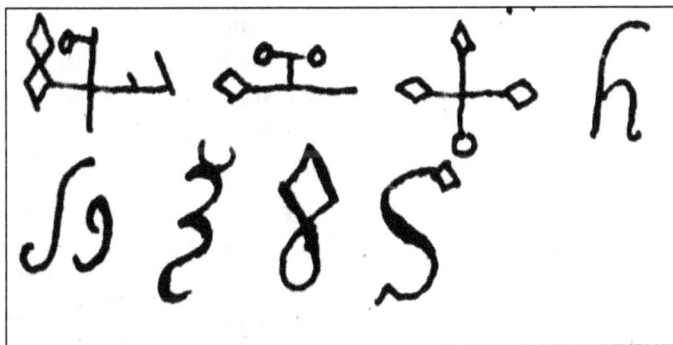

28 - The purpose of these symbols is not given, but taking into account Arthur Gauntlet's use of numerous grimoires and their similarity to symbols found in some Key of Solomon MSS, they may possibly be those carved on the wand used in the preceding charm, For the Accomplishment of the Pleasure of the Flesh.

To gain the love of Man or Woman:

Take a piece of virgin Parchment as broad as your hand and make in it two images The one of thy self the other Of the woman or man Then with the blood of the little finger of thy left hand write on thine own Image thine own name. And on the other his or her name, betwixt the Images write these three names Sathan Lucifer Donskion. You must make it so that when you close the Parchment the Images may be right over one another. Make thine own Image on Friday the first hour that ♀ governs And the other the Friday following In the same hour This done put the Images under your foot three times a day removing it to the other foot. In the Morning the first hour of the day, At 12 a clock at Noon And at night before it be dark Saying at every time As followeth

I Conjure you Sathan Lucifer and Donskion[207] which are Princes, By Baratria[208] which expelled Adam and Eve out of Paradise By his holy Hand and straight way I charge you by the + Father by the Son + and by the Holy Ghost + And by the four Elements. I charge you by things possible and impossible In the part and behalf and by the power which God hath In Heaven In the Earth in the Sea And all deeps And by the holy Trinity And by the

---

[207] This may well be a corruption of Dansiation, who is one of the powers with Lucifer and Sathan in the conjurations of the previously mentioned demon bishops in Sloane MS 3824. See The Book of Treasure Spirits, Rankine, 2009:59-60, 65.

[208] Baratria as a term meant "The act of achieving a judgement through bribery".

proper names of God And by his holy name + Tetragrammaton + I conjure you Sathan Lucifer and Donskion that you go to AB and suffer her not to sleep nor to take any rest nor to eat nor to drink to stand nor to sit nor to lie in any quiet In her heart or mind until she hath accomplished and done my will whatsoever I request her to do. Then say as followeth.

O Lord Jesus Christ King of Glory and power I beseech thee That thou wilt give them leave and licence and power that they may cause her burn in torment love of me And to forsake all others for the Love of me. Then say as followeth.

And again I charge you by all the virtues that ever God made In Heaven In Earth and in the Sea And by the powers of Spirits I charge you by all Angels and Archangels And by all the holy company of Heaven and by the Twelve Apostles, And by all the love that God loved them And they loved God Also I charge you by the blessed virgin Saint Mary The Mother of Our Lord and Saviour Jesus Christ And by the love that God loved her. I charge you by all Martyrs Confessors virgins Patriarchs and Prophets and by the Crown of Thorns wherewith Christ was Crowned And by the bands wherewith he was bound and by the Cross whereon he suffered And by the Lance that wounded his side and the water and blood issued forth, That is to say Blood of Redemption, And water of Baptism. I Conjure you by the Rod of Moses And by all the holy names of God and our lord and Saviour Jesus Christ which the patriarchs and prophets did preach through secrets and signs I Conjure you Sathan Lucifer and Donskion by all virtues and all secret powers that may be named And I beseech the lord Jesus Christ that I may have the love of AB whose name and sign I bare under my foot + fiat + fiat + fiat + Amen +

Then you must have five pieces of Gold to be sent her in the time you be in your work before it be ended And she will love you as long as you live. **Taken out of Virgil.**

The former Experiment

In the first day of ♀ after the change of the ☽ make an Image in virgin Parchment after thine own likeness And the next Friday after make another of the woman and write her in her Image and thy name in the other with the blood of the middle finger of thy left hand These images must be made so as when the Parchment is doubled they may fall Just one upon the other Between the images write these names Sathan Lucifer Dentalion[209] Then fold the parchment together Then the day aforesaid put it under the sole of thy foot within thy shoes And let it lie there for 3 days Every day saying this invocation

I Conjure thee Sathan Lucifer and Dentalion which are the princes of Hell which caused Adam and Eve to offend in Paradise and by your most deceitful wit and art + I Conjure you by the + father + the Son + and the Holy Ghost + And by the 4 Evangelists + I Conjure you by things possible and impossible which God hath made in Heaven in Earth below in Hell in the Sea and all deeps + I Conjure you by the indivisible Trinity by the unspeakable name of God + Tetragrammaton + I Conjure you Sathan Lucifer & Dentalion That you go now unto AB And that you do not let him (or her) to be at rest any manner of ways neither Sleeping nor waking nor eating nor drinking Standing nor Sitting or Dreaming but that you cause his heart always and in all places to be fixed on my love and that he (or She) (60) be so enflamed with my love As Iron is made hot by the fire and that he accomplish all my desire in everything what soever to the uttermost of his power and that you do perform this Let him compel you who only by the word of his mouth that most high hath created all things + **Amen + fiat + fiat + fiat + amen O Lord Jesus Christ** the glorious King I pray and entreat thee to give them licence and power to cause him (or her) to love me without framing any excuse So that he may abide continue and increase in my Love So that he love me most vehemently with a love that cannot be loosed under or broken. Amen.

I Conjure you Sathan Lucifer Dentalion by all the virtues and properties of Christ Jesus our Lord + I conjure you by the Angels and Archangels + I conjure you by the love wherewith God loveth those that are his And by the love wherewith thy have loved him And by the love wherewith Mary the mother of our lord Jesus Christ her Son, And by the love wherewith God loved her + I Conjure you by the love wherewith God loved John the Evangelist And by the love wherewith Christ loved him + I Conjure you by the confessors martyrs virgins widows Innocents and Saints + I conjure you by the blessed virgin Mary the Mother of our Lord Jesus Christ And by the virginity that is in her + I Conjure you by the virginity of all virgins And by all the sufferings of all martyrs and by the

---

[209] This Goetic spirit is described in Sloane MS 3824 as stirring up love, see The Book of Treasure Spirits, Rankine, 2009:160.

merits of all confessors and Patriarchs & by the merits of Prophets and by their names and deeds + I conjure you by the crown of Thorns wherewith God was Crowned and by the pillar to which he was bound + I conjure you by the holy cross on which he was crucified + I conjure you by the Spear wherewith his side was pierced through I conjure you by his water and blood by his wounds out of which flowed forth the blood of redemption and the water of baptism + I conjure you by the Rod of Moses and by the virtue thereof I Conjure you by all the unutterable names of God and utterable in which the Patriarchs and Prophets have Preached and he assisted them + I Conjure you Sathan Lucifer Dentalion by all he Saints and she Saints of God that you cause AB to burn in my love without ceasing and that he be enflamed most vehemently with my love That in regard of his heat of love he shall be able to deny me nothing that I ask or desire + I conjure you by the conjuration before said and by the virtues and powers thereof that he (or she) whether I be present or absent may love me without ceasing + **fiat** + **fiat** + **fiat** + **amen** +

O Lord Jesus Christ I beseech thee give leave to those to persuade AB whose name and figure I bear under the sole of my foot that he may love me + **amen** + **amen** + **amen** +

Then burn the image with frankincense and sweet odours and say thou

Lift up the Gates O ye princes and be ye lifted up O you everlasting gates and the King of Glory shall come in + **Amen**

Finis Probat est[210]

Again the former Experiment:~:

Your Images and all things performed as before with the names written over the heads of the Images and these names between Sathan Lucifer Belzibub and put under the sole of the Right foot. Three times a day, 3 days together say this Conjuration. At ☉ rising At noon At ☉ setting. The 3rd day put it away for thy purpose is sped.

I Conjure you Sathan Lucifer & Belzebub which are the princes of hell which have cast Adam and Eve forth of the Earthly Paradise by your wit and cunning + I Conjure you by the father + and the

---

[210] "The end. It is proven."

Son + and the Holy Ghost + and by the 4 Elements and by all things possible and impossible and by the indivisible Trinity and chiefly by this name of God + Alpha + & + ω + and by the most excellent and unutterable name of God + Tetragrammaton + I Conjure you Sathan Lucifer Belzibub that you give me such a wench maid or damsel AB and that you do not suffer her to be at rest in any condition neither standing nor sitting & Neither by any manner or means in what place soever she shall be until she burns with my unquenchable love she give herself to me of her own accord She give me Gold Silver and all her substance & monies and accomplish my will + **fiat + fiat + fiat + amen + O Lord Jesus Christ** I beseech thee to give them power and ability to tempt her and to make her love me + Amen +

I Conjure you Sathan Lucifer Belzebub by all virtues and powers whichever God made and created + I conjure you by the Angels Archangels and 12 Apostles and by the love wherewith God loved the soul of man by the Confessors by blessed Mary the virgin and by the love wherewith Christ Jesus loved her And by the virtue which he infused into her when he separated himself from her + I Conjure you by all the virgins Patriarchs and Prophets by the Crown wherewith God was crowned by the pillar to which he was bound + I conjure you by the Cross on which God was placed + I conjure you by the Spear with which his side was opened and by the blood which gushed out of the same And by the virtue of Aaron by the Crown of Solomon + I demand of you by all the names of our lord Jesus Christ wherewith the Patriarchs and Prophets have named him + I conjure you Sathan Lucifer Belzebub by all these virtues and all other virtues that you torment such a maid or damsel AB that she may not be at rest in any manner or way until she shall accomplish my will but that she may be hot as being enflamed with the fire and heat of my love + fiat + fiat + fiat +

O Lord Jesus Christ I beseech thee give them power that they may obey me so that I may obtain the love of AB whose name is written in the Image which is put under the middle of my right foot that this may be brought to pass without any prejudice Cross danger or hurt to me + fiat + fiat + fiat + amen

(61)

Of the Circle and his composition: Peter de Abano[211]

There is not[212] one and the self same manner of Circle used for the calling of Spirits. But Places times days and hours are to be observed And the circle to be altered accordingly. It behoveth therefore a man to consider in the making of his circle, In what time of the year, what day and hour he maketh the same, what spirits he would call forth, what Star and region they govern and what functions they have.

Therefore make 3 Circles in breadth 9 feet And which stand distant one from the other one hand's breadth. And write in the middle circle first the name of the hour in which thou makest thy work. In the second place the name of the Angel of the hour. Thirdly the Seal of the Angel of the hour. Fourthly the name of the Angel that governeth that day in which thou workest and his ministers. Fifthly the name of the present time. Sixthly the name of the Spirits governing and ruling in that part of time. Seventhly the name of the head of the Sign reigning in that part of time in which thou workest. Eighthly the name of the Earth according to that part of time in which thou dost thy work. Ninthly and lastly write the names of the Sun and the Moon according to the foresaid reason of time that the middle circle may be fulfilled.

But the times changing the names also must be changed.

In the uppermost and outward circle in the 4 corners write the names of the Angels governing the Air that day in which thou workest. To wit the King and 3 of his ministers, without the circle in the 4 corners place pentagons. In the inward circle write the 4 divine names crosses placed between them. In the middle of this circle to wit at the East write Alpha and at the west Omega And let a cross divide the middle of the circle The circle being thus finished. According to what hereafter is written proceed.

---

[211] This name was added in the second hand.

[212] The following section is taken from the Heptameron with minor copying errors. See The Fourth Book of Occult Philosophy, Agrippa, 2005:60-92.

Of the Names of the Hours and Angels governing them

We must know that the Angels by successive order according[213] as the Planets which they govern, Govern the hours also. And therefore that Spirits which ruleth the day commandeth also the first hour of the day. The second governs the second. And the third the third hour &c They having gone over the hours according to the rule order and government of the Planets begin again in the same order. But of the names of the hours we must first speak.

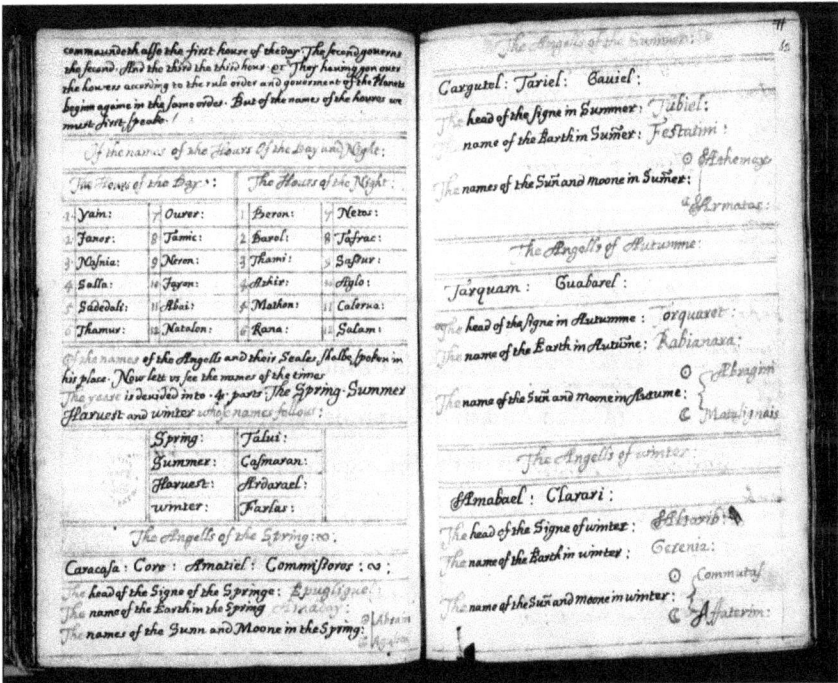

29 – *Example pages from Arthur Gauntlet showing material drawn from the Heptameron, which follows in the text*

---

[213] "according" is repeated here.

Of the names of the Hours Of the Day and Night:							
The Hours of the Day:				**The Hours of the Night:**			
1	Yain:	7	Ourer:	1	Beron:	7	Netos:
2	Janor:	8	Tanic:	2	Barol:	8	Tafrac:
3	Nasnia:	9	Neron:	3	Thami:	9	Sassur:
4	Salla:	10	Jayon:	4	Athir:	10	Aglo:
5	Sadedali:	11	Abai:	5	Mathon:	11	Calerna:
6	Thamur:	12	Natalon:	6	Rana:	12	Salam:

The names of the Angels and their Seals shall be spoken in his place. Now let us see the names of the times

The year is divided into 4 parts The Spring Summer Harvest and Winter **whose names follow:**

Spring:	Talui:	
Summer:	Casmaran:	
Harvest:	Ardarael:	
Winter:	Farlas:	

The Angels of the Spring:~:

Caracasa : Core : Amatiel : Commissoros :~:

The head of the Sign of the Spring: **Epugliguel:**[214]

The name of the Earth in Spring **Amaday:**

The names of the Sun and Moon in the Spring: ☉ **Abraim**

☽ **Agusita**

(62)

The Angels of the Summer:

Cargutel : Tariel : Gaviel:

The head of the Sign in Summer: **Tubiel:**

The name of the Earth in Summer: **Festativi:**

The names of the Sun and Moon in Summer: ☉ **Athemay**

☽ **Armatas**[215]

---

[214] This has been miscopied in the manuscript. The original text gives Spugliguel.

The Angels of Autumn:

Tarquam : Guabarel :

The head of the Sign in Autumn: **Torquaret:**

The name of the Earth in Autumn: **Rabianara**

The name of the Sun and Moon in Autumn: ☉ **Abragini**

☽ **Matasignais**

The Angels of Winter:

Amabael : Clarari:[216]

The head of the Sign of winter: **Altarib:**

The name of the Earth in winter: **Gerenia:**[217]

The name of the Sun and Moon in winter: ☉ **Commutaf**

☽ **Affaterim:**

Of Consecrations and blessings And first of blessing of the Circle:~:

After that the Circle is rightly perfected, Sprinkle it with holy water and say **Sprinkle** me O Lord with hyssop And I shall be clean Thou shalt wash me And I shall be whiter than Snow[218]

The blessing of Fumigations:

O God of Abraham God of Isaac God of Jacob bless these Creatures that they may hold in the force and virtue of their Odours. That the enemy nor Phantasms may not enter into them, Through our Lord Jesus Christ. Afterwards sprinkle them with Holy water.

---

[215] Armatus.

[216] Ctarari.

[217] Geremiah.

[218] Psalm 50:9.

An Exorcism of the Fire upon which the Fumigations are put:

The fire which we use in fumigations let it be put in a new earthen vessel and exorcise it as followeth.

I exorcise thee creature of fire by him by whom all things were made that presently thou cast off from thee (or out of thee) Every Phantasm that may hurt in any kind. **Afterwards say.**

Bless lord this Creature of fire and sanctify it That it may be blessed to the praise of thy holy name That it may not hurt the lookers-on. Through our Lord Jesus Christ.

Of the Garment and Pentacle

Let it be a Priest's Garment If it may be had If not let it be clean linen. **Afterwards** Take this Pentacle following being made the day and hour of Mercury the Moon increasing In Parchment of a Kid's skin. But first say a Mass of the Holy Ghost and sprinkle it with Baptism water.

The Pentacle followeth :∞:

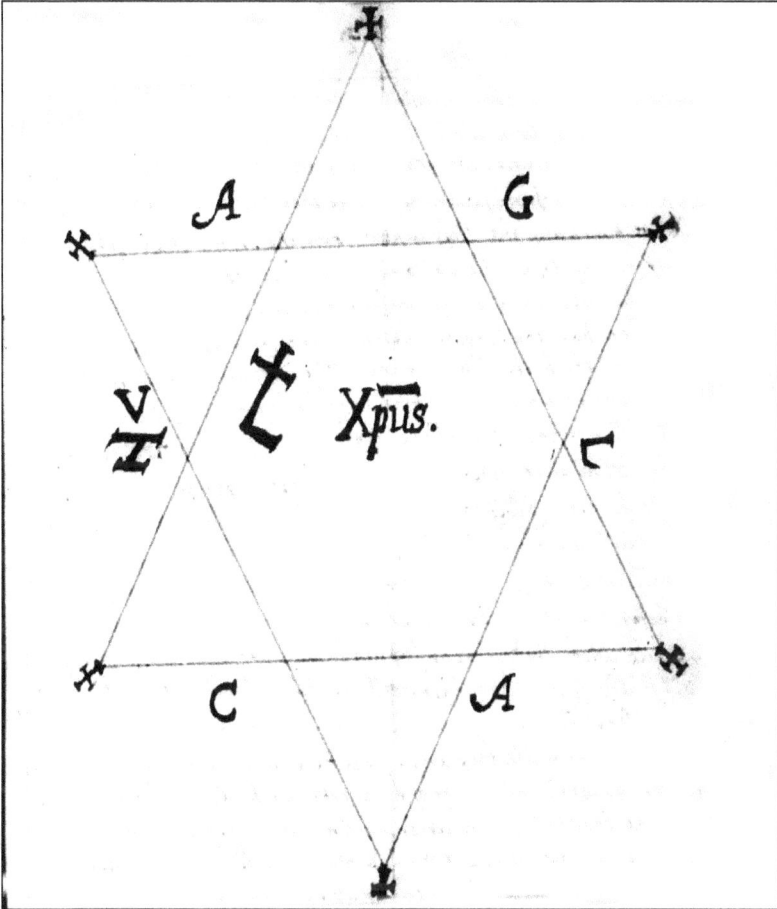

30 - Pentacle design from the Heptameron mentioned in the preceding heading The Pentacle Followeth. Note the divine name AGLA running from the top left clockwise. The figures which resemble a C and V may be simplified versions of the characters for Alpha and Omega, used as a divine name

A Prayer to be said when the vesture is put on :∞:

Ancor, Amacor, Amides, Theodonias, Anitor, **O Lord** by the Merits of thy holy Angels I will put on the vestments of health. That this which I desire I may bring to effect Through thee O most holy Adonay whose Kingdom endureth through all ages forever: **Amen:**

Of the manner of working:

Let the Moon be in the increase Or full if it may be And let it be[219] Let the workman be clean and pure for 9 days before the beginning of the work Let him be confessed And take the Sacrament Let him have his fumigations assigned to that day in which he worketh Also let him have the Holy water from the Priest, The earthen new vessel full of fire, The vestment and Pentacle. And let all these things be duly and rightly consecrated and prepared. Let one of the Scholars have the Earthen vessel full of fire and fumigations Another carry the book Another the vestment and pentacle And let the Master bear a Sword upon which let him say a Mass of the Holy Ghost And in the middle of the sword let this name + **Agla** + be written And on the other side this name + **On** + Let him go unto his consecrated place and say always Letanies[220] And let the Scholars answer him. And when he cometh to the place where he would make the circle let him draw out the lines of the Circle as is before taught. And after he hath so done let him sprinkle the Circle with Holy water saying Thou shalt purge me with Hyssop and I shall be clean Thou shalt wash me And I shall be whiter than Snow

The Master having purified himself with fasting Chastity and abstinence from all luxury 3 whole days before the day of working being clothed in the day of his work with clean apparel, his vestment Panticle fumigations And all other necessary things Let him enter the circle And Call the Angels from the 4 parts of the world which Govern the 7 Planets the 7 days of the week the colours and metals whose names in their places thou shalt see And with bended knee Calling upon and nominating the said Angels let him say

---

[219] There is a space in the text here, the original has "let her not be combust".

[220] Litanies.

O **Angels** above spoken of be you helpers in my petition and assist me in my matters and prayers.[221]

Then thou shalt call upon the Angels that rule the Air in that day in which thou makest thy work and experiment from the 4 parts of the world and implore all the Spirits and names written about in the Circle Saying (64)

O **all you** I adjure you and contest you by the seat of Adonay by Hagios, Ho, Theos, Iscyros, Athanatos, Paracletus, Alpha and Omega. And by these 3 secret names, Agla On Tetragrammaton That this day you do faithfully what I desire **This being done** Read a conjuration assigned to the day in which thou makest thy experiment As hereafter followeth.

But if they be stubborn and refractory and will not obey the conjuration for the day appointed neither the prayers before made Then use these following Conjurations and Exorcisms.

An Exorcism of the Aerial Spirits

We that are made after the Image of God, Granted the power of God and made by his will, we by the power and strong name of God El strong and admirable do Exorcise you (Naming the Spirit and his order) and command you by him which said the word and it was done And by all the names of God. And by the names of Adonay El, Elohim, Zebaoth, Elion, Escerihie, Jah, Tetragrammaton, Saday. The Lord God high we exorcise you and powerfully command you that you appear presently to us here nigh the circle In fair form (to wit) human and without any deformity or tortuosity. Come all ye such because we command you by the name **Y** and **V** which Adam heard and spake And by the name of God Agla which Lot heard and was made safe with his family and by the name Joth Which Jacob heard from the Angel with him and was delivered from the hands of his brother Esau and by the name Anephexeton Which Aaron heard and spake and was made wise And by the name Zebaoth which Moses named and all the Rivers and Moors of the land of Egypt were turned into blood. And by the names Eciriehe Oriston which Moses named and all the rivers brought forth frogs which ascended into the Houses of the Egyptians destroying all things And by the name Elion which Moses named and there was such hail such as was not from the

---

[221] This and other phrases are given in Latin in the original text.

beginning of the world And by the name Adonay which Moses named and there appeared locusts upon the land of Egypt which ate up that which the hail left And by the name Schemes Amathia which Joshua called and the Sun stayed his course And by the name of Alpha and Omega which Daniel named and he destroyed Bell and slew the Dragon And in the name of Emanuel which the 3 children Sidrach Misach and Abednigo in the hot fiery furnace sung and were delivered and by Hagios and the seat of Adonay And by O Theos Iscyros, Athanatos, Paracletus, And by these 3 secret names Agla, On Tetragrammaton I adjure and contest: And by these names And by all other names of our Lord God almighty the living and true God who for your fault cast you from Heaven into the Infernal place of Hell, we exorcise and strongly command by him who spake the word and it was done, And whom all creatures obey, And by that fearful Judgement of God, And by the Sea of Glass which is in the sight of God's majesty sliding and powerful and by the 4 divine Creatures those beasts **T** going before the seat of God's Majesty having eyes before and behind And by the fire standing about his throne And by the holy Angels of the heavens **T** And by the Church of God: And we exorcise you by that chief wisdom of the Almighty God that you appear here to us before this circle unto the doing of our will in all things as it shall please us: By the seat of Baldachia And by this name Primeumaton which Moses named and Dathan Corath and Abiram were swallowed up in the deeps of the Earth. And in the virtue of this name Primeumaton compelling the whole host of Heaven we curse you and deprive you from all office and place and your joy even to the pit of Hell And put and bind you again unto the last day of Judgement into eternal fire even the lake of fire and brimstone unless you presently appear here before us before the circle unto the doing of our will In all things Come by these names Adonay Zebaoth Adonay Amioram come (65) come come Adonay Saday The most powerful and dreadful King of Kings commands you whose power no creature is able to resist And unless ye obey and appear before the circle affably and that suddenly, Let your ruin be weeping and miserableness and remain ye for ever in the unquenchable fire. Come therefore in the name of Adonay Zebaoth Adonay Amioram come come why tarry ye make haste Adonay commands you The King of Kings El, Aty, Titeip, Azia, Hin, Len, Minosel, Achadan, Vay, Vaa, Ei, Haa, Eye, Exe, A, El, El, El, a, Hy, Hau, Hau, Hau, Va, Va, Va, Va.

A Prayer unto God which ought to be said
in the 4 parts of the world in the Circle :∞: :~:

Amorule, Taneha, Latisten, Rabur, Taneha, Latisten, Escha, Aladia, Alpha and Omega, Leyste, Oriston Adonay, My Heavenly and most Clement father have mercy on me, Make bright in me this day the Arm of thy power that I sinner may have licence thine unworthy child against these most stubborn spirits, That I (thou willing) may be made a beholder of thy divine works And may be made shining with all wisdom and always Glorify and do worship to thy holy name humbly I beseech thee and call upon thee that these spirits by thy judgement whom I call upon being convicted and bound may come being called and give true answers concerning those things I shall ask them And that they may give us and defer not those things which shall be commanded them by me or us not hurting any creature not raging nor hurting neither me nor my fellows nor any creature nor frighting no man but grant they may be obedient to my petitions in all things which I shall command them.

Then let him stand in the middle of the circle holding his hand near the Pentaculum. Let **him say**

You that are called by the Pentacle of Solomon give me true answers.

Afterwards say By the seats of Beralense By the seats of Pneumachia and Apologia, By the Kings and Magnanimous powers and Prepowerful Princes, By the Genius of Liachida the minister of the seat of Hell: Primac, this prince in the ninth bond of the Apologian seat, I call upon you And by calling I conjure you And being aided with the virtue of the high Majesty I powerfully command you by him which said and it was done And whom all creatures obey And by this ineffable name Tetragrammaton יהוה Jehovah in whom is all ages of all works at whose voice the Elements fail the Air is shaken, The Sea goeth back The fire goeth out The Earth trembleth And all the companies of Heaven, Earth and Hell quake and are troubled and fall down That presently and without delay all occasions being laid aside ye come from all parts of the world and answer us reasonably concerning all things I shall ask you and that you come peaceably visibly and talkably, which we desire and manifest your selves without delays – ye are conjured by the name of the eternal living and true God Helioren. And you perfecting our commandments persist always and unto the end and intention I have be visible to us and affable and speak with a clear and understanding voice unto us without equivocation or doubtful ambiguity.

Visions and Apparitions:

The foresaid things being rightly performed there will appear infinite visions and phantasms playing on organs and all kinds of musical Instruments And it is made of the Spirits that they might compel the Master's fellows by fear out of the Circle because they can do nothing against the Master. After these things thou shalt see infinite bowmen with an infinite number of Horrible beasts which seem as if they want to devour thy fellows but notwithstanding fear nothing. Then the Priest or the Master holding his hand on the Pentacle let him say

Let your iniquity depart hence by the virtue of the power of God and then the Spirits are constrained to obey the Master And his fellows shall see them no more. (66)

After this the Exorcist holding his hand near the Pentacle shall say

Behold Solomon's Pentacle which I have brought before your presence. Behold the person of the Exorcist in the middle of his Exorcism who is weaponed very well from God without fear Circumspect who hath invocated and called powerfully by force Exorcising you. Come therefore with speed In the virtue of the names Aye Saraye Aye Saraye Aye Saraye Do not defer your coming by the eternal names of the living and true God Eloy Archiman Rabar: And by this present Pentacle which powerfully commandeth upon you And by the virtue of the Heavenly Spirits your Masters and the person of the exorcist you are conjured to come quickly And obey your Master who is called Octimonos.

These things being finished there will be a hissing in the 4 corners of the world and thou shalt see immediately great motions and when thou seest it say.

Why tarry ye why delay you what do ye prepare yourselves and obey your master In the name of the lord Bathat or Vachat overthrowing above Abac coming above Abeor above Aberer.

Then Immediately, they will come in their proper forms and when thou shalt see them nigh the Circle Show them the Pentacle covered over with holy fine linen and uncover it. And say

Behold your conclusion be not made disobedient. And suddenly thou shalt see them in a peaceable form And they will say to thee Ask what thou wilt for we are prepared to fulfil all thy Commandments because the lord hath yoked us under unto these things.

But when the Spirits are appeared then say

Ye are welcome Spirits and most noble Kings for we have called you by him to whom every knee boweth of things in Heaven earth and Hell, In whose Hands[222] the Kingdoms of all Kings are neither is there anything which he is not able to do. Also for as much as we bind you that ye remain affable and visible here before the circle as long as my pleasure is And so constant And not without my licence to depart until you perfect my will by true speech without any deceit by the virtue of that power who hath given the Sea her bounds that she cannot pass, (to wit) God the highest the King and lord who created all things. **Amen.**

Then command what thou wilt And it shall be done After these things licence them to depart, **Thus,**

In the name of the Father of the Son and of the Holy Ghost Go unto your places: And peace be between us and you Be ye prepared to come again being called.

These are those things which Peter of Abano said concerning the Elements or Grounds of Magick.

But that thou mayest the more easily know how to make the Circle **Let it be thus** As suppose we should make it in the spring time The first hour of the Sunday Then shall it be as in the figure following you may behold.

(67)

---

[222] "In whose Hands" is repeated.

It now remaines that wee should serch out dilligently the weeke wherein we worke with every day perticular: ly And the Spirits which Governe them which now shall follow in Order And first of the lords day ·/

31 - Magic Circle copied from the Hepatmeron and placed here in the text. This particular circle is for the first hour of the Lords day, in Spring

It now remains that we should search out diligently the week wherein we work with every day particularly And the Spirits which govern them which now shall follow in Order And first of the lords day.

Considerations for Sunday:

The Angel of the lord's day And his Seal His Planet And the sign of the Planet And the name of the fourth Heaven

---

Michael: Machen:

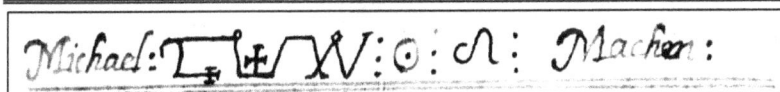

32 - Seal for Michael, and sigils for the Sun and Leo

The Angels of the Sunday:~:

Michael : Dardiel : Hartapel:

The Angels of the Air reigning the Lords Day :~:

Varcan the King: **His Ministers:** Tus: Andas: Cynabal:

The wind that those Angels are under is **The North Wind :~:**

The Angels of the fourth Heaven Reigning on the lords day whom it behoveth to call from the parts of the world.

At the East:~:

Samael: Baciel: Atel: Gabriel: Vionatraba:

At the West:~:

Anael: Pabel: Ustael: Burchat: Suceratos: Capabili

From the North:~:

Aiel: Aniel: or Aquiel: Malgabriel: Sapiel: Matuyel:

From the South:~:

Habudiel:[223] Machasiel: Charsiel: Uriel: Naromiel:~:

The perfume for Sunday is: Red Saunders:~:[224] (68)

---

[223] Haludiel.

A Conjuration for Sunday:

I Conjure and confirm upon you O ye strong and holy Angels of God In the name of Adonay Eye Eye Eye which is he which was is and shall be Eye Abraye and in the name of Saday Cados Cados Cados Sitting high above the Cherubins And by that great name of that God strong and Powerful and Exalted above all Heavens Eye Saraye The maker of Ages who hath created the world the Heaven Earth Sea and all that in them is In the first day And hath sealed them by his holy name Phaa And by the name of the holy Angels who rule in the fourth Host and serve before the most powerful Salamia, That great and honoured Angel And by the name of the Star which is the Sun, And by His Sign and by the great name of the living God And by all the foresaid names I conjure thee O Michael, thou great Angel who art in authority the lords day And by the name of Adonay, The God of Israel who created the world and whatsoever is in it, That thou mayest labour for me And fulfil all my petition according to my will and desire in my business and cause.

Here tell thy cause and business. Tell him farther for what thing thou undertookest this conjuration.

The Spirits of the Air on Sunday are under the North wind and their nature is to obtain by request Gold, Gems, Carbuncles, Riches, Grace, and benevolence, To unloose the enmity of men, To give honours to men, To bring in infirmities or to take them away but how they appear is spoken of elsewhere

Considerations of Moonday

The Angel of the Moonday his Image or seal his Planet and sign of the planet And the name of the fifth Heaven.

Gabriel : Shamain

33 - Seal for Gabriel, and sigils for the Moon and Cancer

---

[224] The Turner translation of the Heptameron gives "red wheat" here.

The Angels of the Moonday

Gabriel: Michael: Samael

The Angels of the Air reigning on Moonday

Arcan the King. His Ministers Bilet: Massabu: Abuzaha

The wind under which the Angels of the Air are is The west wind

The Angels of the first Heaven reigning on Moonday whom it behoveth to call from the four parts of the world.

From the East:~:

Gabriel. Gabrael. Madiel. Deamiel. Janael.

From the west:~:

Sachiel. Zaniel. Habaiel. Bachanel. Corabiel.

From the North:~:

Mael. Vuael. Valnum. Baliel. Balay. Humastrau.

From the South:∞:

Curaniel. Dabriel. Darquiel. Hanun. Anayl. Vetuel.

The fumigation for Moonday is **Aloes:**

A Conjuration on Moonday:

I Conjure and confirm upon you, you strong and good Angels, In the name of Adonay, Adonay, Adonay, Eye, Eye, Eye, Cados, Cados, Cados, Achim, Achim, Ja, Ja, the strong Ja who appeared on the mountain of Sinai with the glorification of King Adonay, Saday, Zebaoth, Anathay, Ya, Ya, Ya, Marinata, Abim, Jeia, who created the Seas Lakes and all waters on the second day Some above the Heavens some on Earth. He hath sealed the Sea by his high name and her bounds that he hath given her, She cannot pass And by the names of the Angels which rule in the first Host which serve Orphamiell that great Angel precious and honoured And by the name of the Star which is the Moon And by the forespoken name I conjure upon you O Gabriel who art in authority on Moonday that for me thou mayest Labour and fulfil all my petition according to my will and desire in my business and cause &c.

The Spirits of the Air of Moonday are under the west wind which is the wind of the Moon. Their nature is to give Silver, To carry things from one place to another to give swift Horses To tell secrets of persons whether they be secrets of present or past. But how they appear is manifested elsewhere.

Considerations for Tuesday

The Angel of Tuesday His Seal His Planet And the Sign ruling the Planet Also the name of the Fifth Heaven.

Samael: Machon

34 - Seal for Samael, and sigils for Mars, Aries & Scorpio

The Angels of Tuesday:~:

Samael. Satael. Amabiel.

The Angels of the Air reigning on **Tuesday:~:**

Samax, King. His Ministers. Carmax. Ismoli. Paffran.

The wind under which these Angels of the air are is **The East wind**

The Angels of the fifth Heaven ruling on the Tuesday whom it behoveth to call from the four parts of the world.

From the East:∞:

Friagne. Guael. Damael. Calzas. Arragon.

From the west:~:

Lama. Astagna. Lobquin. Soncas. Jaxel. Isiael. Irel.

From the North:~:

Rahumel. Hymiel. Rayel. Seraphiel. Mathiel. Fraciel.

From the South:~:

Sacriel. Janiel. Caldel. Osael. Vianuel. Zaliel.

The perfume for Tuesday is Pepper:~: (70)

A Conjuration for Tuesday:

I Conjure and confirm upon you O you strong and holy Angels by the name of Ya, Ya, Ya, He, He, He, Hy, Hy, Ha, Ha, Ha, va, va, va, An, An, A, Aie, Aie, Aie, El, Ay, Elibra, Eloim, Eloim, And by the names of that God who made the water to appear dry and called it Earth. And brought forth Trees and Herbs from it And hath sealed it with his Precious Honoured and Holy name that is to be feared, And by the name of the Angels ruling the fifth Host who serve Acimay the great Angel strong Powerful and Honoured. And by the name of the star which is Mars, And by the foresaid names I conjure upon thee thou great Angel Samael who has the authority to rule the day of Mars and by the names of Adonay the living and true God that thou labour for me and fulfil all my petition according to my will and desire in my business and cause, &c.

The spirits of the Air on Tuesday are under the East wind their nature is to make battle, Mortalities, Slaughters, and burnings, And to give 2000 soldiers at a time Also to give death, Infirmity, or health. But how they appear look elsewhere.

Considerations of Wednesday:

The Angel of Wednesday his Seal, Planet And the Sign ruling that Planet Also the name of the Second Heaven

Raphael: Raquie

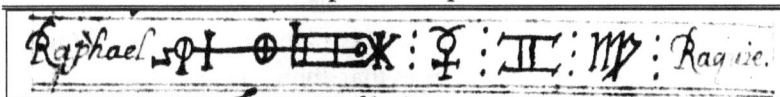

35 - Seal for Raphael, and sigils for Mercury, Gemini & Virgo

The Angels of Wednesday:~:

Raphiel. Miel. Seraphiel.

The Angels of the Air Reigning on **Wednesday**

Mediat or Modiat King. **His Ministers.** Suquinos. Sallales.

The wind under which the said Angels are is **The South wind:~:**

The Angels of the Second Heaven ruling on Wednesday whom it behoveth to call from the four parts of the world.

From the East:
Mathlay. Tarmiel. Baraborat.

From the west:
Jerescue. Mitratron.

From the North:
Thiel. Rael. Jariahel. Venahel. Valel. Abuiori. v

From the South:
Milliel. Nelapa. Babel. Caluel. Vel. Laquel.

The fumigation for Wednesday is **Mastic:~:** (71)

A Conjuration for Wednesday:

I Conjure and confirm upon you, you strong Angels, Holy and powerful In the name of the strong and most to be feared and blessed Ja, Adonay, Eloim, Saday, Saday, Saday, Eie, Eie, Eie, Asamie, Asaraie, and in the name of Adonay the God of Israel who created the great lights to distinguish the day from the night And by the names of all the Angels serving in the second Host before the great Angel Tetra, both strong and powerful, And by the name of the Star which is called Mercury And by the name of his Image which is signed from God most puissant and Honourable by all things aforesaid I conjure upon thee O Raphael, the great Angel who art in authority the fourth day And by the holy name which was written in the forehead of Aaron the Priest of the most high creator, And by the names of the Angels who are confirmed in the grace of their saviour, And by the name of the seat of those creatures which have 6 wings[225] that thou mayest labour for me And fulfil my petition according to my will and desire in my business and cause.

The Spirit of the Air on Wednesday are under the South wind Their nature is to give all Metals all earthly things, To reveal things – present past and to come: To please Judges, To give victories in battle And to re-edify or build again all destroyed sciences, And to teach Experiments, And to change mixed bodies of the Elements conditionally one into another, To give Infirmities or health to exalt

---

[225] This refers to the angels called the Seraphim.

the poor to cast down the high and lofty, To bind or loose a Spirit or Spirits, To open locks. The Spirits have such operations of others but not from their perfect power, but in virtue and science. But how they appear &c.

The Considerations for Thursday:~:

The Angel of Thursday his Seal His Planet and the Sign ruling the Planet Also the name of the Sixth heaven.

Sachiel: Zebul

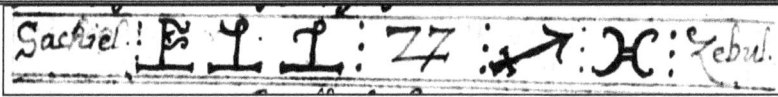

36 - Seal of Sachiel, sigils of Jupiter, Sagittarius & Pisces

Angels of Thursday

Sachiel. Castiel. Asasiel.

The Angels of the Air Reigning on **Thursday**:~:

Suth the King. **His Ministers.** Maguth. Gutriz

The wind under which the foresaid Angels are Is **The South wind:~:**

But because the Angels of the Air are not found beyond the fifth Heaven therefore on Thursday Say in the 4 parts of the world the prayers following.

At the East:~:

O God great high and honoured through infinite ages. I beseech thee.

At the west:~:

O God wise Glorious and Just and divine Clemency I beseech thee holy father that I may fulfil my petition That my work and labour I may perfectly understand O thou which livest and reignest through Infinite ages of ages. **Amen.**

At the North:~:

O God powerful strong and without beginning, I beseech thee.

At the South:~:

O God puissant and merciful.

The perfume on Thursday is **Saffron:~:** (72)

A Conjuration for Thursday

I Conjure and confirm upon you holy Angels by the name of Cados, Cados, Cados, Eschereie, Eschereie, Eschereie, Hatim, ya, strong the confirmer of ages, Cantine, Jaim, Janic, Anic, Calbat, Sabbac, Beresay, Alnaim, And by the name of Adonay, who created fishes and creeping things in the waters And Birds above the face of the Earth flying in the open firmament of Heaven on the fifth day, And by the names of the Angels serving in the Sixth Host before the Pastor Angel that holy great and powerful prince, And by the name of the Star which is Jupiter And by the name of his Seal, And by the name of Adonay, The greatest God and creator of all things And by the names of all Stars And by the force and virtue of them And by the foresaid names I conjure thee Sachiel, thou great Angel who hast authority on Thursday That thou labour for me And fulfil my petition according to my will and desire in my business and Cause &c.

The Spirit of the Air on Thursday are subject to the South wind. Their nature is to get the love of women To make men joyful and merry To pacify strifes, To make enemies mild, To heal the infirm To make infirm the whole, To bring or take away loss. But how they appear &c

Considerations for Friday:

The Angel of Friday, his Seal his Planet The Sign ruling the Planet Also the name of the Third Heaven.

Anael: Sagum

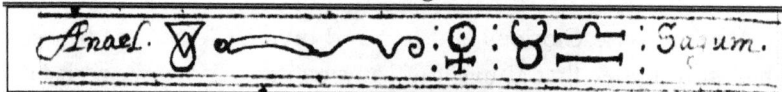

37 - Seal for Anael, and sigils for Venus, Taurus & Libra

The Angels of Friday

Anael. Rachiel. Sachiel.

The Angels of the Air ruling on **Friday**

Serabotes the King. **His Ministers** Amabiel. Aba. Abalidoth. Flaef.

The wind under which these said Angels are is **The west wind**

~

The Angels of the third Heaven Ruling on Friday whom it behoveth to call forth from the four parts of the world.

From the East:~:

Setchiel. Chedusitaniel. Corat. Tamael. Tenaciel.

From the west:~:

Turiel. Coniel. Babiel. Kadie. Maltiel. Hufaltiel

From the North:~:

Peniel. Penael. Penat. Raphael. Raniel. Doremiel.

From the South:~:

Porna. Sachiel. Chermiel. Samael. Santanael. Famiel.

The fumigation for Friday is **Costuo**.[226]

---

(73)

A Conjuration for Friday:

I Conjure and confirm upon you, you strong angels holy and powerful In the name of On, Hey, Heya, Ja, Je, Adonay, Saday, And in the name of Saday, who created 4 footed beasts and creeping things And men on the Sixth day And gave power to Adam over al living creatures, From whence blessed be the name of the Creator in his place, And by the names of the Angels serving in the third host before Dagiel, the great Angel the strong and puissant Prince And by the name of the Star which is Venus, And by her Image which truly is holy And by the aforesaid names I conjure upon thee Anael, who hast the authority the Sixth day That thou labour for me And fulfil my petition according to my will and desire in my business and cause &c.

The Spirits of the Air in Friday are under the west wind Their nature is to give silver To stir up men and make them move inclining to Riot and luxury to make friends enemies as by excess And to make Marriages, To allure Men unto the love of women, To give infirmities and to take them away And to do all things which hath motion.

---

[226] The Turner translation gives Pepperwort. Kostos or Costos (*Saussurealappa*) has a long history of use in incense, see e.g. the Greek Magical Papyri, PGM XIII.17-20.

Considerations for Saturns day

The Angel of Saturns day. His Seal his Planet And the Sign ruling that Planet.

Cassiel

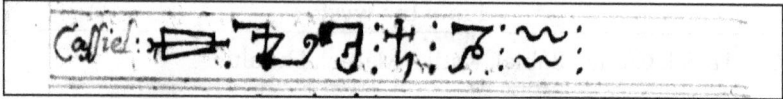

38 - Seal of Cassiel, sigils of Saturn, Capricorn & Aquarius

Angels of Saturns day

Cassiel. Machatan. Uriel.

The Angels of the Air ruling on Saturns day

Maymon the King. **His Ministers** Abumalith. Assaibi. Balidet.

The wind under which the foresaid Angels are is **The South wind.**[227]

It is said in the considerations of Thursday That beyond the fifth Heaven no Angels of the Air rule Therefore use the same Prayers.

At the East:~:

O great and high God honourable through all the world I beseech thee.

At the West:~:

O wise God both Glorious and just And of great Clemency I beseech thee holy father that I may fulfil my petition That my work and my labour this day and perfectly understand it Bring thou this to pass which liveth and Reigneth forever world without end. **Amen.**

At the North:~:

O mighty and strong God and without beginning, I beseech thee.

At the South:~:

O mighty and merciful God.

---

[227] Turner gives South-west wind.

The fumigation for Saturns day is **Brimstone:~:**[228] (74)

A Conjuration for Saturns day:

I Conjure and confirm upon you Caphriel or Cassiel, Machatori and Seraquiel strong and powerful Angels by the name of Adonay, Adonay, Adonay, Eie, Eie, Eie, Acim, Acim, Acim, Cados, Cados, Ina or Ima, Saday, Ja, Sar, the lord the creator of Ages who rested on the seventh day And by him who gave his Children Israel an Inheritance, That they should keep and Sanctify it holy That they might remunerate him in another age. And by the names of the Angels serving in the Seventh host Booel[229] the great Angel and powerful prince And by the name of the Star which is Saturn And by his holy Image And by the foresaid names I conjure thee Caphriel, who hast authority the Seventh day which is the Sabbath day That thou labour for me and fulfil my petition according to my will and desire in my business and cause &c.

The Spirits of the Air on Saturday are under the South wind.[230] Their nature is to sow discord hatred and evil thoughts To give lead at their pleasure To slay something, To cut off some member. But how the appearance is elsewhere shown.[231] (75)

---

[228] Brimstone is another name used for sulphur.

[229] Turner gives Pooel.

[230] Turner gives Southwest wind.

[231] The end of the material copied from the Heptameron.

The fourth Book of the hidden Philosophy or of the Magical ceremonies: written by Cornelius Agrippa

In our books[232] of the hidden philosophy we have not declared so compendiously as copiously the beginning of Magick itself and the reasonableness. And our experiments are sifted out and composed That they might bring forth all wonderful effects. The truth is because they are delivered there more by contemplation than by practice. Also some are not so complete. Some are spoken figuratively (as it were in a riddle) that sometimes those things which with great study diligence and curious searching out we have obtained are expounded to all ignorant vulgars: **Therefore** in this book we have finished the hidden philosophy which is as the complement and key of the books of all Magical works:~ And we will give thee the precepts and most joyful experiments of the undefiled truth and unvanquished magical discipline of the holy Gods: That when thou readest these books of the hidden Philosophy thou mayest desire to know these things greedily Therefore read this book and thou shalt triumph of the truth wherefore touch it within the secrets of thy religious breast and it will pierce with silence. But conceal it with a constant taciturnity.

But know thou this that the names of the intelligences governing every one of the Planets are ordained after this manner For the letters being gathered from the figure of the world from the rising of the body of the Planet according to the succession of the Signs by single degrees. And by those single degrees aspected by the Planet itself made by the degree of the ascendant. After the same manner the names of the princes of the evil Spirits are received by a retrograde or back degree order. Governing under all the Planets by making extension against the succession of the Signs from the beginning of the Seventh house But the name of the supreme intelligence whom many judge to be the soul of the world is gathered from the four bounds of the figure of the world according as I have delivered the reason. And by the opposite manner is gathered the name of the great Devil about the four cadent corners. Likewise thou shalt gather the names of the great spirits governing the powers of the air above the four corners of the succeeding houses So that a casting out is made that the name of

---

[232] This is the start of the material from Agrippa's Of Occult Philosophy or Of Magical Ceremonies. See The Fourth Book of Occult Philosophy, Agrippa, 2005:19-57.

the good Spirit may be picked out according to the succession of the Signs beginning from the degree of the ascendant. But to find out the name of the evil spirit do the contrary.

But know this That the names of the evil Spirits are drawn out by these tables. The names of the good as well as of the bad spirits So that notwithstanding if we enter into the table with the name of the good Spirit of the second order we shall find out the name of the evil Spirit of the order of the Princes and governors. But if we enter the table with the name of a good Spirit of the third order Or with the name of an evil Spirit the governor what way soever they are picked out, either by this table or by the Heavenly figure the names which proceed from these will be the names of the evil Spirits the ministers of the inferior order.

Also this we must know That as often as we enter into this table[233] with the good Spirits of the second order The names themselves are drawn out of the second order. And if under them we draw out the name of the evil Spirit It is that of the superior order of the Governors. And it is the same if we enter with the name of the evil Spirit of the superior order. But if we enter this table with the names of the spirits of the third order Or of the Spirits the ministers as well good as bad. The names of the Spirits the ministers of the inferior order will be picked out.

But many Magicians men not of little authority after this manner would enlarge their tables in Latin letters So that by the same tables as also by the name of the office or of any effect the name of the Spirit as well good as bad was found out. Likewise as above it is delivered by taking the name of the office or effect in the column of the letters in his line under his Star. And the great author of this is Trismegistus who when he delivered his calculation in the Egyptian letters he could not refer them foolishly to other letters of other tongues by reason of the assigned to the Signs. But of all men who have handled to find out the names of the Spirits he was the first that was extant.

Therefore the force and secret and dignity of a master consisteth in disposing of the vowels how rightly and truly the holy names of (76) the Spirits are found out which may bring to pass the name of the Spirit and to whom the right name is appointed. And this artifice is thus performed. First in placing the vowels of these

---

[233] This table is in Book 3, ch.27 of Agrippa's Three Books of Occult Philosophy.

letters which by calculation of the heavenly figure are found out, unto the names of the Spirits of the second order good and bad Governing and Governors shall be picked out And this is thus performed in the good: The Stars being considered which ordain letters and place them in order First the degree of the eleventh house is subtracted from the degree of the Star which is the former in order And that which then remaineth is cast away[234] from the degree of the ascendant And where that number ceaseth there is part of the vowel of the first Letter. Begin therefore to cast away the vowels of those letters according to his number and order. And that which shall happen in the place of the star which is the former in order That vowel is attributed to the first letter. From henceforth thou mayest find part of the second Letter By subtracting the degree of the star which is second in order from the former star and what remaineth cast away from the Ascendant And this is part from which thou mayest begin to cast away vowels and what shall happen above after the Star that is the vowel of the second letter And so consequently thou shalt fetch out the vowels of the following letters Always subtracting the degree of the Star following from the degree of the Star next going before And all casting away and numerations must be made according to the Succession of the Signs in the names of the good Spirits But in the names of the evil Spirits wherein the good the degree of the eleventh house is taken, In them the degree of the twelfth house is taken But the numerations and projections or castings away are all done with the succession of Signs taken their beginning from the degree of the tenth house. But in all these things extracted by the tables the vowels are placed after another manner. For first the how many number of letters is taken appointing the name itself And so it is numbered from the beginning of the column of the first letter or under which the name is extracted And the letter into which this number happeneth is referred unto the first letter of the name extracted by taking a distance of the one from the other according to the order of the Alphabet. But the number of that distance is cast away from the beginning of his column and where it ceaseth there is the part of the former vowel Therefore cast away the vowels themselves from it in his number and order and in the same column: And what shall happen above the first letter of the name that shall be attributed to itself. But thou shalt find the following vowels by taking distance from the foregoing letter unto that that

---

[234] I.e. subtracted.

followeth And so consequently according to the Succession of the Alphabet. And the number of the distance is numbered from the beginning of his column; And where it happeneth there is part of the vowel sought for. Therefore cast away the vowels from it (as it is spoken of above) and those which shall happen above his letters are attributed to the same But if some vowel should happen above a vowel, Let the former give place to the latter: But understand this only of the good spirits: And in the bad thou mayest proceed the same way: unless thou makest numberings by a contrary and returned order And against the succession of the Alphabet And against the order of the columns to wit of the Ascendant.

The name of the good Spirit of every man called his Genius which we have taught to find out in the third book of the hidden Philosophy according to that reason not of little authority, neither is it of a small foundation. But now we will show thee some other way assayed not with vain reasons. Of these one is by taking five places of the Hylegions[235] in the figure of nativity which being noted the characters of the letters in their order and number from the beginning of Aries are cast away And those letters which fall into the degrees of the said places according to the order and dignity of them being disposed and combined do make plain the name of the Genius: There is also another way. Almutel are taken That is domineering Stars above the five said places, And let a projection or casting out be made from the degree of the Ascendant by gathering the letters falling above Almutel which being placed according to their dignity in order ordain the name of the Genius or Spirit of such a man: There is yet another way in much custom with the Ægyptians by making an extent from the degree of the ascendant by gathering the letters. The second Almutel of the eleventh house which house they call the good Devil[236] which being placed according to their dignity do ordain the names of men's Spirits. But after the same manner we find out the evil Genius or spirit of man But that projections are made against order (77) And succession of the signs And wherein the good we cast forth from the beginning of Aries. In the bad we number from the beginning of Libra: wherein the good we number from the degrees of the

---

[235] The five hylegical parts were heavenly positions calculated by reference to the planets and used in medieval astrological charts. They are the Sun, Moon, Ascendant, Mid-Heaven and Part of Fortune.

[236] Turner gives 'daemon'.

Ascendant, In the bad we cast away from the degree of the Seventh house. But according to the Ægyptians the name of the Genius is gathered after Almutel of the twelfth house whom they call the evil Devil. And all these rites which we have delivered from us to others being written in the Third book of the hidden Philosophy may be done by the characters of any language: Seeing in all these (as above it is said) There is A mystical and divine number, order, and figure, From whence it cometh to pass that the same Genius or Spirit of man may be called by diverse names. But others from the name of the same Spirit good or bad are extracted by tables formed unto this.

Therefore the heavenly characters consist of lines and heads. There are six heads according to the six magnitudes or greatness of the Stars unto which also the Planets are reduced. The first magnitude keepeth a star or cross with the Sun. The second with Jupiter holds a circular point The third with Saturn, A half circle triangle round or sharp The fourth keeps with Mars one line passing through another or a Squared right or crooked. The fifth with Venus and Mercury a Girdle or a tailed point ascending or descending. The sixth with the Moon black points all which thou mayest behold in the table following. Therefore placing the heads according to the situation of the Stars in the figure of Heaven, Then the lines are prolonged according to the convenience of their natures, And this thou must understand of the fixed Stars. But in the erections of the Planets the heads being placed according to their aspect among themselves the times are prolonged.

39 - *The six heads attributed to the classical planets, placed here in the text*

But when a Character is to be formed of any heavenly Image ascending in any degree or face of the Signs which consist of the Stars of the same Magnitude and nature Then placing the number of those Stars according to their situation and order their lines are drawn out like the signified image that it may be done copiously.

But the Characters which are drawn out according to the name of the Spirit are compounded by this table following by giving to every letter of the name that which agreeth to itself in the table: Like as it is easily manifest. But in this there is not a little difficulty when as to wit the letter of the name into the line of figures or letters that we might know what figure or what letter is to be taken. But this maybe thus known: For if A letter should happen in the line of letters, Consider how many this letter is in the order of the name as the second or third: Then how many letters the name itself contains, as five, or seven: And multiply these numbers together among themselves, and triple the product. Afterward the whole being gathered together, cast away from the beginning of the letters according to the succession of the Alphabet: And into which of the letters that number happeneth that it is that ought to be put in the Character of that Spirit. But if some letter of a name happen into the line of figures: This shalt thou do, Take the number how many this letter is in the order of the name, and multiply it by the number how many this letter is in the Order of the Alphabet, and being gathered together divide it by nine The residue showeth the figure or number to be placed in the Character. For it may be placed either with a Geometrical figure, or with an Arithmetical figure or number which notwithstanding ought not to be noninary[237] or to exceed the nine corners. **The Characters follow.**

These figures are to be placed under or as the foot of the next table. Of the Good Spirit

A Letter Stichinge.	Joyning to.	Separated.
ſ	ſ	ſ

40 - Addition for the table of Good Spirits, as mentioned immediately preceding by the comment The Characters Follow

---

[237] Nine.

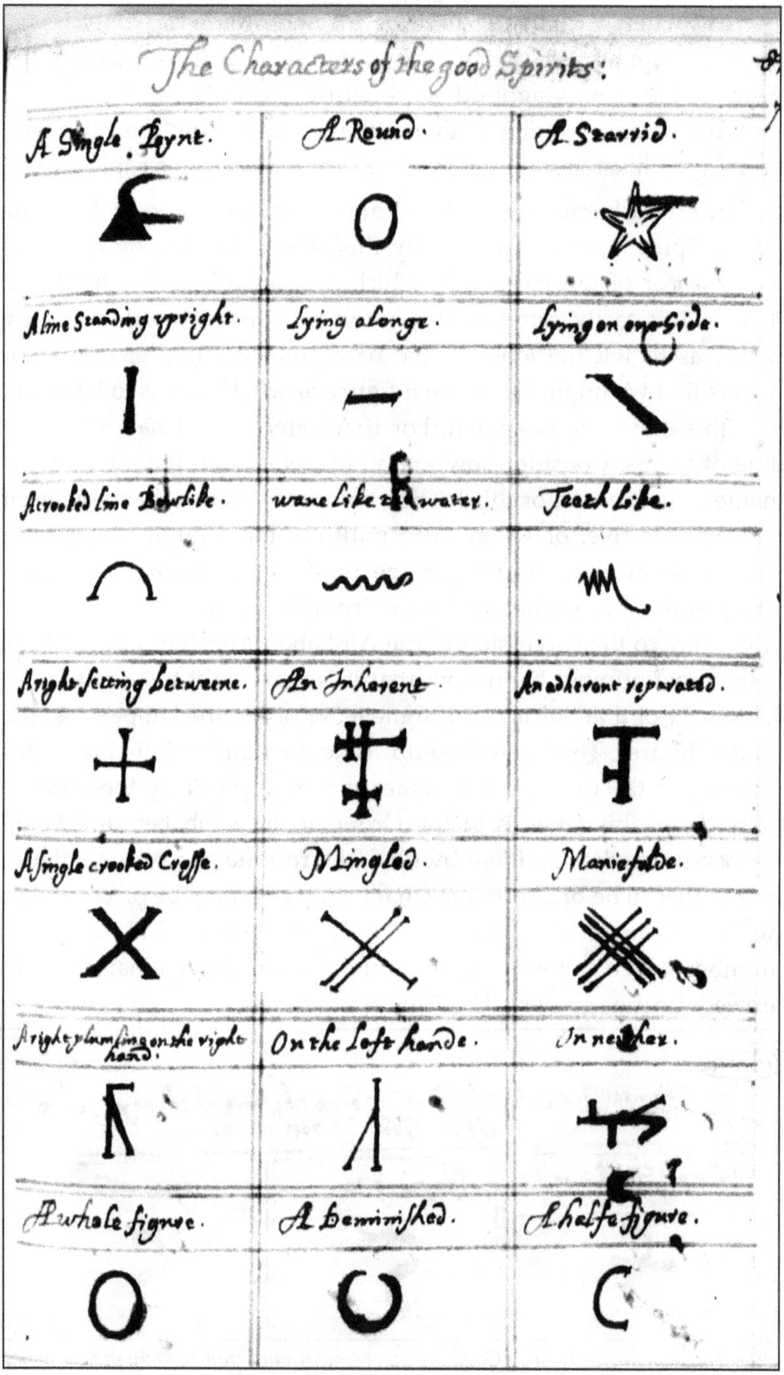

41 - Table of the Characters for Good Spirits

The Characters of the Euill Spirits:

A Right line.	A Crooked.	A bending back.
A Single figure.	Penetrans.	Broken.
A right letter.	Retrograde.	Turned vpside Downe.
A Flame.	The winde.	A Riuer.
A Masse Or Lumpe.	Raine.	Clay.
A flying beast.	Creeping Beast.	A Serpent.
An Eye.	A Hande.	A Foote.
A Crowne.	A Crest.	Horned.
A Scepter.	A Sworde.	A linke Or Torch.

42 - Table of the Characters for Evil Spirits

(79) The Characters which are taken by the revelation of the Spirits have afterward their virtues: Because they are certain little signs lying open ordaining the harmony of the same divinity: Or they are signs of making a covenant and promise of faith or obedience: And those Characters cannot be sought out by any other way. And furthermore there are Characters which are some certain familiar figures and images of the evil Spirits under whose form they are wont to appear and meet with those that call for them And these Images are found out by the Table following, according to the reason of the letters which ordain the name of the Spirit himself, So that if any letter be accounted or reckoned manyfold in the same Spirit the Image of him possesseth the sovereignty or Lordship, the rest after their manner by mixture, So that those that are the former orders the superior part the head of the body is attributed to them according to their figure: But the last occupy the feet and legs; So the middle letters show something to be like the middle part of the body, But if any contrariety shall happen, that letter which is the better in number let it prevail: But if things be equal they shall be mingled together: Moreover if the same name shall obtain some notable token or Instrument from the table of Characters the same also shall obtain it in the Image. But we shall be able to know the dignities of the evil Spirits by those tables of the Characters and Images. For to what Spirit soever shall happen some notable token or instrument from the table of Characters The same possesseth the dignity, If it shall be a Crown it showeth a kingly dignity, If a Crest it shows a Captain's honour, If horns it shows fellowship, If without them the Sceptre or Sword shows rule and authority, Likewise thou shalt find by the table of Images who carrieth before him a kingly dignity, Judge from the Crown comes dignity, From instruments Authority. Lastly they who are very good in human figure they are more worthy than they who agree in the images of beasts. Furthermore the horsemen exceed footmen. And thou shalt judge the excellency of the spirits according to all their mingled dignities, Notwithstanding know this that the Spirits of the inferior order of what dignity soever they be always are subject to the Spirits of the superior order And so it is not inconvenient that kings and captains should be under and minister to them that are before them of a higher order. The Table followeth.

The familiar forms of the Spirits of Saturn: ♄:

They appear as with a very long and slender body, with a wrathful countenance, having four faces, one in the hinder part of the head, another in the forepart of the head and both of them beaked like a bird's bill: In either of their knees appeareth also faces: They are of a black colour shining that one may see through them: Their Motion or moving is the stirring of winds with the shape of an Earthquake. Their sign is white earth, whiter than any snow.

But their particular forms are:

A Bearded King riding on a Dragon **An** Old Bearded Man **An** old Woman with a Staff **A** Hog **A** Dragon **An** Owl **A** Black Garment **a** Hook or Bill **The** Juniper Bush

The familiar forms of the Spirits of Jupiter:

They appear with a Sanguine and Choleric body of a middle Stature with an horrible motion, with a mild visage, and fair speech, Of a Green colour. Their motion is a brandishing or glittering with Thunder Their sign is, There will appear near the circle men who shall be devoured by Lions in shape.

But their particular forms are:

A King riding on a Hart with a glittering Sword **A** Man clothed with a long Garment **A** Maid with a Laurel Crown decked with flowers **A** Bull **A** Hart **A** Peacock **A** Blue garment **A** Sword **The** Box-tree. (80)

The familiar forms of the Spirits of Mars:

They will appear with a long body choleric and with most ill-favoured and deformed looks, Of a brown colour as it were somewhat red with Horns almost like a Harts, and with the nails of a Griffin, They bellow like mad bulls. Their motion is made as it were like unto burning fire. Their Sign in shape is Lightning and Thunder near the Circle.

But their particular forms are:

An armed King riding on a wolf **An** Armed man **A** woman holding a Shield on her thigh **A** Buck Goat **A** Horse **A** Hart **A** Red Garment Wool.[238]

The familiar forms for the Spirits of Sol: ☉:

They appear as with a very large and great body, Sanguine and fat with a Golden colour about the dyed blood. Their motion is the glittering of Heaven, and their sign is to trouble or move sweat in him that calleth them.

But their particular forms are:

A King having a Sceptre riding on a Lion **A** King wounded **A** Queen with a Sceptre **A** Bird **A** Lion **A** Cock **A** Garment of a Saffron colour or Golden **A** Sceptre Tailed

The familiar forms for the Spirits of Venus: ♀:

They appear with a fair body of a middle stature amiable and pleasant in countenance of a white or Green colour Gilt from above. Their motion is like to a most clear Star. For their sign Maids will be seen playing without the Circle who will move the caller into play.

But their particular forms are:

A King with a Sceptre riding on a Camel **A** Maid fairly apparelled **A** Naked maid **A** She Goat **A** Camel **A** She Dove **A** white Garment or Green Flowers **The** Savine herb.[239]

The familiar forms for the Spirits of Mercury: ☿:

They will appear as with a body of a middle stature, Cold, moist, fair, with an affable speech In a human form like to an armed Soldier of a colour shining through. Their motion is like to a silver cloud, for their sign they bring horror to him that calleth them.

---

[238] Turner includes "A Cheeslip".

[239] Sabina cacumina, a powerful abortificant and wart destroyer.

But their particular forms are:

A King riding on a Bear **A** fair young man **A** woman holding a colander or Strainer **A** Dog **A** She Bear **A** Pye-Bird[240] **A** Changeable coloured garment **A** Rod **A** Staff. (81)

The familiar forms for the Spirits of the Moon: ☾:

They will appear as with a very great body large soft and phlegmatic of a colour like to a black and dark cloud with a swollen countenance with red eyes full of water with a bald Head and Boar's teeth: Their motion is to the great storm on the Sea, For their Sign there will appear a great Rain near the Circle.

But their particular forms are:∞:

A King being a Bowman riding on a Buck **A** little Boy **A** woman hunter with her bow and arrow **A** Cow **A** Little Deer **A** Goose **A** Green or silver garment **An** Arrow **Many** feet.

Moreover now let us speak of the Holy Pentacles and Seals. Now the Pentacles themselves are as some certain holy signs to preserve us from evil events and helping us to bind and exterminate the evil Spirits and alluring the good Spirits reconciling them to us. The Pentacles consist of the Characters and names of the good Spirits of the Superior order, Or of the Sacred pictures of the holy letters or revelations: with verses found out either of the Geometrical figures and holy names of God composed according to the purpose of many, Or of all those together, Or of many of them compounded and mixed. But those characters which are profitable for us for the ordaining of the pentacles are those characters of the good spirits. Especially of the good of the first and second order sometimes also of the third And of this kind of Characters which most chiefly is called holy Then those characters which above we have called holy. Therefore whatsoever character of this sort appointed let us compose it about with a double circle In which let us write about the name of his Angel And if we would add some divine name to that Spirit agreeable to his office It shall be of greater power and efficacy And if we would lead about some corner figure to him according to the reason of the numbers That all

---

[240] Magpie.

so may be done. But the holy pictures which form the Pentacle are those which here and there in the holy Scriptures and Prophets as well of the old as new testament are delivered to us. As the figure of the Serpent on the Cross and the like of the which there is great plenty found out in the vision of the Prophets as of Isaac, Daniel, Edras[241] and others As also out of the Revelation, And we have spoken of them in the third book of the hidden Philosophy where we have made mention of these holy things. Therefore place some such picture of the holy Images and compass it about with a double Circle to whom[242] let some divine name be written apt and conformable in effect to the figure itself: Or let some little verse be written about to him taken from part of the body of the holy Scripture which promiseth or prayeth for a desired effect. As if a Pentacle should be made for victory and revenge against enemies as well visible as invisible. A figure may be taken out of the second book of the Machabees: To wit: A hand holding in it a Golden Sword brandished to which was written about a verse containing the same. To wit Take the holy Sword, the gift from God with which thou shalt cut in pieces the adversaries of my people Israel. Or also let this verse of the first[243] Psalm be written about it, In this is the strength of thine arm, there is death before thy face, Or any other like verse. But if it like thee to write about a divine name Take some name signifying a Sword, Anger, The vengeance of God, or the like name agreeable to the desired effect, And if it like thee to write a corner figure. Take according to the reason of the number as we have taught in the second book of our hidden Philosophy where we have spoken of numbers. And so of the like works. And of this kind there are two pentacles of high virtue and great power very profitable and necessary to the consecration of Experiments and Spirits. Of them one is which we have in the first chapter of the revelation to wit. The figure of the Majesty of God sitting in the throne having in his mouth a two-edged Sword as there it is said. To which let it be written about I am Alpha and Omega the beginning and the end, who is, who was, and who is to come Almighty I am the first and the last living and have been dead, and behold I am alive for evermore, and I have (82) the Keys of death and of Hell. Then let these three verses be written about Commit it

---

[241] One of the Apocryphal books.

[242] "to whom" is repeated here.

[243] Turner gives "fifth".

O God to thy virtue,[244] Confirm this O God that workest in us[245] Let them be made as the dust before the wind[246] and the Angel of the lord scattering them. Let their ways be dark and slippery And the Angel of the lord persecuting them. Furthermore let these ten general names be written about it which are + El + Elohim + Elohe + Zebaoth + Elion + Escerchie + Adonay + Jah + Tetragrammaton + Saday +

Another Pentacle whose figure is like a lamb killed whose Horns and eyes are Heaven And under his feet a Book Sealed with seven seals as it is said in the fifth chapter of the Revelation To whom let this versicle be written + Behold the lion of the tribe of Judah overcame, The root of David. I will open the book and loose the seven seals thereof + And another versicle + I saw Satan like lightning fall from Heaven. Behold I give you power to tread upon Serpents and Scorpions And upon all the power of the enemy and nothing shall hurt you + And let the foresaid ten general names be written about it.

But those Pentacles which are ordained of figures and names keep this order, For place some figure conformable to some number unto some sure effect or virtue, Let there be written in all the corners some divine name obtaining the force of the desired thing Notwithstanding it must be so that such a name be of so many letters as the figure appointeth the number Or how many letters of the name conferred together among themselves Do appoint the number of the figure or doth constitute some number which by the number of the figure without any superfluity or diminishment may be parted. For such a name found out one or more or diverse must be written in the figure in all the corners But in the middle of the figure the whole or at least the principal revolution of turning back of the same name shall be placed.

We oftentimes ordain also pentacles by making a certain revolution of some name in the foursquare table with a single circle going about or with a double writing therein some holy versicle agreeable to this name or from which the name is derived. And this is the form of the pentacles according to their distinct manners

---

[244] Psalm 67:29.

[245] This verse is drawn from a thanksgiving hymn recited after the liberation of a demoniacally possessed person from Renaissance Italy.

[246] This verse is drawn from Saint Adelbert's curse or charm against thieves, Book 12, ch. 17 of Scot's Discoverie of Witchcraft.

which we may multiply and mingle together unto a greater efficacy and to the intention and extension of virtue among themselves with others. As if prayer should be made for the destruction of enemies, we must remember how god destroyed the face of the Earth in the deluge of waters, Sodom and Gomorrah by rain of fire and brimstone, The Host of Pharaoh in the red sea And the like, If there be any other curse found in the holy Scriptures. So by praying against the danger of waters, Let us remember the safeguard of Noah in the deluge, The Children of Israel's safe passage over the red Sea, And also Christ walking with dry feet upon the waters And preserving the ship being in danger to be drowned and the like. Lastly when with these we call upon some holy names of God, To wit those which are significant to our desire And those which are profitable to the purposed desire. As for the destruction of enemies we call upon the names of the wrath, vengeance, fear, justice and the strength of God. But for the avoiding of some peril or evil we call upon the names of God's mercy, defence, salvation, fortitude, Goodness and the like names of God. Also when we pray God to grant us that which we desire, That name we may set between some good Spirits one or more whose office is that we desire. Also oftentimes we humbly beseech God to send some evil Spirit to constrain men whose name also we insert or place between: And this is rightly done, if the work tendeth to evil as unto revenge, punishment, or destruction. Furthermore if any versicle in the Psalms or other part of Scripture be found agreeable to our desire we place that between in our prayers: But make a prayer unto God: Sometimes it will be convenient to make a prayer after that To the executor whose ministry we desire in our former prayer whether he be one or more whether he be an Angel or Star whether a Soul of one of the heroical men And such ought the prayer to be compounded according to the delivered rules by us in the second book of our hidden Philosophy, where we have spoken of the compounding of Enchantments. (83)

Thou must know also that there are three sorts of bonds. For the first bond is when we Conjure by natural things, The Second is composed of the mysteries of religion As by Sacraments Miracles and the like, The third is ordained by divine names and holy Seals. And by these bonds not only the Spirits, But also whatsoever Creatures else are bound: As the living creatures, Tempests, Fires, Plagues, And the force of armies &c. Oftentimes we use the aforesaid bonds not only after the manner of conjuration but also by way of Prayer and thanksgiving. Furthermore it assaileth to conjure much of the like sort If so be they are found agreeable to holy Scriptures: As in the conjuration of Serpents, we remember the curse of the Serpent In the Terrestrial Paradise, the lifting up of the Serpent in the desert, And also that versicle, Thou shalt walk upon the Asp and the Basilisk &c. Superstition is of very much force in these by the translation of some Sacramental rite to that which we intend to bind or hinder, As the rite of Excommunication, of burials, funerals, and the like.

It is convenient that we should speak of consecration which is made by a man, And instruments necessary for this Art in all things And this virtue is perfited[247] especially in two things: To wit, By the virtue of the person himself consecrating, And by the virtue of the prayer itself by which consecration is made. For in the person there is required holiness of life, and power of hallowing which both are attained by Dignification or by being made worthy and by instruction in the beginnings or principals of religion: Afterward this is also required that the person himself know undoubtedly and of a firm belief that this virtue and power is in himself, But of part of the prayer itself by which consecration is made there is required the same holiness which is either in the prayer itself: As many holy prayers which are found in holy Scripture or such as are appointed by the ordination of the church from virtue of the Holy Ghost: Or there is holiness in a Prayer not by itself But by commemoration or remembering again of holy things, Or the commemoration of the holy Scriptures, histories, works, miracles, effects, Graces, Promises, Sacraments and Sacramental things and the like: which will be seen to attain to the consecrated thing, Some similitude properly or improperly, Add hereto the invocation of the holy and divine names with the figuring of the holy Seals and the like, which tend unto sanctification and satisfaction to God: As are the holy waters, Sprinklings about, the Anointings of the holy oil, Sweet Suffumigations, these added to a religious life. Know this also that in every consecration the blessings and consecrations of water, oil, fire, and fumigations, with the wax or Lamps, those blessed Lights go before, For without light no Sacrament is rightly performed. This also is to be known and firmly to be observed that if a thing be consecrated in profane things into which some pollution may happen, then the exorcism and satisfaction of those things ought to go before the consecration: which things as they are

---

[247] Perfected.

effected by virgins are more apt to receive the influence of divine virtues. It is also to be observed that in the end of every consecration after the prayer duly pronounced, the consecrator himself ought by words in the presentence to bless by drawing in his breath the thing to be consecrated in the divine virtue and power And he must remember his own virtue and authority So may it be done more rightly and with a firm mind. Now therefore I will place and give thee some example of these things by which the way shall easily lay open unto thee to the considering the whole in a key. So in the consecration of water are remembered how God placed in the firmament in the midst of the waters How he in the terrestrial paradise placed a fountain of waters from whence by the four holy rivers the universal orb of the world is watered. Also how he made the waters of his Justice an instrument to destroy the Giants[248] by the general flood upon all the Earth And in the destruction of Pharaoh's host in the red Sea Also how he brought forth his own People with dry feet through the midst of the Sea and through the midst of Jordan And how miraculously he brought forth water out of the rock in the wilderness and brought forth a fountain of living water out of the Tooth of the Jawbone of an ass at the prayer of Samson[249] Also how he placed the waters Instruments of his mercy and salvation in the doing away of original sin. Also how Christ was Baptised in Jordan who by this cleansed and sanctified the waters, Moreover the divine names that are conformable to this are to be called on, As for (84) example That God is a living fountain He is the water of life The flood of mercy and the life. So in the Consecration of fire we remember how God created the fire an instrument of his justice for punishment revenge and satisfaction of Sins. Also how he shall come to judge the world by fire Also how God appeared to Moses in a bush of fire burning Also how he went before the Children of Israel in a pillar of fire And how nothing might be offered Sacrificed or Sanctified according to the law without fire Also how he appointed the fire that should not go out to be kept in the tabernacle of the covenant: And the same being put out he kindled wonderful again And from another place hath conserved it to lay hid not put out under the water, And the like of this sort, Therefore the names of God which are conformable unto this must be called on As we read in the Law

---

[248] Genesis 6:2-4.

[249] Judges 15:19.

and the Prophets for God is a Consuming fire And if there be any names among the divine names which soundeth fire Or names like it As the Glory of God The light of God, The brightness of God &c.

So in the consecration of Oil and fumigations we remember holy things pertaining to this which we read out of Exodus Of the oil of anointing And the holy names of God conformable to these Such is the name Christ which signifieth anointed And if there be any the like in holy mysteries Such as that of the Apocalypse or revelation[250] concerning the two Olive trees distilling holy oil into the lamps burning before the face of God and the like. But the blessing of light and wax and the lamps is taken from fire And from that altar which mingled the fuel of the flame together And the like As that of the Seven candlesticks and lamps burning before the face of God. These are the consecrations which are necessary first of all in all Sanctimony and ought to go before without which nothing can be duly performed.

But we will show thee the consecrations of places Instruments and the like. Therefore thou shalt take out that Prayer of Solomon[251] in the dedication of the Temple as thou art about to consecrate any place or circle, Furthermore thou shalt bless the place with blessed water and fumigation, remembering in blessing the mysteries what they are, The sanctification of the throne of God, The mountain of Sinai The Ark of the Covenant The Holy of Holies the Temple of Jerusalem Also the sanctifying of the Hill Golgotha by Christ Crucifying The Sanctifying of the Sepulchre of Christ Also the mountain of Jabor by the transfiguration and ascension of Christ and the like. Call upon divine names agreeable to these places, As the place of God The throne of God The seat of God, God's tabernacle God's Altar God's habitation and the like names of God which are meet to be written In the Circle or Consecrated place.

But in Consecrating Instruments whatsoever things serving to this art Thou mayest go on the same way Sprinkling them with holy water And performing them with hallowed fumigations according with holy Oil By assigning some holy Seal by blessing with prayer By remembering holy things out of the Scriptures and religion and divine names which seem conformable to the thing considered As for Example In Consecrating the Sword, we remember that of the Gospel He which hath two coats &c and that

---

[250] Revelation 11:4.

[251] II Chronicles 6:12-42.

of the Machabees in the second book[252] How there was wonderfully and divinely sent a Sword to Judas Machabear And if there be any the like in the prophets: s that Take to you the two edges swords.

After the same manner thou shalt consecrate the experiment and books And whatsoever the like is in holy Scripture Pictures and the like by sprinkling perfuming anointing, Sealing and blessing the commemoration, by remembering Sanctifications from the Mysteries, As the Sanctification of the Tables of the Ten Commandments which were delivered to Moses from God in the Mountain of Sinai Also the Sanctification of the old and new Testament The Sanctification of the Law of the Prophets and Scriptures which were published by the Holy Ghost Moreover we must remember the holy names of God conformable to those As God's Testament, God's Book, the book of Life, The book of the knowledge of God, of the wisdom of God and the like. After the same manner the consecration of the person is performed.

But there is as yet another rite of consecration of great wonder and much efficiency And this is from the kinds of superstitions whereas to wit the rite of consecration or conferring together some sacrament is transferred to that thing which we would consecrate. (85)

Also it is to be known that a vow, oblation and Sacrifice have the force of consecration as well real as personal And they are as certain covenants and agreements between those names for whom they are made, And as who make them, Sticking strongly for our desire and wished effect. As for example, when our things, As fumigations, anointing, rings, images, looking Glasses, and those things which less partake of the matter, as powers Seals, Pentacles, enchantments, prayers, pictures, Scriptures, we vow offer and Sacrifice them to certain names As more at large you may see in the Second book of Hidden Philosophy.

There remains with those Magicians who use very much the ministry of the Devils, a certain rite of calling Spirits by a book consecrated before which is rightly called the book of Spirits: Of that now there are a few things to be spoken: This book is consecrated, being the book of evil Spirits after its name and manner rightly composed, To which book the Spirits within written have vowed obedience at hand by their holy Oath Therefore this book is made of most pure paper, which not as yet is put to any

---

[252] An Apocryphal book.

use, Many call it virgin paper, And the book is written within after this manner, The image of the Spirit is placed on the left hand, but on the right hand is his character with his oath written above containing the name of the Spirit and his dignity and place with his office and power But many have composed this book otherwise or they have omitted the characters or image, Notwithstanding it is more powerful to neglect none of those things that are delivered. Furthermore the circumstances of places, times, hours are to be observed according as to those Stars to which those Spirits are under might seem to agree in their seating rite and order, The book which this is written well bound let be adorned and conserved distributively with his registers and Seals lest any time it should come in peril of working to be opened without purpose in any place after the consecration. Furthermore it shall be kept as reverently as it may. For the reverence of the mind would lose his virtue by pollution and profanation.

The little book composed according to the manner now delivered thou mayest go on to consecrate it two manner of ways, The one is that all and singular the Spirits which are written in the book be called unto the Circle according to the right and manner which we have taught above, And let the book to be consecrated be placed without the circle in a Triangle. And first let all the Oaths written in the little book be read in the presence of the Spirits: Then let the book be consecrated be laid without the circle in the Triangle, the same writ down and all and singular the Spirits will be gathered together where their images and characters are pictured to set their hands and to confirm and consecrate it with a special and common Oath which being done let the book be received and kept shut as is said above and let the Spirits be licensed according to the due rite.

There is also another way more easy of consecrating the book of the Spirits and it is of much force unto every effect: unless it be in the opening of this book the spirits do not always come into sight, And this way is such as followeth. Make a book of the Spirits as above is described but at the end of the book Let the invocations or prayers and bonds and most strong Conjurations be written wherewith every Spirit whatsoever may be bound. Then let this book be brought together in 2 tables or plates of metal wherein let there be written in the inside the holy pentacles of God's majesty which we have described above out of the Revelation, Of which let the first be put in the beginning of the book, The second at the end of it. After this manner the book being perfected in a clear and fair time before midnight Let the little book be carried unto the circle where ways do meet according to the art we have already taught: And there first open the book and consecrate it according to the rite and manner we have already spoken concerning consecration which being done let every of the Spirits be called which are written in the book after this manner and placing by conjuring them thrice by the bonds described in the book that they may come unto that place within three days space to perform their obedience and to confirm it in the said consecrated book. Then that little book being rolled up in white and clean linen buriest in the midst of the circle and there shut it up fast, And then destroying the circle because the Spirits shall be licensed do then depart before the Sun rising. But on the third day about midnight return or reform or make new the circle, And with bended knees make thy prayer and give thanks to God. (86) And precious fumigation being made open the hole and take forth the book and keep it not opening it. Then the spirits being licensed after their manner and the circle destroyed depart before the Sun rising. And this is the last rite of consecrating, It is profitable for all writings and Experiments which are directed to the Spirits, by placing this book between two holy plates of metal of the Pentacles, as above is already showed.

But he that is about to work by the consecrated book let him do it in a clear time and fair sky little troubling the Spirits And let him place himself towards the region of the Spirit. Then let it be opened under a right register, And let the Spirit be called on by his oath, The same written down and confirmed, And by the name of the character and Image, for that which thou desirest, and if need be, Conjure him by the bonds which are placed at the end of the book: And obtaining thy desired effect Thou shalt license the Spirit to depart.

Now concerning the invocation of Spirits as well good as bad Good Spirits are called upon as by diverse ways, and diverse ways they meet with us. For the watchful they speak openly or offer themselves to our sight Or they inform us in dreams and sleeps of our desired things by an oracle. Whosoever therefore would call upon a good Spirit that he might have sight and conference with him must observe two things especially, Of the which the one is about the disposition of the caller, The other concerning those things which are put to the prayer outwardly for the conformity of calling the Spirit. Therefore it behoveth the caller himself now to be religiously disposed throughout many days unto such a mystery. First he ought to be contrite and confessed inwardly and outwardly and rightly to satisfy God, every day washing himself in holy water. Furthermore that the caller doth keep himself throughout these whole days, Chaste, abstinent, with a mind altogether untroubled and that he separate himself[253] from all external and secular business whatsoever as much as he can. Also he must observe fastings these days according as it shall seem to him to be able to perform, And daily also Let him make his prayers from the East Sun, even to the west to God and the Angels to be called on , in the place of his invocation being clothed with a holy and linen vestment. Seven times let him do it without interruption or being let in his business. But the number of days of preparation is commonly a whole Month of the Moon: But another number observed with the Cabalists is forty days.

But about those things which concern this rite of Calling. The first is That a clean place be chosen, Chaste, fast shut, quiet, and remote from all noise, Subject to no other sights. Here first he must exorcise and consecrate, And in this place let there be set a table or altar covered with white linen clean, placed towards the East, And upon it from either part, Let there be two consecrated waxen candles set burning whose flame in all these days must not be wanting. In the middle of the Altar let the plates of metal[254] or holy pages be placed as is above said covered with fine linen which unto the end of those days is not to be uncovered Also thou shalt have the precious fumigation provided and ready prepared, And the pure oil of anointing, both being consecrated, lay them up. Also the censer being placed at the head of the Altar which being kindled and the fire blessed thou shalt perfume every day as often as thou prayest. Thou shalt also have a long Garment of white linen shut before and behind which may cover the whole body and feet which thou shall bind with the like Girdle, Thou shalt also have a headpiece like a mitre made of fine linen In which former part let the plate of metal be fastened[255] being Gold or Gilded with the inscription of the name Tetragrammaton all which things after their manner are blessed and consecrated. But go not into the holy place unless first thou art washed and clothed with holy vestments And thou must go in barefooted, when thou art entered in sprinkle it with holy water, then thou shalt perfume upon the Altar,

---

[253] "himself" is repeated.

[254] i.e. Pentacles.

[255] i.e. attached to the headpiece.

Afterward with bended knees thou shalt worship before the Altar as we have said. But at the end of these days Thou shalt fast more strictly the last day and thou shalt be fasting the day following, At the Sun rising thou mayest (87) enter into the holy place after the rite already spoken of. First sprinkle thyself, then perfuming, thou shalt sign thyself in the forehead with holy oil, and anoint thy eyes, doing all these consecrated things with some prayer. Then thou shalt uncover the holy plate and with bended knees worship before the Altar as above: And make an Angelic Invocation, they will appear to thee whom thou desirest whom being received thou shalt license with a benign and chaste conference.

Thou shalt make thy place for the calling of Some Spirit after this moment either in metal like in fashion or in new wax with shapes and colours conformable mixed: Or Let it be made in fair paper with agreeable Colours: But let the outward figure of it be foursquare, Circular, or Triangular, or of the like sort according to []256 of the number In which let the divine names as well general as special be written But in the centre of the plate an [H]exagon or

Starred like Six blazers thus shall be described In the middle of which shall be written the name and character of the Star or Spirit his governor to whom the good Spirit to be called is subject About this starlike figure shall be placed so many pentagons or five streamed Stars257 as the Spirits be whom we call together. And if we have called upon one alone notwithstanding let there be four pentagons depictured In which let the name of the Spirit or Spirits with his or their characters be written But this table ought to be made the moon increasing in those days and hours which then agree to the Spirit. And if we take a fortunate Star with this it will be the better, which table made after this manner let it be consecrated according to the rule above delivered. And this is the table after his manner general for the calling of all whatsoever good Spirits, yet we may make special tables agreeable to every spirit that manner which we have said concerning the holy Pentacles.

Now we will tell thee another rite and more easier for this thing to wit Let a man who is about to receive some Oracle from the good Spirits be Chaste, clean, and Confessed, then having a clean and neat place covered all over with white linen, On the lords day

---

256 Blank space in the text.

257 Pentagrams.

in a new moon Let him enter into that place clothed with white and Clean vestments and let him exorcise the place and bless it and make a circle in it with a blessed coal And let him write in the outmost Circle The names of the Angels but in the inward let him write the high names of God And let him put within the circle at the four corners of the world Censers for the fumigations. Then let him enter the place fasting and washed and let him begin to pray towards the East This whole Psalm Blessed are the immaculate or pure in the way &c[258] perfuming and in the end praying to the Angels by the said divine names That they may be worthy to enlighten and reveal that which thou desirest and do this for six days continually being washed and fasting every day, And on the Seventh day which is the Sabaoth[259] likewise be washed and fasting and then enter the circle and perfume and anoint thyself with holy oil of anointing, anointing thy forehead and both thy eyes and in the palms of thy hands and upon the feet Then with bended knees Say the Psalm aforesaid with the divine and Angelical names The which being said arise And begin from the East to the west within the said Circle to walk it about until thou art giddy in the brain and fall down in the Circle when rest And presently he will be taken up in an ecstasy And he will appear unto him who will inform him of all things. Also it is to be known that in the Circle there ought to be four Holy Candles burning at the four parts of the world, which never through the whole week must want light. Also the fast must be such that he abstain from all things having a sensible life And those things which come from them[260] And let him drink pure flowing water only Neither let him take meat until the Sun setteth. Let his washing be such that early in the morning before the Sun rising he wash himself being naked all over in a (88) flowing water or river, let the fumigation and oil of anointing be as we read in Exodus[261] and in other places of Scripture. He must have on his forehead a Golden plate with this name Tetragrammaton written thereon as is above said Always as often as he entereth into the Circle.

But unto the Oracles which are taken from every Spirit by a dream they also conduct natural things to us and their commixions:

---

[258] Psalm 119.

[259] Is given as Sabbath in Turner. This is an interesting mis-copying.

[260] I.e. animals and animal products such as dairy foodstuffs.

[261] Exodus 30:22-25.

As are fumigations and anointing and meats or drinks which thou must take out of the first book of the hidden Philosophy. But that he may be always willing and ready to receive an Oracle of Dreams let him Make him a Ring of the Sun or Saturn unto his fashion, and let him also make an Image of excellent efficacy unto his effect which ring and image being laid under his head while he sleepeth It will warrant true dreams virtually concerning whatsoever things the mind had before deliberated. The tables of numbers likewise confer to the Oracle being rightly formed under their constellations And these things thou mayest know out of the second book of the hidden philosophy. Also the holy tables and papers add to the oracle being made and consecrate especially to this effect. Such is the table of Amadel of Salomon[262] and the table of the revolution or turning back of the name Tetragrammaton and those of the like sort, of diverse figures numbers pictures which are written to these with the inscriptions of the holy names of God and Angels whose composition is taken from diverse places of holy Scripture from the Psalms and versicles and other places of foretelling Revelation and Prophecy. Holy prayers and imprecations as well to God as to the holy Angels and nobles do conduct the matter to the same effect: of which prayers the imprecations are composed as above is shown according to some religious likeness of miracles, Graces, and the like which we intend to do making mention of them as out of the Old Testament concerning Jacobs, Josephs, Pharaohs, Daniels and Nebuchadnezzars dreams, if out of the New Testament concerning Josephs dream and the dream of the Three Magicians of John the Evangelist sleeping upon the lords breast and whatsoever the like is found in religion, miracles and revelations, As the revelations of the cross to Helene, the revelation of Constantine and Charles the great, the revelation of Bridget, Cyrill, Methodius, Mechtildis,[263] Joachim,[264] Merlin and the like being compounded according to the which deprecations if that one went to sleep with firm intention having these things in readiness undoubtedly they are wont to bring to pass a powerful effect. But he which knoweth how to conjoin those things which we have now spoken of he will receive most true Oracles of Dreams. But let him do this observing those things which are spoken for this purpose the book of our secret or

---

[262] The Art Almadel, which forms Book 4 of the Lemegeton.

[263] St Mechtildis of Hefta, was a 12th century German Benedictine abbess.

[264] Blessed Joachim of Fiore, a 12th century Italian mystic and theologian.

hidden Philosophy. Therefore is he willing to receive an Oracle, let him abstain from eating any supper or drinking drink, otherwise being well disposed his Brains being free from troubling vapours. Also let him have a clean and neat chamber exorcised and hallowed if he will, Then let him begin to perfume in it with convenient perfumigation. And let him anoint with ointment And the Ring being put on his finger Taking with him some Image or holy table or holy paper let him put it under his head. Then after he hath prayed let him enter into his bed and thinking upon the thing that he desireth to know, So let him sleep, for so undoubtedly he shall receive most true Oracles by dreams. Let it be done when the Moon runneth by that sign which was in the ninth house of nativity, Also when she runneth through the Sign of the 9th house of the revolution of nativity. And when she is in the ninth Sign from the sign of perfection. And this is the manner by which we may observe whatsoever Sciences and arts Suddenly and Completely with the true enlightening of our understanding although the inferior familiar spirits whatsoever help us to this effect, yea oftentimes the evil Spirits informing us and our senses inwardly and outwardly.

And if we would call some evil Spirit to the Circle First it behoveth to consider and know his nature to which of the Planets he soundeth like and what offices are distributed to him from that Planet. These things being known let him look out a place fit for invocation according to the nature of the Planet and quality of the offices of the said Spirit, That if their Power be over Seas, fountains and rivers Then let a place be chosen on the Sea shore and so of the rest, Then let him seek out and find a fit time as well for the quality of the Air, That it be fair, clear, quiet, and ft for the Spirits to take to them bodies: as for the quality and nature of the Planet and Spirit, that he be fortunate or unfortunate on his day or time wherein he governeth, Sometimes in the night, Sometimes in the day as the Stars or Spirits require. These things considered let a circle be made in the chosen place as well for the defence of the caller as for (89) the confirming of the Spirit, And in this circle the general divine names of God are to be written and those which stand for our defence, And with them the divine names also which govern that Planet and office of that Spirit, Also there shall be written within the circle the names of the good spirits which rule over and can constrain that Spirit whom we intend to call, And if we would more amply fortify our circle, let us add Characters and Pentacles agreeable to the work. And then if we will we may make a figure cornered within or without the circle having written therein the numbers convenient as they agree among themselves to our work, which truly are to be known for the numbers and figures sake of which in our Second book of the hidden Philosophy we have sufficiently declared. Afterward let him provide, lights, fumigations, ointments medicines[265] for the Eyes, made according to the nature of the Planet and Spirit, which things partly agree to the Spirit because of the natural and heavenly virtue, partly also they are set abroad to the Spirits view for a religious lifes sake or a Superstitions. Then let him provide the holy and consecrated things as well for the defence of the caller and his fellows, as also being necessary for the binding of the Spirits and constriction: Such are the holy papers, plates, pictures, pentacles, swords, sceptres, vestments, of matter and colour agreeable and the like, Then all these things prepared the master standing within the Circle with his fellows, First let him consecrate the circle and all things which he useth which being done with gesture and countenance convenient let him begin to pray with a loud voice after this manner, First let him make his prayer to God, Then let him pray to the good Spirits And if he would read any prayers of Psalms or Gospels for his defence they ought to go before, Then his prayers being ended call upon the Spirit whom he desireth from all parts of the world with a meek and fair enchantment with the commemoration of his authority and virtue, And then let him rest a little while looking round about to see if any Spirit appear. And if the Spirit tarry, Let him reiterate his invocation as is above said unto three times, And if he be Stubborn that he will not appear, Let him begin to conjure him with a divine power So that the conjuration be agreeable to the nature and office of that spirit, Saying it three times over making it stronger and stronger by rebukes, reproaches, curses, and punishments, And by suspending him from his office and power, and suchlike but after every time of conjuring let him rest awhile. And if any Spirit appear let him turn himself calling the Spirit and receiving him gently. First let him inquire his name, demanding whether he be called by any other name, Then let him proceed farther to ask of him what he would. And if in any thing he be stubborn or lie bind him by conjurations convenient, And if thou doubtest him that he is in a lie, Then make the figure of a Triangle without the circle with the holy Sword or the figure of Pentagons and compel the Spirit to enter therein. And

---

[265] i.e. herbs.

if thou shalt take any promise which thou wouldst fortify with an oath, The holy Sword being stretched out of the circle let the Spirit swear putting his hand upon the Sword, Then obtaining by request what thou desirest of the spirit thou shalt license him with mild words by commanding him that he hurt nobody, And if he will not depart, compel him by stronger conjurations, And if need be by exorcisms driving him out and making contrary fumigations. And when he is gone go not out of the circle but stay awhile making thy prayers and thanksgivings to God and the good Angels for their defence and conservation: Then everything in particular being done in order thou mayest depart. But if thou art frustrated of thy hope and no spirits appear despair not for this thing: but leaving the circle thou mayest return by other courses doing as at first. And if thou judgest thyself to err in anything, then thou mayest by adding or diminishing correct thine error. For often times the constancy of reiteration doth increase authority and virtue and brings terror to the Spirits, and maketh them humble unto obedience. And therefore some are wont to make a door in the circle whereby they may go in and out, which they shut and open at their pleasure, And fortified with holy names and pentacles Also this is to be known when no Spirits appear, and when the master being rested shall deliberate to give over, because he cannot depart without the license of the Spirit, for many neglecting this are in peril unless they are fortified with some higher defence for very often the Spirits come although they appear not by reason of the terror in the caller or in things which he useth or in the work itself. But such a license is not given simply but by reason of dispensation with (90) suspending them until they are ready to obey in those things. But without circle they are called into sight by that way which is delivered in the consecration of the book.

But when we intend to follow and practice some effect by the evil spirits where there is no need of their appearance then that fabrication being made which existeth to us as the instrument or subject of an experiment. As is a image, or a Ring, or a writing, or some Character, or candle, or sacrifice, or any the like Then let him write the name of that Spirit with his character according as the experiment shall require, Or by writing with some blood, or otherwise a conformable fumigation for the spirit: Also oftentimes making our prayers unto God and the good Angels we do call that evil spirit by conjuring him with the divine power.

There is another kind of Spirits as we have said in the third book of the hidden Philosophy not so hurtful, Neighbour to men,

So that they are affected with the same passion of men And rejoice in human conversation, and dwell willingly with them, But others inhabit groves and woods: Others are joyful with the company of diverse living creatures at home and abroad: Others dwell about fountains and green meadows: Therefore whosoever would call these spirits it is necessary to be done in the place where they tarry, with odoriferous perfumes with sweet sounds, with the instruments of music made especially for this purpose Adding Songs and Enchantments and pleasing verses with promises[266] and promises. The obstinate are compelled to this by threatnings and Comminations by blasphemies, mocks, reproaches, and chiefly by threatening to turn them out of these places where they are conversant. Afterward if need be thou mayest exorcise, For the chiefest thing that it behoveth to observe in the invocation of these Spirits, Is to have a constant mind and boldness without any fear. Lastly when thou art about to call these spirits thou oughtest to prepare a table in the place of invocation, cornered with clean linen, on which thou shalt put new loaves of bread, And aquavit or milk in new earthen vessels, and new knives: And make a fire in which thou shalt perfume, But go and call at the head of the Table, and let there be seats round about for the Spirits as shall please thee. And those Spirits thou shalt invite by calling unto the drink and meat. And if perchance thou fearest some ill Spirit, write about the Circle and let part of the table within the Circle wherein thou shalt sit calling, Let the rest be without the Circle.

In the third book of our hidden Philosophy we have taught how and by what means the Soul is joined to the body, and what happens to the Soul after death: Know therefore that beyond these things which are spoken, Those Souls love their forsaken bodies after death, even as some kindred alluring them Even as they are the Souls of hurtful men which violently have forsaken their bodies: and Souls wanting their due burial which as yet wander in the troubled and moist Spirit about their carcasses. Now these Souls the means being known by which sometimes they were joined to their bodies, the means being known they are easily allured by the like vapours, liquors and savours. From hence it is that the souls of the dead are not called forth, without blood, Or the putting of some part of the forsaken body & we perfume with fresh blood in the calling forth of Shadows, with the bones of the dead,

---

[266] Turner gives praises.

and flesh, with Eggs, Milk, honey, Oil and the like which attribute a fit means for the souls to assume their bodies, we must know that if we would call forth the souls of the dead It ought to be done in those places in which such Souls especially are known to be conversant: or for some kindred sake alluring them into the forsaken body: Or for some affections sake in lifetime, Sometime impressed, drawing the said Soul unto certain places or things or persons: Or for the hellish natures sake of some place fit for the purging or punishing of Souls: which places are chiefly known by experience of visions, nightly invasions, and the like prodigies and sights. Therefore the most aptest places for these things are Churchyards and these places are better than those wherein the execution of Criminal judgement is made, And these are better than those wherein there is a public slaughter of men in late years, And better is that place than these where some carcasses not as yet satisfied for sins, neither duly buried is violently cast underground in latter years. For the satisfaction itself of the places A holy rite also is duly added to the burial of the bodies oftentimes it forbiddeth (91) the souls themselves to come there and repelleth them to the place of judgement. And from hence it is that the Souls of the dead are not called forth easily, unless it be the souls of them whom we know to be evil and have perished by some violent death whose bodies want due burial. Although unto such places as we have spoken of it would be less safeguard or profit to go to, it sufficeth us to take some principal part of the forsaken body for whatsoever place to be chosen and with it to perfume and perfume[267] the rest of the rites. It is also to be known that because certain lights of the Soul are Spiritual; therefore the Artificial lights if chiefly they are made of certain things agreeable composed according to a certain rule with inscriptions of names and signs agreeable, it doth much help for the calling forth of the souls. Furthermore these things which are spoken do not always suffice for the calling forth of the Souls by reason of the natural portion of the mind and reason: which is above heaven and the fates, and known to the only region. Therefore it behoveth us to allure the said Souls by beyond natural and celestial virtues duly administered as by those things which move the harmony itself of the Soul as well imaginative as reasonable and intellectual: as are voices, songs, Sounds, Enchantments, and those things which are of

---

[267] Probably a mis-copying, as Turner gives perform, which makes more sense.

religion, as prayers, conjurations, exorcisms, and the rest of the holy things which commodiously may be added to these.[268]

Thus endeth the fourth Book of Cornelius: Agrippa:

An invocation to call a Spirit into A Crystal:

First say this prayer O lord God Holy father and lord God Almighty which hast created all things of nothing And haddest them in mind before they were made, which art from everlasting to everlasting, under whose power Heaven and Earth Hell the Sea and all that in them is be subject and yield all reverence and obedience vouchsafe to hear me thy unworthy servant **A** And confirm O Lord my God that thou hast wrought in me hold forth thy right hand over me, help me for Jesus Christ his sake And send me grace and power to see the Spirit **B** In this Crystal stone visible to my sight let there be so much light only and only so sufficient light O Lord which saidest Let light be made and it was made, That I may perfectly see and behold the said Spirit aforesaid And that he may be made obedient unto me by thy mighty power That he may show me the truth of all such questions as I shall demand of him without all leasing[269] falsehood or deceit To the uttermost of his office. Grant this, O Heavenly Father for Jesus Christ his sake thy dear Son. **Amen.**

Then say as followeth I **A** a Christian man do warn thee Spirit which art called **B** By + the Father + the Son + and the holy Ghost + And by all the Angel Archangels Thrones Dominations Potentates and Powers And by all the Celestial company Patriarchs Prophets Apostles Martyrs Innocents virgins and confessors And by the virginity of the blessed virgin Mary And her elect Child Jesus Christ, By the four Evangelists Matthew Mark Luke and John, By the three Kings of Collen[270] By the head of St John Baptist, By the death and passion of our Lord and Saviour Jesus Christ, By the power that he hath given to all Christian men and women And to me **A** Christened, And by all the venerable names of almighty God, And these his most excellent names + Tetragrammaton + Jesus + Agyos + Panton + Sabaoth + Sother + Emanuel + Adonay + I warn

---

[268] The end of the material from Of Magical Ceremonies.

[269] An old word for lying.

[270] The three Magi who attended the birth of Christ.

thee Spirit + By all holy Churches of Christ's belief And by the mystery of all mysteries The body and blood of our Lord and Saviour Jesus Christ that thou come hastily and presently into this fair Crystal Stone visible to my sight In most delectable manner and fair form of a child of twelve years of age without any hurt doing to me or any other creature Not avoiding my sight until thou hast certified me of all such questions as I shall ask or demand of thee faithfully justly and truly without any leasing falsehood deceit or delay As thou shalt answer it at the dreadful day of doom, On pain of thy damnation Come hastily and presently as aforesaid not departing my sight till I license thee, Come Come hastily and tarry not + In the name of the father + and of the Son + and of the Holy Ghost + Come

Having thy desire license him to depart as followeth: B I license thee to depart to the place which God hath appointed thee to rest in being always prest[271] and ready to come when I call thee, Go in peace and the peace of God be between thee and me and all other creatures now and evermore **Amen** finis.

Another Conjuration to make a Spirit appear in a Crystal Stone: Looking Glass, or such like:~:

I do conjure thee B + by the Father + And the Son + And the holy Ghost + The which is the beginning and the ending The first and the last, and by the latter day of Judgement That thou **B.** do appear in this Crystal Stone or any other instrument As my pleasure to me and to my fellow Gently and beautifully in fair form of a boy of twelve years of age, without hurt or damage of any of our bodies or Souls And certainly to inform and show us without any guile or craft All that we do desire or demand of thee to know By the virtue of him which shall come to judge the quick and the dead and the world by fire. **Amen.**

Also I Conjure and Exorcise thee B. by the Sacrament of the Altar and by the substance thereof by the wisdom of Christ by the Sea by his virtues by the Earth and by all things that are above the Earth and by their virtues By the Sun and the Moon by Saturn Jupiter Mars Venus and Mercury and by their virtues And by the Apostles, Martyrs, Confessors, And the virgins and widows and the Chaste And by all Saints of men and women (93) and Innocents

---

[271] An old word for prepared.

And by their virtues, By all the Angels and Archangels, Thrones, Dominations, Principates, Potestates, Virtues, Cherubims and Seraphims, And by their virtues And by the holy names of God + Tetragrammaton + El + Ousion + Agla + And by all the other holy names of God and by their virtues, By the Crucifixion, Passion and Resurrection of our Lord Jesus Christ, By the heaviness of our Lady the virgin And by the Joy which she had when she saw her Son rise from death to life that thou **B** do appear in this Crystal Stone (Or any other instrument) At my pleasure to me and to my fellow Gently and Beautifully and visible In fair form of a Child of twelve years of age without hurt or damage of any of our bodies or souls And truly to inform and show unto me and to my fellow without fraud or guile all things according to thine Oath and promise to me whatsoever I shall demand or desire of thee without any hindrance or tarrying And this conjuration be read of me three times upon pain of eternal condemnation to the last day of Judgement **fiat fiat fiat** Amen.

Being appeared bind him with some strong bond fit for the purpose

Being Bound make your demands Saying I charge thee **B** by the Father to show me true visions in this Crystal Stone, If there be any Treasure hidden In such a place **B** And wherein it lyeth And how many foot from this piece of earth, East, west, North, Or South &c

Having your desire License him to depart &c

The manner to shut a Spirit into a Crystal Stone
that will show thee anything thou desirest:~:

Provide a Clear Crystal Stone and wrap him in virgin Parchment and write on the back side of the Parchment + Osimimilis + Orebon + Makalice + Askariel[272] + Baylon + Offriel + Cokiel + Taketh + Bariel + And upon the side that the Stone is wrapped in write + Cerberus[273] + Glumfogro + Frodissma + Hundalgunda + Memibolo + Tamandundiceth + Lundrmqnusa + Then say presently wrapping the Stone within the Parchment as followeth.

---

[272] Askariel is a spirit called into the crystal stone in other MSS, see Bod e mus 253, fo.92-96.

[273] The Greek mythic multi-headed dog who guarded the underworld.

I conjure you Devils by the name of the most highest God + Tetragrammaton + And by all the names of God And by all the Signs and characters which are placed in the firmament, And by all holy suffrages both in Heaven and in Earth That you send into this stone one Spirit in fair form and shape of a man or woman expert in knowledge of secret things which are present past and to come, which shall show all things which I shall desire or crave without lying deceit trouble or any other error And that I may have answer of him at all hours and places according to my desire.

This done Go into the field or Garden In some secret place and there with a knife with a black haft draw the circle following and put the Stone and Parchment into the Ground a cubit[274] from the circle and a cubit deep And say the conjuration aforesaid Then leaving the Stone in the Earth depart for that night The next morning before Sun rising take up the Stone But look not on it nor open the Parchment But say this Conjuration following

O thou Spirit appearing in this Stone according to my desire And to fulfil my will, I Conjure thee bind thee and exorcise thee And also command thee by the living God true holy Omnipotent and eternal God which is + Alpha + and Omega + the first and the last The beginning and ending of all things God of Gods King of Kings and lord of lords Of whom and by whom all things are made unto which all creatures obey Armies or Companies of Holy Angels do fear (94) and tremble at him And unto him all reverence is done and knees are bowed In Heaven earth and in Hell below And by his virtue and Omnipotency and the fearful and terrible day of doom And by all which may be spoken of God Or Earth Or Men Or Angels Or minds can think And by all which God hath done In Heaven and Earth And in all the Sea and bottomless places To the laud and praise and great Glory of his most holy name, That thou move not nor depart from this Stone But to remain still peaceable and quietly I bind thee by thy head and Prince *Maros* that thou show and speak to me at all times and in all places whatsoever and wheresoever when I will without lying falsehood craft or deceit by him which shall come to judge the quick and the dead and the world by fire.

---

[274] A cubit is the first recorded measure, from ancient Egypt. The size varied over the centuries, with an English cubit being 45.72cm.

Then take the Stone and depart and keep it Secret and unlooked on the space of Twelve hours after Then look on it at thy pleasure.

Beware you work not when the Moon is new Nor at the full.

The Circle for the foresaid Experiment:~:

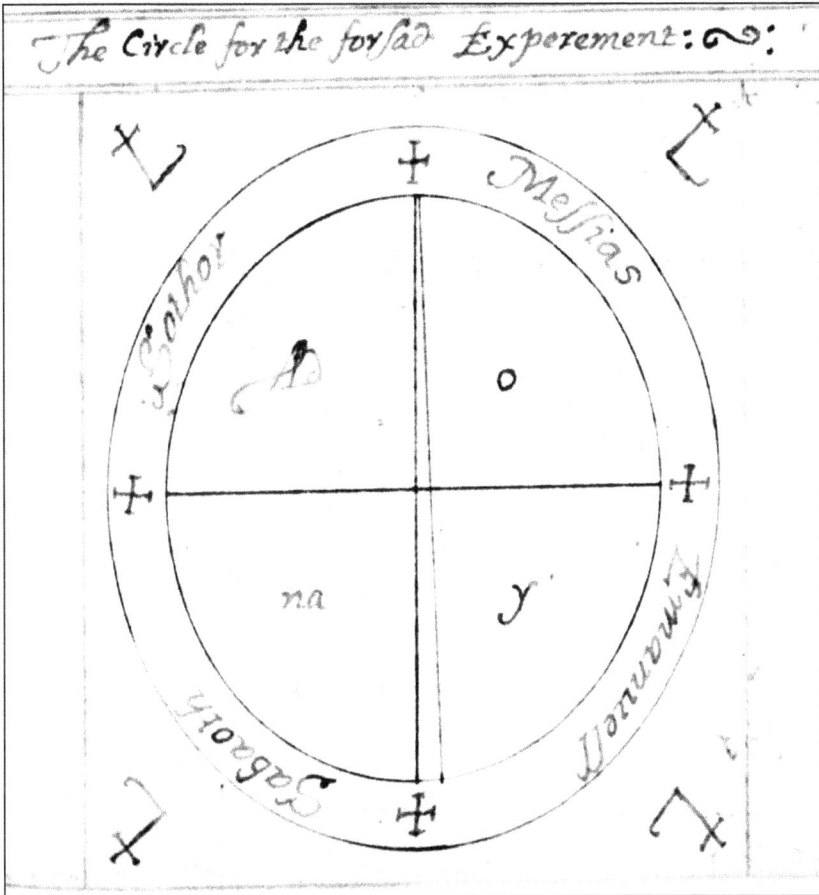

43 - *Magic Circle for the Angelic conjurations into a crystal, as described by the preceding title* The Circle for the forsaid Experiment. *Note the divine name Adonay in the centre, and Messias, Emanuell, Sabaoth and Sothor around the edges*

How to include a Spirit in a Crystal Stone Beryl
Glass or into any other like Instrument:~:

First thou in the new of the Moon being clothed with all new fresh and clean array and Shaven And that day to fast with bread and water And being clean confessed Say the seven Psalms[275] and the litany for the space of two days with the prayer following.[276]

I desire thee O lord God my merciful and loving God the giver of all graces The giver of all Sciences Grant that I thy well-beloved servant **A** Although unworthy may know thy grace and power good lord against all the deceits and craftiness of the Devils And grant me power good lord to constrain them by this art for thou art the true and lively and eternal God which livest and reignest ever one God through all worlds. **Amen**

Thou must do this five days and the sixth day have in a readiness five bright Swords And in some secret place make one circle with one Sword, And then write this name *Sitrael*, which done Standing in the Circle thrust in the sword into the name Then with another Sword do the like and write *Malanthon* then with another and write *Thamaor* with another *Falaur* and with another *Sitrami* and do as you did with the first, All this done turn thee to *Sitrael* and kneeling say this having the Crystal stone in thine hands.

O Sitrael Malantha Thamaor Falaur and Sitrami[277] written in these circles appointed to this work I do conjure you And I do exorcise you by the father by the Son And by the Holy Ghost By him which did cast you out of Paradise And by him which spake the word and it was done And by him which shall come to judge the quick and the dead and the world by fire That all you five infernal Masters do come unto me to accomplish and to fulfil all my desires and requests which I shall command you Also I conjure you you Devils and command you I bind you and appoint you By the

---

[275] The seven Penitential Psalms are given in the C15th Book of Abramelin and were also used by Dr. John Dee before his operations. These Psalms are 6, 31, 37, 50, 101, 129 & 142.

[276] This section is copied from Book XV, Ch. 12 of Scot's Discoverie of Witchcraft.

[277] The five infernal kings of the north, subsequently included in Harley MS 6482 in the Jupiterian Sixth Table of Enoch (1699-1712), and Codex Gaster 1562 (1693-95).

lord Jesus Christ the Son of the most high God And by the blessed and Glorious virgin Mary And by all the Saints both of men and women of God And by all the Angels Archangels Patriarchs and Prophets Apostles Evangelists Martyrs and Confessors virgins and widows and all the elect of God Also I conjure you and every one of you you Infernal Kings By Heaven By the Stars By the Sun and by the Moon And by all the Planets By the Earth Fire Air and Water and by the Terrestrial Paradise and by all things in them contained And by your Hell and by all the Devils in it And dwelling about it And by your (95) virtues and power And by all whatsoever And with whatsoever it be which may constrain and bind you Therefore by all their foresaid virtues and powers I do bind you and constrain you unto my will and power That you being thus bound may come unto me in great humility Ad to appear in your circles before me visible in fair form and shape of Mankind Kings and to obey unto me in all things whatsoever I shall desire And that you may not depart from me without my license And If you do against my precepts I will promise unto you that you shall descend into the profound deepness of the Sea[278] Except that you do obey unto me In the part of the living Son of God which liveth and reigneth In the unity of the Holy Ghost by all world of worlds **Amen.**

Say this true Conjuration five courses. Then shalt thou see come out of the North part Five Kings with a Marvellous company which when they are come to the circle They will alight down of their Horses And will kneel down before thee saying Master Command us what thou wilt and we will out of hand be obedient unto thee, unto whom thou shalt Say See that ye depart not from me without my license And that which I will command you to do let it be done truly surely and faithfully and essentially And then they all will swear unto thee to do thy will And after they have sworn say the conjuration Immediately following.

I conjure Charge and Command you and every of you *Sitrael Malanthon Thamaor Falaur* and *Sitrani* you infernal Kings to put into this Crystal Stone One Spirit learned and expert in all arts and Sciences by the virtue of this name of God + Tetragrammaton + And by the Cross of our Lord and Saviour Jesus Christ And by the blood of the Innocent lamb which redeemed all the world and by all their virtues and powers I charge you you noble Kings that the said Spirit may teach show and declare unto me And to my friend at all

---

[278] Note the threat using the sea, recalling the brazen vessel of Solomon.

hours and minutes both night and day the truth of all things both bodily and Ghostly in this world whatsoever I shall require or desire declaring also to me my very name And this I command in your part to do and to obey thereunto as unto your own lord and Master.

That done they will call a certain Spirit whom they will command to enter into the Centre of the circled or round Crystal. Then put the Crystal between the two Circles And thou shalt see the Crystal made black. Then Command them to command the Spirit in the Crystal not to depart out of the Stone till thou give him license And to fulfil thy will forever.

That done thou shalt see them go upon the Crystal both to answer your request and to tarry your license. That done the Spirits will crave license. Then say **Go you to your place appointed** of Almighty God + In the name of the Father + And of the Son + And of the Holy Ghost + Amen +

Then take up thy Crystal and look therein Asking what thou wilt and it will show it unto thee.

Let all your Circles be nine foot every way and made as followeth

Work this work in Cancer, Scorpio, Pisces in the hour of the Moon or Jupiter

When the Spirit is enclosed If thou fear him bind him with some bond in such sort as is elsewhere expressed. **Finis.**

This figure or type proportional following Showeth what form must be observed and kept in making the figure whereby the former secret to be effected.

(96)

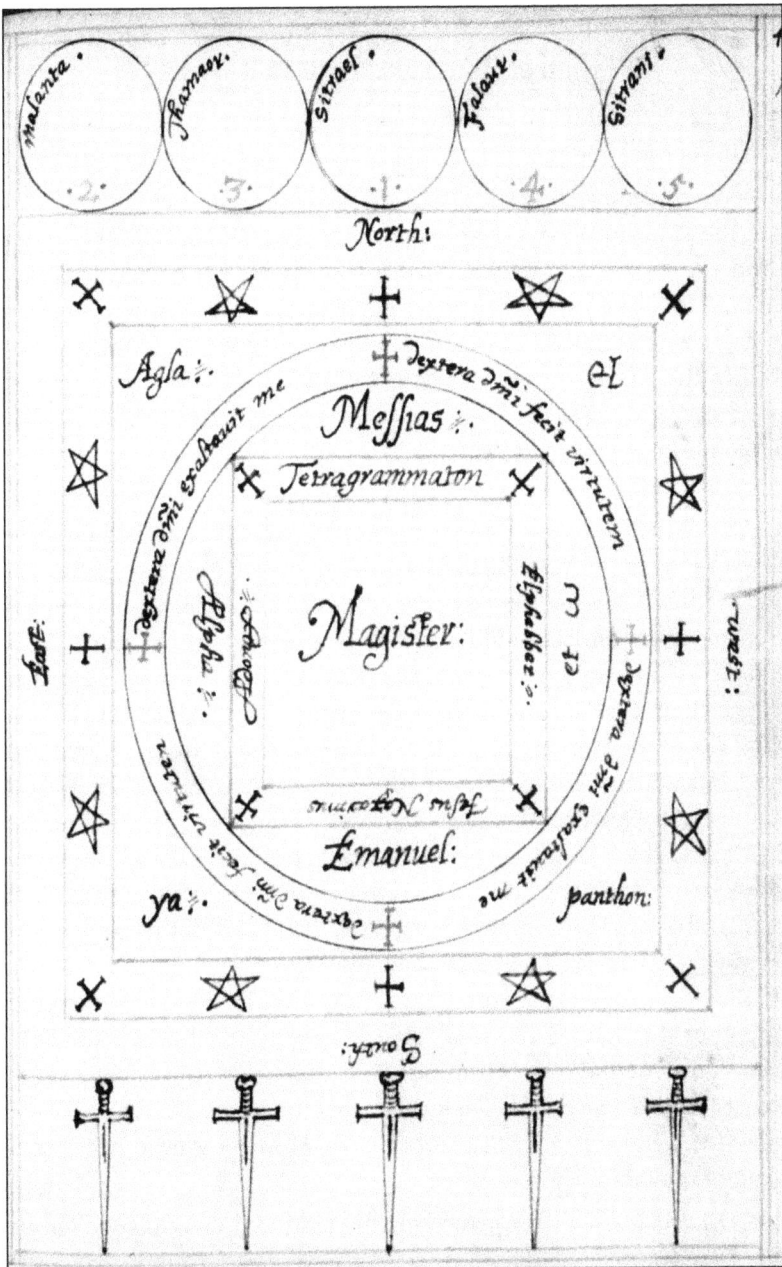

44 - *Magic Circle referred to in the immediately previous heading: This figure or type proportional following, originating from Scot's Discoverie of Witchcraft. Note that East and West have been inaccurately transposed*

(97)

How to call a Spirit into a Crystal Stone which shall declare the truth of all things thou shalt demand:~:

Take a Crystal Stone such a one as is without crannies and filth the bigger the better.[279]

When thou wilt work look thou be not polluted with lechery or sin the space of Seven days before. The cleaner thou be the better And the sooner thou shalt have thy purpose. Look thou be clean bathed and clean shaved The nails of thy hands and feet pared And being clean confessed Have on clean clothes in which Sin was never committed. **Then say this Orisons following**

O Lord Jesus Christ let thy virtue power and mercy appear with haste Establisheth all things by thy right hand, The God of Abraham The God of Isaac The God of Jacob The God of Ely The God of Tobi And thou God of all the Twelve Tribes of Israel which didst save and deliver the three Children out of the fiery furnace, to wit, Sidrack Misack and Abedmerno, Margaret from wild beasts Susana from punishment and the false accusation. O Lord Jesus Christ as thou deliverest Daniel out of the den of Lions Him that was sick of the Palsy from his bed or couch, The woman of Canaan from her bloody issue And as thou freest the defeated rulers son and healed and cured him of diverse and sundry maladies And puttest the Devil to flight And raised to life the Son of the chief ruler And the son of the widow woman And Lazarus that was four days dead And appearest to Moses in the fire of the bush And gavest the law in the mount Sinay And then betook thyself into the Trinity, vouchsafe I beseech thee to send these Spirits Alkates, Walkates, Muron, Matriton, Busto and Vallo, That they may appear to me in this Jewel of Crystal That they may be obedient unto me and show me the truth Of things past present and to come And of what things soever I shall ask them they being bund unto me And may fulfil my will + In the name of the Father + And of the Son + And of the Holy Ghost + Amen +

O Lord Jesus Christ which art the truth who wouldst be led by the false Jews before Pilate And be accused by false witnesses + O Lord Jesus Christ the King of Nazareth that wouldst be scourged by the Jews And be condemned by the Governor of Caesar the King And to be led upon the Mount of Calvary And in the said place wouldst be lifted up and crucified upon the Cross + O lord Jesus

---

[279] i.e. flawless and polished.

Christ which art the King of Glory + The Father + The Son + And the holy Ghost + which shall come to judge the quick and the dead and the world by fire + O King of Kings and lord of lords which art the salvation and safeguard of the world The Saviour of the world And the redeemer of the world I earnestly beseech thee That thou wouldst vouchsafe to give me leave to have and to see And to bind all Spirits of the Air Of the Earth And of Hell beneath which do appertain to this office, Alkates, Walkates, Muron, Matriton, Busto and Vallo, By all thy holy names + Messias + Sother + Emanuel + Sabaoth + Adonay + Otheos + Eracon + Craton + Ysus + Salvator + Alpha + et ω + Primus + et nominus + Principium + et finis + O lord Jesus Christ which art the son of the everliving God Grant thy Servant **A** virtue and power to bind and try all Spirits of the Air the Earth and Hell that they may obey me and accomplish my will and desire Through thy great power and by thy holy name + Tetragrammaton + O lord Jesus Christ full of infinite virtues which didst destroy our death By thy death And repaid our life by thy Resurrection + O almighty and everlasting God which didst cast seven devils out of the body of Mary Magdalene + O omnipotent eternal God which didst suffer holy Thomas thine Apostle not believing that thou wert crucified and rose again to touch thy wounds + O lord Jesus Christ that wert crucified who after a wonderful manner went up from Galilee into Heaven and sittest in heaven at the right hand of God the father from whence thou shalt come to Judge the quick and the dead and the world by fire, Grant me that I may see and bind the hindrances of diabolical deceits of every Spirit of the Air external and infernal on Earth or in Hell below by thy Holy name which is blessed for ever and ever. **Amen**

That wheresoever they shall be they may accomplish my will + In the name of the Father + And of the Son + And of the Holy Ghost + Amen.

Then say In the name of the Holy trinity the father of truth I hold this Jewel of Crystal. **Then call as followeth.**

I conjure you Alkates, Walkates, Muron, Matriton, Busto and Vallo, which do dwell in Besto, I conjure you and command you and every one of you and your fellows &c **Call them and bind them &c**

Then wrap up the Stone in a clean linen cloth &c

When thou wilt have thy purpose brought to pass touch the ring[280] with thy spittle And thou shalt have the love of any woman thou wilt. Finis. (98)

An Experiment of A Spirit called Baron which telleth of Treasure. He will bring A woman to thee And do diverse other things :~:

[281]**Three days before you work** abstain from the use of women And use moderate diet, wash thyself and pare thy nails both of thy hands and feet And keep the parings in a linen Cloth And put them in thy bosom

This may be done winter or Summer Any hour of the day or Night in any secret place or Chamber **At the first time** have three fellows with thee But if thy Heart serve thee It is better alone.[282] **Make your Circle** with your Sword, Or have it in Parchment as you list when you have once spoken with him you need no more Circle Except ye list.

First have in a readiness Barons Characters thus made in parchment Make them in two lines as followeth

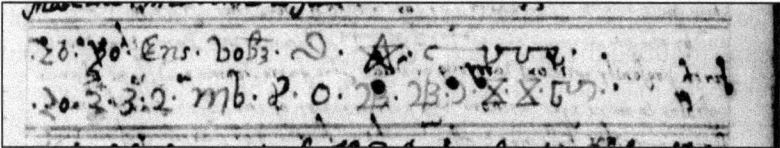

45 - Baron's Characters, as mentioned immediately preceding

Hold those Characters in thy Hand Saying the **:51: Psalm** folio:[283] three times: concluding at the end of the Psalm with **Glory be to &c**

Then say this Conjuration following:

---

[280] This may be copied from somewhere else, or should read crystal, as there is no earlier reference to a ring.

[281] This conjuration is found in Folger Vb.26 (1) fo.96-96v

[282] i.e. if you are seeking to attract a woman.

[283] The page number for the earlier full version of Psalm 51 was not filled in here.

I Conjure thee thou Spirit Baron by the Almighty God + The Father + The Son + And the Holy Ghost + I also Conjure thee Baron By the living God by the true God And by the holy God By God the Holy Ghost By God the Lord Jesus Christ And by that Great God which did cast down thee and thy fellows from Heaven for your sinful deeds[284] And by the holy virgin Mary mother of our lord Jesus Christ By his holy Cross and Passion which redeemed us out of your power And as I trust to be saved and obtain the Joys of Paradise Even as this is true and most true That our Lord Jesus Christ took flesh and blood of the virgin Mary and in the same flesh the third day did wonderfully rise again from the dead And so did ascend into heaven and sitteth on the right hand of God the father in the glory of the Judgement seat from whence he shall come Thee Spirit Baron me and all creatures both quick and dead to judge Therefore by his wonderful coming at that fearful day of doom and by all Angels and Archangels of God Dominations Potentates Principates Cherubim and Seraphim And by all the virtues of Heaven I Conjure thee Baron by the love Death and passion of Jesus Christ our lord and Saviour By his Glorious resurrection and ascension, And by his holy Cross whereon he was hanged by the nails wherewith he was fixed to his Cross By the Spear wherewith Longis pierced his side and blood and water issued out By the crown of Thorns which he wore on his head And by the seven degrees of S[285]   of the Holy Ghost And by all things in Heaven Earth and Hell to be feared. And also and moreover I Conjure thee Baron by the Milk of the virgin Mary which our lord did Suck with his own Mouth which is called + Alpha + et Omega + Saday + Emanuel + Sabaoth + Messias + Sother + Adonay + Athanatos + Panton + Craton + Ysus + Yskyros + Mediator + Leo + Rex + Fimitas + unitas + Jesus Nazarenus + On + El + Tetragrammaton + Also I exorcise thee and adjure thee Baron by the four rings of Solomon And by his bond which did bind thee and thy fellows And by the faith and obedience which thou dost owe to thy Creator our Lord which is above thee By the four Elements and by the great name of God + Agla + I Conjure thee Baron that thou come forth presently without tarrying or delay In fair form and shape of a man visible to mine eyes without any perturbation of the Air Earth Water or Fire or any other Element And without hurting or harming of me or any

---

[284] This makes Baron's nature as a fallen angel clear.

[285] The text has a space here after the "S".

other creature Barn House or any thing created And without tempest of wind rain Hail thunder lightning or such like But quietly and peaceably come and do my will And it being fulfilled quietly with my license to depart By all afore rehearsed quickly and speedily come and obey me and fulfil my desire, So and so many times do I adjure thee Baron by virtue of our lord Jesus Christ the Son of the everliving God And the most pure and merciful God And by that Angel which at the day of Judgement shall blow the Trumpet And shall say Come Come Come Also by the divine Trinity of the + Father + Son + and Holy Ghost + And by the bodies of the Saints which were asleep and rose again at the time of the death and passion of our Saviour Jesus Christ By Aarons rod that he divided the Red Sea By the Ark of the covenant and Throne of the living God, I Conjure thee Baron to come By these holy names of God + Ya + Semephoras + And by those blessed names of God + Adonay + Sother + which being pronounced made all Stones of Earth By his holy name + Ya + which being pronounced the wicked shall be condemned and the just saved Moreover I adjure thee Baron by the great works of the lord my God (99) That is the firmament The Sun the Moon the Stars And the Creation of Mankind The Earth with all creatures therein contained The Seas most wonderful with the strange and diverse manner of fishes in the same And by him that is the mighty + Jehovah + The Saviour of the world even my Lord Jesus Christ the anointed King who is + Alpha + et omega + Show thyself immediately as I have said not terrifying me nor any other creature but come in likeness of a man or child of nine years of age upon pain of eternal damnation + Come + Come + Come + fiat + In the name of the Father + And of the Son + And of the Holy Ghost + Amen +

An Experiment of A Spirit called Bealphares:

This Spirit will appear to thee In the likeness of a fair Man or a fair woman and will come to thee at all times He will tell thee of hidden Treasures He will bring thee Gold or Silver He will transport thee from one Country to another without any harm of body or Soul.[286]

He that will do this work Shall abstain from lecherousness Drunkenness and from false swearing And do all the abstinence

---

[286] This conjuration is drawn from Book XV, Ch.13 of Scot's Discoverie of Witchcraft.

that he may do And namely three days before he go to work. In the third day when night is come and when the Stars do shine and the Element is fair and clear He shall bath himself and his fellow if he have any all together in a quick wellspring. Then he must be clothed in clean white clothes And he must have another private place And bare with him Ink and pen wherewith he shall write this holy name of God Almighty in his Right hand + Agla + And in his left hand this name following ✝ Ⅱ ℮ ▽ ℮ ✝ [287] And he must have a dry thong of a lions or of a Harts skin And make thereof a Girdle And write the holy names of God all about And in the ends + A + and Ω +

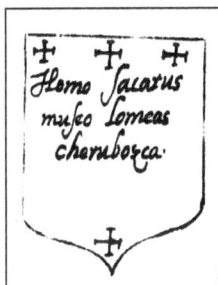

46 - *Lamen for the conjuration of Bealphares, mentioned in the text following.*

And upon his breast he must have this present figure written in virgin Parchment And it must be sowed upon a piece of new linen and so made fast upon thy breast And if thou hast a fellow to work with thee He must be appointed in the same manner. You must have also A bright Knife that was never occupied[288] And he must write thereon On the one side of the blade + Agla + And on the other side of the blade of the Knife ✝Ⅱ ℮ ▽ ℮✝ And with the same Knife he must make a circle as hereafter followeth The which circle is called Salomons circle, behold the figure of the Knife written on the one side On the other side write ✝Ⅱ ℮▽℮✝ The circle being made go into it And close again the place where thou wentest in with the same Knife Then say

---

[287] Joseph Peterson has pointed out the likelihood of this being a stylised form of the divine name IHVH.

[288] i.e. never used, virgin.

An experiment of A Spirit called Bealphares.

This Spirit will appeare to thee In the likenes of a faire Man or faire woman and will com to thee at all tymes Hee will tell thee of hidden Treasures He will bring thee Golde or Silver He will transport thee from one Country to another without any harme of body or Soule.

He that will doe this worke Shall abstaine from Lecherousnes Dronkennes And from false swaring And doe all the abstinencie that he may doe And namely three dayes before he goe to worke. In the third day when night is come and when the Starrs doe shine and the Ellement is faire and cleare He shall bath him selfe and his fellow if he have any all together in a quick wellspring. Then he must be clothed in cleare white clothes And he must have another privie place And bare with him Inke and penn wherwith he shall wright this holy name of God Almighty in his Right hand ✝ Agla ✝ And in his Left hand this name following ✝ ∏ ℇ ▽ ℇ ✝ And he must have a dry thonge of a Lions or of a Harts skin And make therof a Girdle And wright the holy names of God all about And in the ends ✝ A ✝ and ✝ S ✝

And uppon his brest he must have this present figure written in virgin Parchment And it must be sowed uppon a peece of new linnen and so made fast uppon thy brest And if thou hast a fellow to work with thee He must be appointed in the same manner. You must have also A bright Knife that was never occupied And he must wright theron On the one side of the blade ✝ Agla ✝ And on the other side of the blade of the Knife ✝ ∏ ℇ ▽ ℇ ✝ And with the same knife he must make a circle as hereafter followeth The which circle is called Salomons circle. behold the figure of the Knife written on the one side On the other side wright ✝ ∏ ℇ ▽ ℇ ✝ The circle being made goe into it And close againe the place where thou wentest in with the same Knife Then say ✝ Per crucis hoc signum ✝ fugiat procul omne malignum. Et per idem signum ✝ salvetur quodque benignum. ✝ And make fumigations

Homo Sacatus
museo Lorncas
cherubozca.

✝ AGLA ✝

47 - Page showing the Conjuration of Bealphares, with the lamen and knife, as recorded in the prior text

+ Per crucis hoc signum + fugiat procul omne malignum. Et per idem signum + salvetur quodque benignum +[289] And make fumigations (100) to thy fellow or fellows with Frankincense Mastic lignum aloes then put it in wine And say with good devotion In the worship of the high God almighty altogether that he may defend you from all evils

And when he that is Master will close the Spirit He shall say towards the East with meek and devout devotion These Psalms and prayers following here in order.

The 22 Psalm:

1. **O my God my God** look upon me why hast thou forsaken me: and art so far from my health And from the words of my complaint.

2. O my God I cry in the day time but thou hearest not And in the night season also I take no rest.

3. And thou continues holy O thou worship of Israel.

4. Our fathers hoped in thee They trusted in thee And thou didst deliver them.

5. They called upon thee and were helped They put their trust in thee And were not confounded.

6. But as for me I am a worm and no man A very scorn of men and the outcast of the people.

7. All they that see me laugh to scorn They shoot out their lips and shake their head saying.

8. He trusted in God that he would deliver him Let him deliver him if he will have him.

9. But thou art he that took me out of my mothers womb Thou wast my hope when I hanged yet upon my mothers breasts.

10. I have been left unto thee ever since I was born Thou art my God even from my mothers womb.

11. O go not from me for trouble is hard at hand And there is none to help me.

12. Many Oxen are come about me For Bulls of Basan close me in on every side.

---

[289] "By this sign + of the cross. May you flee far from all evil, and by the same + sign may you be blessed all that is good."

13. They gape upon me with their mouths as it were a ramping and roaring lion.

14. I am poured out like water and all my bones are out of joint. My Heart also in the midst of my body is even like melting wax.

15. My strength is dried up like a potshard And my tongue cleaveth to my gums And thou shalt bring me into the dust of death.

16. For many dogs are come about me And the counsel of the wicked laid siege against me.

17. They pierced my hands and my feet I may tell all my bones They stand staring and looking upon me.

18. They part my Garments among them And cast lots upon my vesture.

19. But be not thou far from me O Lord Thou art my succour Hast thee to help me.

20. Deliver my soul from the Sword My darling from the power of the dogs.

21. Save me from the lion's mouth Thou hast heard me also from among the Horns of the Unicorns.

22. I will declare thy name unto my brethren In the midst of the Congregation will I praise thee.

23. O praise the lord ye that fear him Magnify him all ye of the seed of Jacob, And fear him all ye seed of Israel.

24. For he hath not despised nor abhorred the low estate of the poor he hath not hid his face from him But when he called unto him he heard him.

25. My praise is of thee in the great congregation My vows will I perform in the sight of them that fear him.

26. The poor shall eat and be satisfied They that seek after the Lord shall praise him, your heart shall live forever.

27. All the ends of the world shall remember themselves and be turned unto the lord and all the kindreds of the nations shall worship before him.

28. For the Kingdom is the lords And he is the Governor among the people.

29. All such as be fat upon Earth Have eaten and worshipped.

30. All they that go down into the dust shall kneel before him And no man hath quickened his own Soul.

31. My seed shall seek him They shall be counted unto the Lord for a Generation.

32. They shall come And the Heavens shall declare his righteousness: unto a people that shall be born whom the lord hath made.

Glory be to the Father &c

Then say the :51: Psalm :3: times

Have mercy upon me O God &c. As you shall find it in **Pag :50:**[290] concluding with **Glory be to the Father &c**

Then say this verse O lord leave not my soul with the wicked Nor my life with the bloodthirsty **Then say** Pater Noster + Ave maria + and credo &c.

Then say O lord show us thy mercy and we shall be saved. Lord hear our prayers and let our cry come unto thee. **Let us pray.**

O Lord God almighty as thou warnst by thine Angel the three Kings of Collen + Jasper + Melchior + and Balthazar + when they came with worshipful presents towards Bethlehem + Jasper brought Myrrh + Melchior Incense + Balthazar Gold + worshipping the high King of all the world Jesus Gods Son of Heaven The second person in Trinity Being born of the Holy and clean virgin St Mary Queen of Heaven Empress of Hell And lady of the world At that time the holy Angel Gabriel warned and bade the foresaid three Kings that they should take another way for dread of peril That Herod the King by his ordinance would have destroyed these three noble Kings That meekly sought out our Lord and Saviour. As wittily and truly as these (101) three noble Kings turned for dread and took another way So wisely and so truly O Lord God of thy merciful mercy bless us now at this time for thy blessed passion

---

[290] Gauntlet is reminding himself or the reader of the folio reference in the MS, which was changed to fo.47-48 when the MS was renumbered.

save us and keep us altogether from all evil And thy holy Angel defend us. **Let us pray.**

O Lord King of all Kings which containest the throne of Heaven and beholdest all deeps weighest the Hills And shuttest up with thy hand the Earth Hear us most meek God And grant unto us being unworthy according to thy great mercy to have the verity and virtue of knowledge of hidden treasures by this Spirit invocated Through thy help O lord Jesus Christ To whom be all honour and Glory from worlds to worlds everlastingly. **Amen.**

Then say these Names:

+ Helie + Helyon + Esseire + Deus eternus + Eloy + Clemens + Heloy + Deus sanctus + Sabaoth + Deus exercituum + Adonay + Deus mirabilis + Jao + Veray + Anepheneton + Deus ineffabilis + Sodoy[291] + Dominator + Dominus + On fortissimus + Deus + The which wouldst be prayed unto of sinners. Receive we beseech thee sacrifices of praise And our meek prayers which we unworthy do offer unto thy divine Majesty. Deliver us and have mercy upon us And prevent with thy holy spirit this work And with thy blessed help to follow after That this our work begun of thee may be ended by thy mighty power. **Amen. Then say**

+ Homo + Sacarus + museolameas + cherubozca +

Being the **figure** upon thy breast aforesaid, **The Girdle** about thee **The Circle** made, Bless the Circle with Holy water and sit down in the midst And read this Conjuration as followeth, Sitting back to back at the first.

The Conjuration:~:

I exorcise and Conjure Bealphares the practicer and preceptor of this art by the maker of Heaven and of Earth And by his virtue And by his unspeakable name + Tetragrammaton + And by all the holy Sacraments And by the holy majesty and deity of the living God **I Conjure and Exorcise thee Bealphares** by the virtues of all Angels Archangels Thrones Dominations Principates Potestates Virtutes Cherubim and Seraphim and by their virtues And by the most truest and specialist name of your Master That you do come

---

[291] This is clearly a miscopying and should be the divine name Saday.

unto us In fair form of Man or womankind here visible before this circle And not terrible by any manner of ways This circle being our tuition and protection by the merciful goodness of our Lord and Saviour Jesus Christ And that you do make answer truly without craft or deceit unto all my demands and questions by the virtue and power of our lord and Saviour Jesus Christ. **Amen**

When he is appeared bind him with this bond following.

The Bond:∞:

I Conjure thee Bealphares by God the Father By God the Son And by God the Holy Ghost And by all the Holy company in Heaven And by their virtues and powers. I charge thee Bealphares that thou shalt not depart out of my sight Nor yet to alter thy bodily shape that thou art appeared in, Or any power shalt thou have of our bodies or Souls Earthly or Ghostly but to be obedient to me And the words of my Conjuration that Is written in this book. **I Conjure thee Bealphares,** by all Angels and Archangels Thrones Dominations Principates Potestates Virtuts Cherubim and Seraphim and by their virtues and powers I Conjure and Charge bind and constrain thee Bealphares by all the royal words aforesaid and by their virtues that thou be obedient unto me And to come and appear visible And that in all days hours and minutes wheresoever I be being called by the virtue of our Lord Jesus Christ The which words are written in this book Look ready thou be to appear unto me and to give me good counsel, How to come by Treasure hidden in the Earth or in the water, How to come to dignity and knowledge of all things That is to say Of the Magick Arte, And of Grammar, Dialectic, Arithmetic, Geometry, And of Astronomy, And in all other things my will quickly to be fulfilled. I charge thee upon pain of everlasting condemnation.

Fiat. Fiat. Fiat. Amen.

When he is thus bound Ask him what things thou wilt and he will tell thee And give thee all things thou wilt request of him without any sacrifice doing to him and without forsaking thy God that is thy maker

When the Spirit hath fulfilled thy will and entreaty Give him license to depart as followeth.

A license for the Spirit to depart:∞:

Go unto the place predestinated and appointed for thee where thy Lord God hath appointed thee until I shall call thee again Be thou ready unto me and to my call as often as I shall call thee upon pain of everlasting damnation. (102)

And if thou wilt thou mayest recite two or three times the last conjuration until thou do come to this term. **In throno.**

If he will not depart then say. In throno that thou depart from this place without hurt or damage of any body Or of any deed to be done, That all creatures may know that our Lord is of all power most mightiest and that there is none other God but he which is three and one living for ever and ever. **And the Malediction** of God the Father Omnipotent The Son and the Holy Ghost descend upon thee and dwell always with thee Except thou depart without damage of us or of any Creature, or any other evil deed to be done And then to go to the place predestinated. And by our Lord Jesus Christ I do else send thee to the great pit of Hell (Except I say) that thou depart unto the place whereas the Lord God hath appointed thee And see thou be ready to me and to my call at all times and in all places at mine own will and pleasure day or night without damage or hurt of me or any creature upon pain of everlasting damnation. **Fiat. Fiat. Fiat. Amen. Amen.**

The peace of Jesus Christ be between us and you + In the name of the Father + And of the Son + And of the Holy Ghost + Amen + **Per crucis** hoc + signum **Fugiat** procul omne malignum, **Et per** idem + signum **Salvetur** quodque benignum.[292]

In principio erat verbum &c In the beginning was the word &c as followeth in the first chapter of S[t] Johns Gospel stopping at this word, Full of grace and truth. **To whom** be all Honour and Glory world without end. **Amen.**

At the first calling Sit back to back when you call the Spirit.✤ **This** Spirit Bealphares being once called and bound shall never have power to hurt thee.

Call him in the hour of ♃ or ♀ the ☽ increasing.

---

[292] "By this sign + of the cross. May you flee far from all evil, and by the same + sign may you be blessed all that is good."

✤ & for the fairies make this Circle with Chalk on the Ground as is said before

Bealphares or Bialphar is an excellent Carrier, he telleth of hidden Treasures in the Earth, or of things stolen or lost, & is true in all his doings, he cometh forth out of the East, for so he hath before called from the East & he appeared, very dutiful to God properly & soberly.[293]

---

[293] This added footnote is in a different hand, the same hand found on fo.37.

A type or figure of the Circle for the

Master and his fellows to sit in:

Showing how and after what fashion it should be made[294]

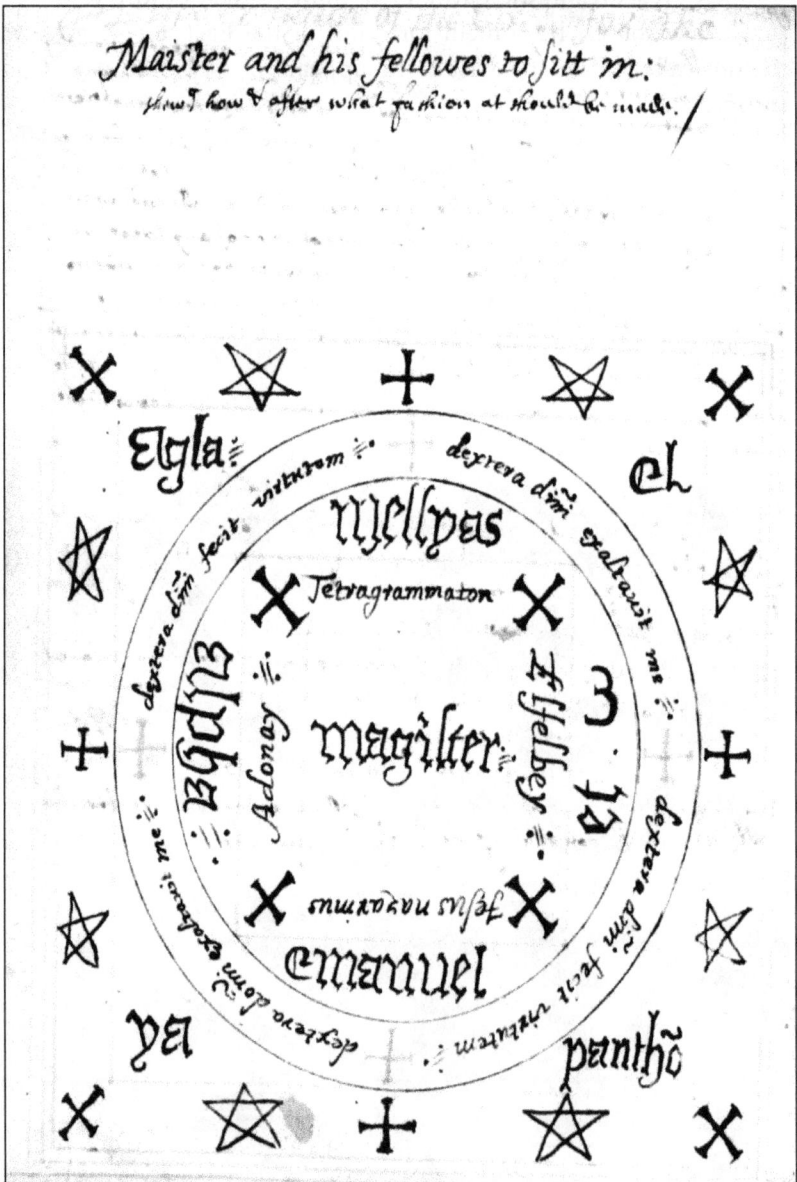

48 - Magic circle as per title above, originating from Scot's Discoverie of Witchcraft

(103)

---

[294] This final line is in the second hand.

To have the Spirit of a dead body:~:

Go to the Grave of a man or woman the ☽ Increasing The first night after the body is buried And make a Circle Then stand in it And say as followeth

O Asariel Aerell or Asaciell the King of the dead Or the keeper of the bones of the dead **I conjure thee** by our Lord Jesus Christ which was conceived of the Holy Ghost Born of the virgin Mary Suffered under Pontius Pilate And by all those names of God almighty + Saday + Aglay + Adonay + Alpha + Omega + The first and the last And by the unutterable name of his + Tetragrammaton + And by that great name + Jehovah + And by all other names of the Allmighty known or unknown And by all the Sacred words that our God spake And by all the holy deeds And merits of Jesus Christ the son of God And by all things that may be said or spoken of God, That thou presently appear unto me, Or presently that thou suffer (or permit) The Spirit of this **A.B.** whose body lies here for the present Or all his time To appear unto me And that he yield me his Service and obedience quietly and gently And that he obey and do my will without deceit Or double meanings God binding him fast thereto **Amen** so be it + so be it + so be it +

After calling the dead say the invocation following

O thou A.B. whose body lies here **I conjure thee** by all these names of the living God + On + Agla + Som + Emanuel + Sabaoth + Harmur + Ioth + Jehovah + Salvator + Agios + Athanatos + Otheos + Theor + And by all other holy names of God The father almighty And by him which made the Heaven and doth contain and support the firmament and doth behold the deep by his beholding it which is King of Kings and lord of lords which doth weigh the Hills which doth shut up the Earth with his fist which made his Angels spirits and Ministers of flames of fire which bringeth forth winds out of his treasuries which smote the first born of Egypt from Man even unto the Cattle which separated the light from the darkness which made two great lights The Sun and the Moon which only doth great wonders **That** wheresoever thou be thou come unto me and appear presently unto me without any violence wrath noise or terror And that thou tell me the truth of whatsoever I shall ask of thee without any lying deceit double meaning doubtfulness guile or complaint or gainsaying And that you yield your service and obedience peaceably and gently and that you obey me in all things without hurt of my Soul or body So that you do whatsoever I would have you to do

And I promise you in the word of God And by the faith of thee and me That I will cause to be celebrated five Masses on the holy feast of blessed Mary the virgin for forgiveness and pardon of thy Soul from year to year while I live. If I shall be able I will not do it on the feast of any other for forgiveness of thy sins **Amen** fiat + fiat + fiat +

This done depart and come again the second night And so the third doing in all respects as at the first And the third night thou shalt have appearance And when thou hast appearance Say this conjuration viz

I Adjure thee AB and Conjure thee by all the holy words and names which thou ever heardest in thy lifetime And by the virtue of the great head of our Lord Jesus Christ And by the virginity of blessed Mary his Mother And by all their virtues And by all things afore named and Spoken of **I Conjure and charge thee** not to depart from me nor from my sight until thou hast obeyed my will in all things and hast accomplished my desire and art licensed by me as thou believest or trustiest to be saved and not to be damned in the day of doom & Judgement. **Fiat + fiat + fiat +** Amen.

Then make your demands what you will in manner following.

I conjure thee Adjure thee and charge thee Spirit of **AB** by the same virtue by which thou camest hither By the same by which thou Obeyest me And by all the virtues and powers of Our + Lord Jesus Christ + And by this unutterable name + Tetragrammaton + And by all the holy names of God the Father And by all the things before mentioned and by the living God + The Father + The Son + and the Holy Ghost + Three persons and one God **That** thou presently make haste and forthwith bring the Book of Magick science and art written in such a hand And with such letters that I may read it well And in such a tongue That I may well understand it And under the Kings of the world dedicated to the Princes of the Air So that when I open it and read in it All the Spirits in the Air and Earth &c[295] (104)

---

[295] The conjuration ends abruptly here. There is space at the bottom of the page for another two lines of text, so the conjuration either was not recorded fully or has a very sudden end!

Another Experiment of the Dead

[296]**First** fast and pray iii [3] days And abstain from all filthiness: **Go** to one that is new buried Such a one as killed himself wilfully.[297] Let no person see thy doings but thy fellow And about 12 of the Clock at night Go to the place where he was buried And say with a bold faith and hearty desire To have the Spirit come that thou doest call for, Thy fellow having a Candle in his left hand, And in his Right hand a Crystal Stone, The Master having a Hazel wand in his Right hand And these names of God written thereupon + Tetragrammaton + Adonay + Agla + Craton + Then strike iii [3] Strokes on the Ground And say as followeth.

Arise A **Arise** A **Arise** A **I conjure thee** Spirit A by the resurrection of our lord Jesus Christ That thou do obey to my words And come unto me this night verily and truly As thou believest to be saved at the day of Judgement, And I will Swear to thee an Oath by the peril of my Soul That if thou wilt come unto me this night And show me true visions in this Crystal Stone, And fetch me the fairie Sibilia[298] that I may talk with her visible And that she may come before me as the conjuration leadeth And in so doing I will give thee an alms deed And pray for thee A to my Lord God whereby thou mayest be restored to thy Salvation at the resurrection day To be received as one of the Elect of God to the everlasting Glory **Amen.**

The Master standing at the head of the Grave His fellow having in his Hands the Candle and the Stone Must begin the Conjuration as followeth, And the Spirit will appear to you in the Crystal Stone In a fair form of a child of 12 years of Age. When he is in feel the Stone And it will be hot, And fear nothing. For He or She will show many delusions to drive you from your work. Fear God but fear him not, This Conjuration following is to constrain him.

I Conjure thee Spirit A by the living God The True God And the holy God And by their virtues and powers which have created thee and me and all the world **I conjure thee** A by these Holy names of God + Tetragrammaton + Adonay + Algramay + Saday + Sabaoth + Planaboth + Panthon + Craton + Neupmaton + Deus +

---

[296] This conjuration is taken from Book XV, Ch.8 An experiment of the dead in Scot's Discoverie of Witchcraft.

[297] i.e. a suicide.

[298] Spelled Sibylia in Scot.

Homo + Omnipotence + Sempiturnus + Ysus + Terra + unigenitus + Salvator + via + vita + Manus + Fonce + Origo + Filius + And by their virtues and powers And by all their names by the which God gave power to man both to speak or think So by their virtues and powers **I Conjure thee** Spirit A, That now immediately thou do appear in this Crystal Stone visible to me and to my fellow without any tarrying or deceit **I conjure thee** A by the excellent name of + Jesus Christ + A + and + Ω + the first and the last For this holy name of + Jesus + is above all names For in this name of + Jesus + every knee doth bow and obey both of Heavenly things Earthly things And infernal And every tongue doth confess that our Lord + Jesus Christ + is in the glory of the father Neither is there any other name given to man whereby he must be saved. Therefore in the name of + Jesus of Nazareth + and by his nativity resurrection and Ascension And by all that appertaineth unto his passion And by their virtues and power **I conjure thee** Spirit A that thou do appear visibly in this crystal Stone to me and to my fellow without any dissimulation **I conjure thee** A by the blood of the innocent Lamb + Jesus Christ + which was shed for us upon the Cross for all those that do believe in the virtue of his blood shall be saved **I Conjure thee** A by the virtues and powers of the royal names and words of the living God by me pronounced, That thou be obedient unto me and to my words rehearsed. **If thou** refuse this to do I by the holy Trinity and their virtues and powers do condemn thee Thou Spirit A Into the place where there is no hope of remedy or rest but everlasting horror and pain daily Horribly and lamentably thy pain to be there augmented as the stars in the Heaven and as the Gravel or Sand in the Sea Except thou Spirit A do appear to me and to my fellow visibly Immediately In this Crystal Stone And in a fair form and shape of a Child of 12 years of age And that thou alter not thy shape. I charge thee upon pain of everlasting condemnation **I Conjure thee** Spirit A by the Golden Girdle which girded the loins of our lord Jesus Christ So thou Spirit A be thou bound Into the perpetual pains of Hellfire for thy disobedience And unreverant regard that thou hast to the holy names and words and his precepts **I Conjure thee** A by the two edged Sword which John saw proceed out of the Mouth of the Almighty And so thou Spirit A be torn and cut in pieces with that Sword And to be condemned into everlasting pain where the fire goeth not out And where the worm dieth not **I Conjure thee** A by the Heavens And by the Celestial city of Jerusalem And by the Earth And by the Sea And by all things contained in them And by their virtues and powers I

Conjure thee A by the obedience that thou doest owe unto thy principal prince And except thou Spirit A do come and appear in this Crystal Stone visibly in my presence here immediately as it is aforesaid **Let** the great curse of God The anger of God The shadow and darkness of death and of eternal condemnation be upon thee A for ever and ever because thou hast denied thy faith thy health and Salvation for thy great disobedience Thou art worthy to be condemned Therefore let the divine Trinity Thrones Dominions Principates Potestates Virtutes Cherubim and Seraphim And all the souls of Saints both of men and women Condemn thee for ever And be a witness against thee at the day of Judgement because of thy disobedience And let all creatures of + our Lord Jesus Christ + Say thereunto **Fiat fiat fiat** Amen.

And when he is appeared in the Crystal as is said before, Bind him with this bond.

I Conjure thee Spirit A that art appeared to me in this Crystal Stone to me and to my fellow **I Conjure thee** by all the royal words aforesaid the which did constrain thee to appear therein and their virtues I Charge thee Spirit by them all that thou shalt not depart out of this Crystal stone until my will being fulfilled thou be licensed to depart **I Conjure** and bind thee Spirit by the Omnipotent God which commanded the Angel St Michael to drive Lucifer out of Heaven with a Sword of vengeance And to fall from Joy to pain And for dread of such pain as he is in I charge thee Spirit A that thou shalt not go out of the Crystal stone Nor yet to alter thy shape at this time Except I command thee otherwise But to come unto me at all places (105) And in all hours and minutes when and wheresoever I shall call thee by the virtue of our Lord + Jesus Christ + Or by any invocation of words that is written in this book and to show me and my friends true visions in this Crystal Stone of any thing or things that we would see at any time or times. And also to go and fetch to me the fairie Sibilia that I may talk with her in all kind of talk as I shall call her by any Conjuration of words contained in this book **I Conjure thee** Spirit A by the great wisdom and divinity of his + Godhead + my will to fulfil as is aforesaid I Charge thee upon pain of condemnation both in this world and in the world to come **Fiat fiat fiat** Amen.

This done Go to a place fast by And in a fair parlour or Chamber Make A Circle with Chalk according to Art, Also make another Circle for the Fairie Sibilia to appear in iiii [4] foot from the circle thou art in And make no names therein Nor cast any holy thing therein But make a Circle round with Chalk And let the Master and his fellow sit down in the first Circle The Master having the book in his hand And his fellow having the Crystal stone in his right Hand Looking in the Stone when the fairie doth appear The Master also must have upon his breast this figure following written in parchment. And begin this work in the new of the ☽ and in the hours of ♃ the ☉ and the ☽ to be in one of the inhibiters Signs as ♋♐♓

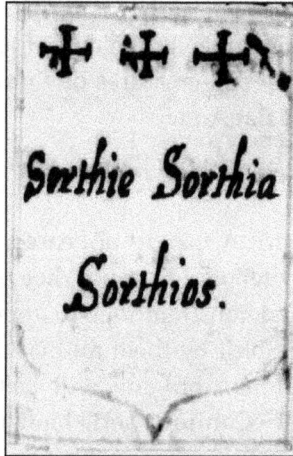

49 - Parchment figure mentioned in the preceding text to be placed upon the breast

This bond following is to cause the Spirit in the Stone to fetch unto thee the fairie Sibilia

All things fulfilled begin this bond as followeth and be bold for doubtless they will come before thee before the conjuration be read vii [7] times.

I Conjure thee Spirit A In this Crystal Stone by + God the Father + by God the Son Jesus Christ + And by God the Holy Ghost + Three persons and one God and by their virtues **I Conjure thee** Spirit that thou do go in peace And also to come again to me quickly and to bring with thee into that Circle appointed Sibilia fairie that I may talk with her in those matters that shall be to her Honour and Glory And so I charge thee declare unto her **I Conjure thee** Spirit A by the blood of the innocent lamb The which redeemed all the world by the virtue thereof I charge thee thou Spirit in the Crystal Stone That thou do declare unto her this Message **Also I Conjure thee** Spirit A by all Angels and Archangels Thrones Dominations Principates Potestates Virtutes Cherubim and Seraphim and by their virtues and powers **I Conjure thee** A that thou do depart with speed And also to come again with speed And to bring with thee the fairie Sibilia to appear in that Circle before I do read the Conjuration in this book Seven times This I charge with My will to be fulfilled upon pain of everlasting condemnation **Fiat fiat fiat** Amen.

Then the figure aforesaid pinned on thy breast Rehearse the words therein & say *Sorthie Sorthia Sorthios* Then begin your Conjuration viz

This Conjuration is to cause the Fairie Sibilia to appear.

I Conjure thee Sibilia O gentle virgin of fairies by the mercy of the Holy Ghost and by the dreadful day of decree And by their virtues and powers **I Conjure thee** O gentle virgin of fairies And by all the Angels of ♃ and their characters And virtues And by all the Spirits of ♃ and ♀ and their Characters and virtues And by all the Characters that be in the firmament And by the king and Queen of fairies and their virtues And by the faith and obedience that thou bearest unto them **I Conjure thee** Sibilia by the blood that ran out of the side of + Our lord Jesus Christ crucified And by the opening of heaven And by the renting of the Temple And by the darkness of the Sun In the time of his death And by the rising up of the dead In the time of his resurrection And by the + virgin Mary + mother of our + Lord Jesus Christ + And by the unspeakable name of God + Tetragrammaton + **I Conjure thee** O Sibilia O blessed and beautiful virgin by all the royal words aforesaid **I Conjure thee** Sibilia by all their virtues to appear in this Circle before me visibly In the form and shape of A beautiful woman In a bright and vesture white adorned and garnished most fair and to appear to me quickly without deceit or tarrying And that thou fail not to fulfil my will and desire effectually For I will choose thee to be my blessed virgin And will have common Copulation with thee Therefore make haste & speed to come unto me And to appear as I said before **To whom** be honour and Glory for ever and ever **Amen**

The which done and ended If she come not repeat the Conjuration till they do come For doubtless they will come.

When she is appeared Take your Censer And Incense her with Frankincense then bind her as followeth

I do Conjure thee Sibilia by + God the Father + God the Son + And God the Holy Ghost + Three persons and one God And by the blessed + virgin Mary + Mother of our + Lord Jesus Christ + And by all the whole And holy Company of Heaven and by the dreadful day of doom And by all Angels Archangels Thrones Dominations

Principates Potestates Virtutes Cherubim and Seraphim and their virtues and powers **I Conjure thee** and bind thee Sibilia that thou shalt not depart out of the Circle wherein thou art appeared Nor yet to alter thy shape Except I give thee license to depart **I Conjure thee** Sibilia by the blood that ran out of the side of our + Lord Jesus Christ + Crucified and by the virtues thereof **I Conjure thee** Sibilia to come to me And to appear to me at all times visibly as the Conjuration of words leadeth written in this book **I Conjure thee** Sibilia O blessed virgin of Fairies By the Opening of Heaven And by the renting of the Temple And by the darkness of the Sun (106) at the time of his death And by the rising of the dead In the time of his Glorious resurrection And by the unspeakable name of God + Tetragrammaton + And by the King and Queen of fairies and by their virtues **I Conjure thee** Sibilia to appear before the Conjuration be read over iiii [4] times And that visibly to appear as the Conjuration leadeth written in this book And to give me good Counsel at all times And to come by treasure hidden in the Earth And all other things that is to do me pleasure And to fulfil my will without any deceit or tarrying. Nor yet that thou shalt have any power of my body or Soul Earthly or Ghostly Nor yet to perish so much of my body as one Hair of my Head **I Conjure thee** Sibilia by all the royal words aforesaid and by their virtues and powers I charge and bind thee by the virtue thereof to be obedient unto me and to all the words aforesaid And this bond to stand between thee and me upon pain of everlasting Condemnation **Fiat fiat fiat** Amen.

Now followeth A license for Sibilia to go and come at all times.

I Conjure thee Sibilia which art come hither before me by the commandment of thy lord and mine that thou shalt have no power in thy going or coming unto me Imagining any evil in any manner of ways In the Earth or under the Earth of evil doings to any person or persons **I Conjure** & command thee Sibilia by all the royal words and virtues that be written in this book That thou shalt not go to the place from whence thou comest but shalt remain peaceably invisible And look thou be ready to come unto me when thou art called by any Conjuration of words that be written in this book (To come I say) at my commandment And to answer unto me truly and duly of all things my will quickly to fulfil. **Vade in pace**[299]

---

[299] "Go in peace".

+ In nomine Patris + Et filii + Et Spiritus Sancti + And the holy + cross be between thee and me or between us and you And the lion of Judah The root of Jesse The kindred of David be between thee and me + Christ cometh + Christ cometh + Christ giveth power + Christ defend me + And his innocent blood + from all perils of body and Soul Sleeping and waking. **Fiat fiat fiat** Amen.

50 - Magic circle for conjuration given in the preceding text, originating from Scot's Discoverie of Witchcraft

(107)

A Bond:~:

I Conjure thee Spirit **A** In the name of (   )[300] by all the virtues And by all the powers of the divine virtues and powers that thou be obedient to me In all my commandments. I conjure thee

---

[300] Blank space here in the text.

thou Spirit by the name of God And by the death of our Lord upon the holy Cross And by these and all they which are alive and dead And by the maker of the world And by the maker of Heaven and Earth And by him that did cast thee down into Hell And by his Cross And by his Passion and by his Ascension That thou grant to me According to thy power whatsoever I shall Ask or demand of thee That thou obey my sayings And that through my Petition to God thou do subdue thyself in his name that hath created thee I do Conjure thee by the invocation of our Lord Jesus Christ the undefiled lamb which hath commanded thee (   )[301] of the holy Angels and Archangels compel thee **A** Michael Gabriel Uriel and Raphael compel thee **A** All Patriarchs Abraham Isaac and Jacob And all other Prophets compel thee **A** All holy virgins And all Saints And all the elect people of God Compel thee. Therefore all the above named Saints pray for me In this hour In this month And in this minute And that he may quickly grant unto my petition And I pray by the death and Passion of our Lord Jesus Christ son of the living God And by the merits of his Passion And by the Intercession of our blessed Lady the virgin Mary being the Mother of Jesus Christ And all the Saints That you will grant me the divine grace and power upon one of these *Andragias*[302] *Saturnion Sathan Conuociell* that you do obey me and my sayings And that whatsoever I shall call him straight away by the power of these let him come and fulfil my will. I **B** the Son of **C** In the power and virtues of our Lord Jesus Christ the which is + Alpha + and + Omega + the first and the last the beginning and the ending. I do Conjure thee Spirit **A** and I call thee by God which Spake the word and all things were made by him whom all creatures do obey And by whom the company of Celestial Angels, Terrestrial and Infernal do tremble quake and fear, And by his virtues and almightiness And by these holy names + On + Ely + Eloy + Adonay + Tetragrammaton + Messias + Sothell + Emanuell + Sabaoth + Agios + Otheos + Iskiros + Otheos + Eleyson + ymas + And that you come quickly without any let visibly in a mans likeness I do conjure thee I do constrain thee I do call upon thee to come to my presence I do Conjure thee **A** And inform thee **A** And in constraint I do make a witness And in a witness I do compel thee Manfully I do Command thee by the name of God + Tetragrammaton + by whom all the

---

[301] Another blank space, a likely substitution based on earlier textual examples would be "by the virtues".

[302] Possibly a corruption of Andras, the 63rd Goetic Spirit.

world was made That thou come before this Circle in my presence and obey my sayings And that thou wilt be in his name which hath created thee And that justly condemned thee if I do Adjure thee In his name whom all things In Hell do fear to whom still the powers of Heaven do fear Saints and Orders be Subjects and fear And do honour And with unfeigned voice and unceased do praise and cry out + Holy + Holy + Holy + Lord God of Sabaoth + Heaven and Earth are full of thy Glory + Hosanna in Excelsis + Let the word that was made flesh command thee And let Jesus of Nazareth King of the Jews Command thee the which hath made thee Come quickly to me and obey my sayings And bring to pass all things whatsoever I shall ask of thee And will know of thee Or will have of thee* Or will know of thee Because by how much the more slack thou art By so much the more I do command thee In the virtue of the above named That so much the more thy punishment may increase from day to day unless thou come quickly without any stay And that thou do diligently whatsoever I shall will thee Command thee Ask of thee Or any would have bring to pass according to thy power He doth bind and command thee which sitteth in the highest beholding the depth and bottom of the waters and of all other things whatsoever, To whom is and shall be All Praise Power Honour Glory Might and Majesty both now and for ever + which doth Reign Rule Govern command in perfect Trinity being a Glorious and fearful God world without end + Amen + fiat +

The God of Angels The God of Archangels The God of Patriarchs The God of Prophets The God of the Apostles The God of Martyrs The God of Confessors The God of virgins The God and father of our Lord and Saviour Jesus Christ I call upon thy holy name Thy excellent Majesty I do openly require and heartily pray thee that thou wilt vouchsafe to help keep and defend (108) me against this spirit **A** That wheresoever he (or they) do lie when he (or they) do hear thy holy name, He (or they) may come to me quickly and swiftly arising out of his (or their) places And let him (or them) come speedily, He doth command thee to be thrown down headlong from the seat of Heaven Into the lowest place of the Earth, Hear therefore **A** and fear thou being bound and lying fast Come in the virtue and power of the Holy Ghost And of our blessed Lord Jesus Christ I do Conjure thee by the unspotted Lamb which doth command thee Hear therefore and see and fear the word of God and be thou ready and obedient to me in all my business that are to be done.

If thou do not these things I **B** a Christian man in the virtue & strength the virtue and power of Almighty God and of all his Saints I do condemn thee **A** into Hell and into everlasting fire even until the last day of Judgement, Let this therefore be done Let it be done Let it be done + fiat + fiat + fiat + Amen + Amen + Amen + unless thou come thee quickly to me And answer me truly and justly in all points and questions whatsoever I shall ask of thee I Conjure thee **A** thou Spirit not in my felicity but in the virtue and power of my Lord Jesus Christ And the holy Ghost that thou be Subject to me in all things whatsoever I bid and command thee to do, Or bring to pass so far as in thy power is to do, I do Conjure thee **A** and bind thee **A** by virtue of the unity of God almighty and by Jesus Christ almighty of Nazareth the undefiled lamb proceeding of the highest the Holy Ghost Conceived and born of the virgin Mary whom Gabriel did show to come whom when John did see He cried with a loud voice saying Behold the lamb of God which taketh away the sins of the world. I Conjure thee and constrain thee And command thee that without any stay thou do come to me always and that thou do so come to me with any hurt or detriment of my Soul and body and of all other things. I Conjure thee by all the above named Sacraments And by all holy things And by all holy writings And by all things that are both in Heaven above and in Earth below and in the water under the Earth And all things also where either alive or dead And by him that cast thee down from Heaven. I Conjure thee and command thee by the name and by the power of all Spirits And by the Characters of the firmament And by all the seals of Solomon And by all Angels and Archangels And by all the Celestial Images Into the Curse and confusion and hurt of the pains that thou art in from day to day that thou shalt have no rest nor cease from thy continual labour pain and torment in the place where thou art now And that thou be deprived from all thy offices case and comfort And from all thy fellowship and temptation Binding thee by the words aforesaid of the commemoration And I forbid thee and confound thy name for ever by thy days of thy Life And by the power which God hath over thee always O Spirit **A** I Conjure thee by the holy God that if thou wilt not come quickly to me that thou go down to Hell And let Heaven and Earth Excommunicate thee and let all the creatures in them contained curse thee thou **A** And let the holy name of God And the twelve names the which thou knowest to be of great power And the four and twenty Seniors curse thee And the fifteen names of God which are most to be named shall curse thee and cast thee **A** down into the pit of Hell in fire and in Brimstone the which cannot be taken away nor suffered By the word and holy name of God And by the excellentest most pleasant and most strongest power which cannot agree Neither is it meet or fit to none but only to God Almighty as thou knowest well enough This hour let him cast thee away being full of Anguish and trouble hurt wrath hatred and pain let him cast thee down into the furnace of Hellfire In the which prison of damnation whereas there is no order but continual fear dwelleth + Let it be done + Let it be done + Let it be done by the power and virtue of almighty God without any end + Amen + fiat + unless thou come the quicklier and apace to me and speak to me And fulfil and perform and obey me and all my sayings and commandments whatsoever + In the name of the Father I say come + In the name of the Son come + In the name of the Holy Ghost come + Come I say unto thee come + I tell thee come + Come In the name of the great God and Trinity Creator of all Creatures Come to me I Say in this hour In the name of the holy Trinity In a fair shape of a Child of ten years of age without the hurt or perishing of any body or thing and without any hurt or peril to the health of my body or Soul And that thou go not away from me until thou hast fully (109) satisfied me my will and sayings And until thou be licensed by me. I Conjure thee thou Spirit And do constrain thee by the Holy Ghost and by the same God which hath created all things and is + Alpha + and + Omega + the first and the last The beginning and the ending And by him which is King of Kings And Lord of Lords And by him which said let it be done and it was done And by him whom all creatures do obey And through him all Angels and Archangels do tremble and fear And all the company of Heavenly things and Earthly things And the terrible things in Hell do tremble quake and fear And by his virtues and his omnipotent power And by the fearful day of Judgement And by all things which may be spoken of or thought of God And by all things the which God hath made And will make or do the Laud and Glory of God and by his name And by the unspeakable name of + Christ + Jesus + Messias + Sother + Emanuell + Sabaoth + Adonay + Alpha + et + Omega + Theon + Iskiros + Otheos + Agla + Yseray + Tetragrammaton + Anepheneton + Ineffenefatall + And by the Seven Seals of the wise Solomon Through which Solomon hath bound thee and thy fellows In a vessel of Glass by the most mightiest and strongest names of God All we do compel you strongly and mercilessly by that you do obey us through him which spake the word and it was done.

I Conjure and Constrain thee **A** by the name of + ya + ya + and in the name + ya + ya + the which Adam did speak. &c as it is before in folio.

51 - Page of text from MS showing William Bacon's conjuration of Sathan, immediately following

The Roman Secret touching the Spirit called Sathan by which the Romans did understand of things present past and to come: By W. Bacon

The Spirit of this invocation doth appear in a Basin and to be wrought every day except the Lords day and the double feast days.

First beware that thou be not defiled with luxury nor wrapped in any deadly sin but steadfast in faith belief and trusting in the lord. And be thou fasting And have a fair Chamber and take with thee a fair and bright well burnished basin And have thou iiii [4] wax Candles And make them fast on the brim of the Basin upon every candle write these names + Moses + Aaron + Jacob + Usion + Tetragrammaton + Moriaton + Then take the Sword and write upon it these words + Jesus Nazarenus rex iudeorum + Jesus of Nazareth King of the Jews the Son of the living God have mercy upon me + And make the Circle with the Sword And sitting in the midst of the

Circle Turning thee first towards the South putting the basin out of the Circle over against thee And perfuming the Basin with Mastic and Lignum Aloes Say the Gospel In the beginning was the word &c which done Sign thyself with the Cross Saying By the Sign of the Cross let everything that is evil be driven from hence. Then say this Conjuration.

I Conjure thee Sathan by the Father + the Son + and the holy Ghost + By holy Mary mother of our lord Jesus Christ and by all the Martyrs And Confessors And all the holy virgins and widows by the Crown of Christ by his head and by his teeth and ears and by his face and nose by his mouth and eyes by his tongue by his arms by his nails by his thumbs by his fingers Sinews and veins by his legs feet and the Soles of his feet by all his members in which he hath vouchsafed to suffer torments for the redemption of mankind by the wounds of Christ by all the torments of his passion and by all the torments of martyrs and Saints of God by the nativity of our lord Jesus Christ and by the circumcision of Christ and by the baptism of Christ by the passion of Christ by the death of Christ by the (110) resurrection of Christ by the ascension of Christ by the coming of Christ in the day of Judgement by the dreadful day of Judgement in which every human and Christian Creature shall appear in the 30th year of his age by the 20 beasts sitting before the throne of God having eyes before and behind And by the wisdom of Solomon I Conjure thee Sathan by the virtue of all these and by the merits of he Saints and she Saints of God that thou appear in this basin in the likeness of a white Monk that thou tell and show me the whole truth and virtue of that thing whereof I shall examine thee without deceit or fraud faithfully + fiat + fiat + fiat + Amen +

Then put out the Candle that stands towards the South and turn thyself towards the west setting the Basin towards thee putting and perfuming the basin as aforesaid. Then say

I Conjure thee Sathan by all these names of God + focnertu + forden + feon + fugorifedus + folo + diry + fumel + Mebon + Magon + Mesias + Alrararay + Adonay + Sabaoth + Sother + Sabn + Sponsus + And all the names of them that be dead and their bodies And by the Seal of God By these names I Conjure thee Sathan that thou enter into this vessel In the likeness of a white monk and tell and show me the whole truth of what I shall demand of thee without deceit or falsity + fiat + fiat + fiat +

Then extinguish the Candle and turn thy self towards the North having the Basin right before thee And Suffumigate the basin as before. Then say as followeth

I Conjure thee Sathan by the Rod of Moses And by the Tables of Moses and by the nine Celestial Candles and by the similitude or picture figure likeness of the 3 spirits by Daniel the prophet by holy Peter holy Paul and by these names of God + Agla + Aglay + Aray + Mara + Mandra + Mory + Motion + Motcory + Matary + Matulia + Nata + Nazary + By the East and west by the South and by the North by the 4 plagues and the 4 Elements and by the 12 signs of the firmament that thou Sathan without any deceit tell me the truth without feigning counterfeiting or lying touching all my things matters that I shall require of thee + fiat + fiat + fiat

Then put out the Candle that stands towards the north And then turn thyself towards the East with the Basin and suffumigate it as before and say

I Conjure thee Sathan by the bonds of Solomon and by the person of Solomon and by the Seal (Signet) of W Bacon and by the Seal of Raimond which is called Chath Malentes by holy Michael And by that holy salutation wherewith Holy Gabriel saluted the blessed virgin Mary Saying Hail Mary full of Grace the lord is with thee blessed art thou amongst women and blessed is Jesus the fruit of thy womb + Amen + And by every good thing which may (can) be in heaven and in Earth And by all the Heavens and by the virtues in them and by the book of life and by that holy Spirit which God Jesus Christ sent upon the Earth And by these holy words which he spoke hanging upon the Cross + Consumatum est + It is finished + And by all the words which I cannot utter speak or which I may (or is not) lawful not utter And by all these names and by their virtues (efficacy) I Conjure thee Sathan that thou appear to me In the form or figure of a Monk in white without any hurt or without any fear or astonishment to me or us and that thou tell me the whole truth of things that I shall demand of thee omitting all impure (filthy) deceit and falsity + Amen + And if thou wilt not do my commandment and precept and obey my Statutes I loose thee from all thy office discharge, seeing that it is so into the depth of waters until the day of Judgement by the authority of him which shall come to judge the quick and the dead And the world by fire + fiat + fiat + fiat

Then put out the fourth Candle and suffumigate the Basin as aforesaid which done say

By the virtue of all these And by the virtue of all the names of God + fiat + fiat + fiat + Amen +

Then the Spirit will appear to thee in manner as aforesaid And let him declare the truth of every thing that thou shalt inquire of him when thou wilt have him depart, Say,

Depart Sathan to the place predestinated where the lord thy God hath appointed thee until I shall call upon thee another time (elsewhere) under pain of everlasting damnation and Curse of God the father (111) almighty + The father + the Son + and the Holy Ghost + except thou depart and retire thee soon to the place appointed for thee by the lord and ordained thee without doing any hurt to me or my fellows And except thou come quickly when I call thee If by any means thou canst And make haste without delay and that thou appear without harm either without the House or in the fields when I call upon thee enjoying the benediction of thy prince + Amen + fiat + fiat + fiat + Amen

---

To burn or Curse A Spirit ~:~:~:

If a Spirit will not appear write his name in virgin parchment and kindle a new fire and put therein Brimstone and other filthy things Saying **I Conjure thee** fire by him of whom the world is Sustained that thou burn this Spirit after that sort that they may feel it perpetually Amen.[303]

And then holding the Parchment with the name over the Smoke thou shalt say N because thou hast not obeyed the commandments of the lord neither wouldst appear unto me which am his eternal servant Answer my why I shall not excommunicate thee and curse thy name here written to the devil wherefore in the name of God And in the name of our lord Jesus Christ and of all the Saints be thou Cursed and excommunicated and like as this name written is burnt with material fire and is perfumed with filthy things even so by the virtue of God I throw N into the deepest pit of Hell and brimstone where thou shalt remain unto the day of Judgement and never shall there be remembrance of thee before the

---

[303] This curse is copied from that found in Additional MS 36674, a 16th century Key of Solomon text. The second paragraph beginning "And then holding the parchment" has been added and is not in the earlier MS. A more complete version is found in Sloane MS 3847, also 16th century.

face of the living God which shall come to Judge the quick and the dead and the world by fire Amen.

Then cast the parchment into the fire saying Cursed and blasphemed be thou forever. Let there be no rest to thee any day or any night nor any hour because now thou hast not been obedient unto the words that are spoken of the mighty maker of all things by whose power every creature is compelled to obey with trembling and by that same virtue and power Thunder and lightning is ordained to destroy thee + Ameneton + Foahat + Sother + Sememphoras + Alma + Alephe + Bethe + Gimel + Dalathe + Stee[304] + Sayn + Cheeth + Teeth + Yed + Chaphe[305] + Ros + Shin + Sin + Tau + we curse thee and deprive thee of all thy power and Strength by the virtue of these names, sending thee to everlasting punishment to burn in fire and brimstone world without end + Amen + fiat + fiat + fiat + Amen +

52 - *Two lines of figure of unknown meaning, recorded here in the text*

The Consecration of a wand or Rod:

Take a hazel wand of a years growth And bathe it in the fire and consecrate it with these words

Purify me O God and I shall be clean That no ill thing shall abide near me. Then write these names of God + Alpha + et + Omega + on both sides of the Rod and Jesus Christ at the end forward and in writing these names with the blood of a lamb of an Ewe Consecrate the wand as followeth

---

[304] This is clearly a miscopying of Heh, and the sixth Hebrew letter, Vav, is missing here from the sequence of the Hebrew alphabet given.

[305] The letters Lamed to Qoph are not included here, where they mostly were in Additional MS 36674. The corruption of the letters given suggests the writer was not familiar with Hebrew. The names and letters have suffered some corruption from the earlier text, where they read "Ameteñeton, Io, Ahac, Pater, Semiphoras, Alleluia, Aleph, Beth, Gymel, Daleth, he, [Vau,] sayn, Cleth [Cheth], Teth, Jod, Caph, Lamed, Mem, [Nun,] Samech, Ain, Pe, Tsade, Coph, [Resh,] Sin, Tau". Note the original also had missing Hebrew letters in the sequence (indicated by []).

Strengthen me O lord God Almighty Creator of all things As thou didst the Rod of Moses That parted the sea in sunder That the children of Israel passed through safe[306] work in me the same virtue O God and I shall be so strong that no ill Spirit shall abide me Sanctify me O God of Sabaoth And let thy name be Glorified in me That as the Rod of Moses did strike the hard stone and water gushed out[307] So sanctify thy name that wheresoever it is writ or spoken all evil and unclean Spirits may be excluded + fiat + fiat + fiat + Amen +

Write these words on a Hazel wand for a defensative[308]

+ Tetragrammaton + Adonay + Secamon + Sadu ay + Sicamosey + Sepatate + Abriell[309] + Joell[310] + Finis + (112)

How he ought to Order him self that would call:

It behoveth him to be Holy and Chastely affected and to approach purely and cleanly neither must he be defiled or polluted or his Soul with Sin nor carry about the cockatrices of Sin marked in his breast or Heart It behoveth him altogether to separate his mind and purge Ill from every disease, From dullness or blockishness Idleness Malice envy hatred and all passions of that sort which accompany him as the Rust doth Iron. This may be effected if we free ourselves from all moving and from all carnal and Earthy affairs Let the mind be purged by cleanness by abstinence by permitence[311] by alms deeds And the Soul is to be healed by Studying of Religion If from day to day we read any thing out of the Sacred Scripture, we must be pure and abstinent when we receive our meat and keeping a holy & moderate table And leading our lives in all temperance. Moreover we must mark the situation of the place Motion and aspects of the planets in their Signs and

---

[306] Exodus 14:21.

[307] Exodus 17:6.

[308] Something which serves to protect or defend.

[309] Abriel is the name of a spirit serving Dorochiel, the Prince said to rule the North-West in the Theurgia Goetia and Steganographia.

[310] An angel mentioned in The Testament of Solomon as controlling the demon Onoskelis.

[311] Permission.

degrees how all these things agree, with the length and breadth of the Element But of all these the ☾ is specially to be heeded, For if the ☾ be not in a good aspect nothing is well accomplished.

Of the Bonds of Spirits:[312]

The bonds of Spirits are 3-fold either in the elementary world where we adjure the Spirit by inferior and natural things known to them or opposite to them As by the Flowers Herbs By things that have life, Snow Hail Ice fire and the like.

The second bond is In the Celestial world whom we adjure by the Heavens by the Stars and by the motions and beams of these and the like And this Bond doth work against the Spirits after a manner of a certain admonition & example.

The Third Bond is in the intellectual and divine world which is accomplished by Religion As when we adjure by the Sacraments by miracles by the divine names by the holy Seals and other mysteries of religion And this bond is the greatest and most strongest of all other workings with command & power against the Spirit. (113)

Of Perfumes ~:

A perfume made of Hempseed and of the Seeds of Fleawort and violet roots and Parsley and (Smallage)[313] maketh to see things to come **And** is available for Prophecy.

A perfume made with Coriander, Saffron, Henbane and Parsley (Smallage) and White Poppy ana[314] bruised and Pounded together If any shall dig Gold or Silver or any precious thing the ☾ being joined to the ☉ in the lower heaven let him perfume the place with this suffumigation.

---

[312] This section is an abbreviated version of Ch. XXXIII of Book 3 of Agrippa's De Occulta Philosophia.

[313] Wild celery.

[314] Middle English word meaning "Of equal quantity".

A perfume of the Planets. Myrrh, Gostu,[315] Mastic, Camphor, Frankincense, Sanders, Opoponax, Lignum Aloes, Alum, Euphorbium, Storax or Thimyam[316] ana 1 oz.[317]

A perfume of ☉[318] yellow amber ½oz Musk 12 grains Lignum Aloes 36 grains Lignum Balsam and the berries of Laurel ana[319] 46 grains Of Gilleflowers[320] Myrrh and Frankincense ana 1oz with the blood of a white Cock make pills in the quantity of ½ dram

A Perfume of ☾ Take of white Poppy seeds 1oz of Male frankincense ½oz Of Camphor 1oz with the blood of A Goose made in balls

A perfume of ♄ Seeds of Black Poppies and the Seeds of Hoyseami[321] ana 2oz The Root of Mandragoras 1½oz The stone Lapis Lazuli[322] ½oz Myrrh 3 grains with the Brains or blood of A Bat in balls the quantity of 1oz

A Perfume of ♃ Seeds of Ash 2oz Lignum Aloes 2oz Storax, Benjamin 1oz Lapis Lazuli 1oz Of the very tips of the feathers of the Peacock Let them be incorporated with the blood of a Stork or of a

---

[315] This is almost certainly a miscopying of Costum.

[316] Probably Thyme.

[317] The measurements are in symbols representing ounces and drams (or drachms). An ounce (oz) = 28g; a dram = ⅛oz = 3½g; 480 grains = 1 ounce, so 1 grain = 0.0583g or 1g = 17.14 grains. Gr. is the abbreviation for grain.

[318] These recipes are based on those found in De Occulta Philosophia Book I, ch. XLIV, The compositions of some fumes appropriated to the planets, but with omissions of some of the ingredients, and including proportions which are not given in Agrippa.

[319] The term 'ana' means 'equally' or 'in equal parts'.

[320] Another name for carnation.

[321] Another name for Henbane.

[322] Probably a transcription error, as Agrippa gives Lodestone, with lapis lazuli for Jupiter as also seen here.

Swallow or the brain of a hart let there be made a trochisk[323] in the quantity of a Groat.[324]

A Perfume of ♂ Euphorbium, Bedelum[325] 1oz Ammoniac roots of both sorts of Eleborus[326] ana the lodestone 2 drams Brimstone 1 dram let it be incorporated with the brain of a Crow and with Mans blood of a black Cat make Trochisks 1 dram

A Perfume of ♀ Musk 38 grains Amber 21 grains lignum aloes 1oz Red Roses 2oz Red Coral 2oz mingle it with the brain of a Sparrow and the blood of a Boar. Make a Trochisk in quantity ½ dram

A Perfume of ☿ Mastic 1oz frankincense 2oz Gilleflowers, pantaphile[327] 2oz ac Lapidi Achate.(With Agate Stone)[328] Incorporate it with the brain of a fox or a weasel and with the blood of A Pie[329] make Trochisk in quantity ½ dram (114)

A Perfume of every Planet ♄ Costum ♃ Nucis Muscate[330] ♂ Lignum aloes ☉ Mastic ♀ Crocum ☿ Cinnamomum ☾ Mirtum[331] ana 1oz

Lunarn[332] avro suffimigacion conficim ex Capiti rana an facto it Oculis tauri, & semeni papavis albi ad thuri & Camphora, quae incorporabuntur cum sanguine menstruo vel sanguim Anserim.[333]

---

[323] A tablet or lozenge

[324] An old English silver coin, supposed to weigh 6.2g, by the 17th century the weight had dropped to 2.1g.

[325] Bidellium is a resin similar to myrrh.

[326] Hellebores.

[327] Cinquefoil.

[328] "With Agate Stone", written in the second hand.

[329] Magpie.

[330] Nutmeg.

[331] Myrtle.

[332] This following section is in Latin in the second hand, I have transcribed it direct including errors, and included the English translation of the

Sunt priteria suffitus ♄ ois odorifera radicor, ut costi Uharba thurib.[334]

♃ is suffitus odoriferi quique fructus , ut nux moseata ut Gariophilli.[335]

♂ omni odoriferum lignum sandalorum, cuprissi, Balsami, & ligni aloes.[336]

☉ gumi, thus masticki, Benzac, storax Ladanum atque ambra & musk.[337]

♀ sunt floris, rosae violae, crocus & consimilis.[338]

☿ omne Carticro lignoy & fructuum & Cinamonum, Cassia ligna, Macim, corticum Citri & lauri grana & quoque etiam odorifera semina.[339]

☽ habit ce suffitu digitalium oium folio et folium Indum et folia myrti & lauri.[340]

Sciam quotrivia iuxta magoy fintructiam, et quod in oium oyi bono cut sunt amor benevolentia & similia suffumigum debit esse bonum ridolinum & preiosum. In malo autem oyi, cut sunt odium, ira, Calamitas & similia suffumigium debit elsi feetidum & vile.[341]

---

appropriate paragraphs it is drawn from in Agrippa's De Occulta Philosophia, Book 1, ch. XLIV.

[333] For the Moon we make a suffumigation of the head of a frog dried, the eyes of a bull, the seed of white poppy, frankincense, and camphor, which must be incorporated with menstruous blood, or the blood of a goose.

[334] Besides to Saturn are appropriated for fumes all odiferous roots, as pepperwort root (the reference in Latin has been changed to costus) etc and the frankincense tree.

[335] To Jupiter odoriferous fruits, as nutmegs, cloves.

[336] To Mars all odiferous wood, as sanderswood, cypress, lignum balsam and lignum aloes.

[337] To the Sun, all gums, frankincense, mastic, benzoin, storax, laudanum, ambergris and musk.

[338] To Venus flowers, as roses, violets, crocus (saffron) and such like.

[339] To Mercury all the peels of wood and fruit, as cinnamon, lignum-cassia, mace, citron peel, and bayberries, and whatsoever seeds are odoriferous.

[340] To the Moon the leaves of all vegetables, as the leaf Indum, the leaves of the myrtle and the bay tree.

[341] Know also, that according to the opinion of the magicians, in every good matter, as love, goodwill, and the like, there must be a good fume,

Habit ilia duodecim signa Zodiaci suoo suffitum, ut ♈
myrrhum, ♉ Costu, ♊ Mastickium, ♋ Camphora, ♌ Thus, ♍
Sandalos, ♎ Galbanum, ♏ Opopanaem, ♐ Lignum Aloes, ♑
Balsam, ♒ Euphorbium, ♓ Thymiama. Potentissimum autem
suffitum de seribit Hermes en septem aromatica iuxta y du
planetary virtum conflatum recipit namque à ♄ Costu à ♃ nucrum
moscatum à ♂ le Lignum Aloes, à ☉ Mastickum à ♀ Crocum, à ☿
Cinomonum, à ☽ Myrtum.[342]

odoriferous, and precious; and in every evil matter, as hatred, anger,
misery, and the like, there must be a stinking fume, that is of no worth.

[342] The twelve signs also of the Zodiac have their proper fumes, as Aries
hath myrrh, Taurus costum (pepperwort in Agrippa); Gemini, mastic;
Cancer, camphor; Leo, frankincense; Virgo, sanderswood; Libra, galbanum;
Scorpio, opoponax; Sagittarius, lignum aloes; Capricorn, balsam; Aquarius,
euphorbium; Pisces, red storax. But Hermes describes the most powerful
fume to be, viz that which is composed of the seven aromatics, according to
the powers of the seven planets, for it receives from Saturn, costum
(pepperwort), from Jupiter, nutmeg, from Mars, lignum aloes, from the
Sun, mastic, from Venus, saffron, from Mercury, cinnamon, and from the
Moon, the myrtle.

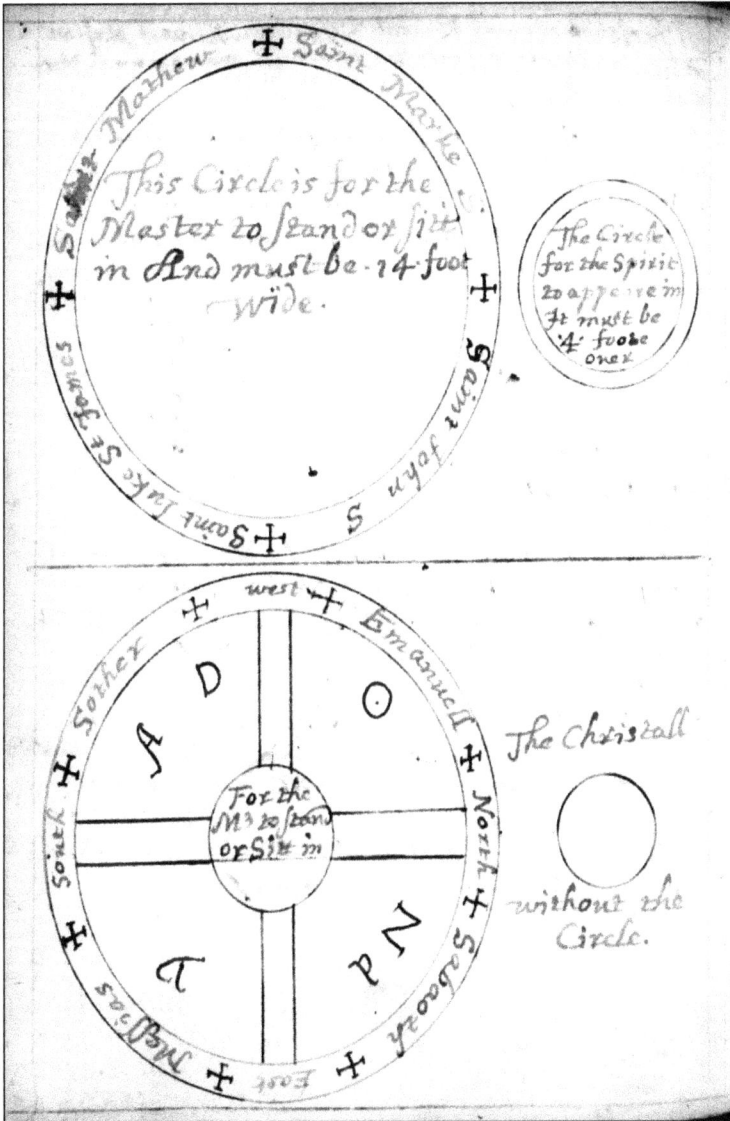

53 - Magic circles recorded here in the MS. The top circle contains the text:
"This Circle is for the Master to stand or sit in And must be 14 foot wide"
The smaller circle to the right says:
"The Circle for the Spirit to appear in It must be 4 foot over"
The second circle has the text "For the Master to stand or sit in" in the centre, and
"The Crystal without the Circle" around the smaller circle

(115)

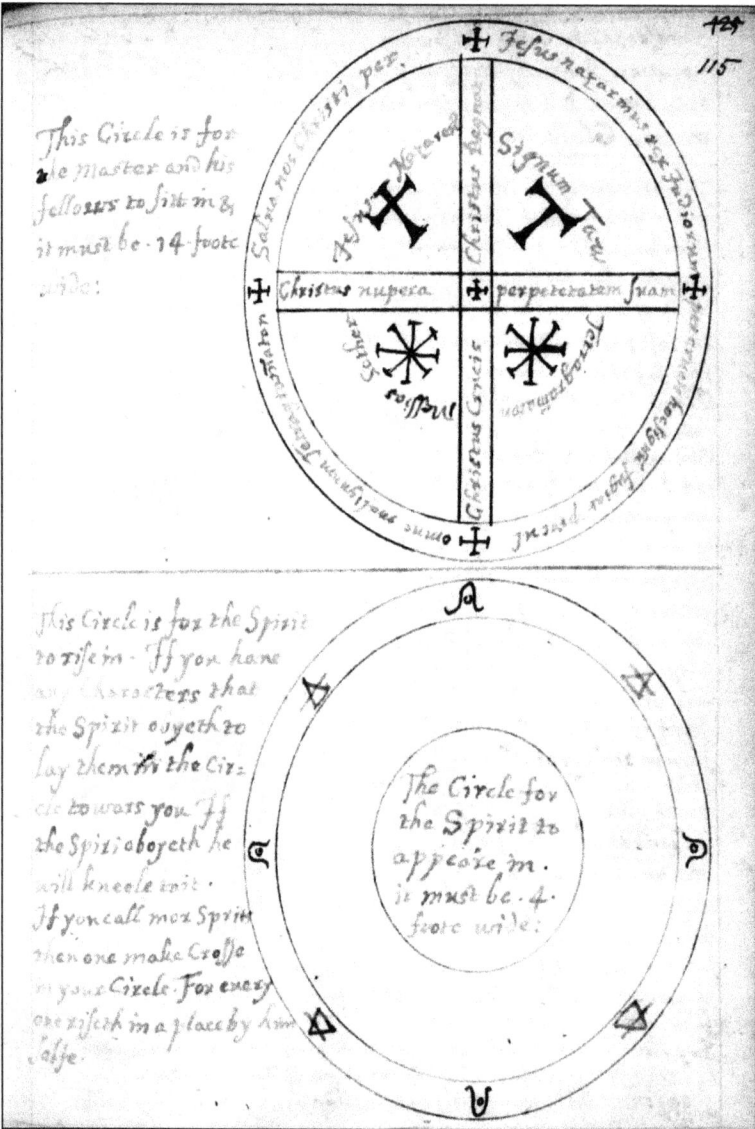

54 - More magic circles. The text to the left of the top circle says:
"This Circle is for the Master and his fellows to sit in & it must be 14 foot wide"
The text to the left of the bottom circle says:
"This Circle is for the Spirit to rise in. If you have any Characters that the Spirit obeyeth to lay them in the Circle toward you If the Spirit obeyeth he will kneel to it. If you call more Spirits than one make Cross in your Circle. For every one riseth in a place by himself."
The text inside the circle says:
"The Circle for the Spirit to appear in, it must be 4 foot wide."

Whosoever hath this following figure And shall use the invocation Presently Presently[343] shall Oberion Come in likeness of a Beautiful man like a Soldier personally in the air or in a Glass:~:[344]

The first day of the Moon Increasing and Ascending when she shall be strong and in the hour of ☾, Take a sheet of lead or of Silver And the Graven Image of the foresaid Spirit and his Sign above his head and his name in his forehead And the sign of the ☉ in the right part about the arm and the name of the Angel of the ☉ which is *Scorax*[345] And the sign of the ☾ in the left part and the name of the Angel of the ☾ which is *Carmelion*[346] Then say this invocation

O Lord O you Angels of the ☉ and of the ☾ *Scorax* and *Carmelion* I Conjure and exorcise you by the virtue and power of the name of the Son of God which is + Alpha + and + Omega + and by this wonderful name which is + Elli + and by him which hath framed you And by the figures which are written in this plate In the unity and omnipotence of the Creator and by this most high name which is + Tetragrammaton + which at what time soever by calling upon or Invocating *Oberion* whose Image is here graven and the name of the sign thereof are drawn forth in this sheet and that you make *Oberion* to obey me and to appear in the Air In the likeness of a Boy of 7 years of age and that he perfectly and truly fulfil my desires so far forth as he is able without any fraud or deceit whatsoever in all things fiat + fiat + fiat + Amen +

Then in the day of ♂ following write the name of his counsellor in the Sheet which name is *Raberion* on the right side and his Sign so as it appear plainly. Then say this Invocation.

---

[343] "Presently" is repeated in this title.

[344] A derivative version of this conjuration may be found in Wellcome MS4669 from 1796, where the name Oberion has been corrupted to Ebrion. Otherwise the details are almost identical. See A Collection of Magical Secrets, Skinner & Rankine, 2009:46

[345] Interestingly Scorax is the name given to the gum of the olive tree, see Lexicon Chymicum, Johnson, 1657:181.

[346] Carmelion is the name of a plain to the north of Galilee, described by Burchard of Mount Sion, a German Dominican monk who travelled Palestine in the late thirteenth century in his work Descriptio Terrae Sanctae. It is also an old form of chameleon. Whether either of these are the origin of this name I cannot say.

I Conjure thee o Spirit *Kaberion*[347] by all things in heaven and Earth in Hell and by King Solomon which hath brought thee under yoke and by all the Signs and Seals and Rings and by the 4 Elements that support the whole world and by the Serpent lifted up in the wilderness That thou counsel thy lord *Oberion* to put himself wholly to me In the shape of a boy of 7 years of age and to his power to fulfil my desire in all things.

So be it + So be it + So be it +

Say this thrice in the day and once in the night Then on the third day to wit on the day of ☿ write the name of his Counsellor which is *Seberion* as it manifestly appeareth in his sign. Say this (116)

I exorcise thee thou *Seberion* and command thee by this name Obriun or Obyron which befits no man to name save he that is in peril of death and is employed in this art And by all the Spirits as well Superior as inferior that without delay or any complaining you advise and counsel your lord Oberion to show himself familiarly to me in all things and at all times. So be it.

Afterward you may read the names of the 4 Angels Saying this[348] (117)

A prayer to be Prayed before that prayer of healing or any other thing thou shalt take in hand

---

O Eternal God and most blessed father Allmighty the creator and maker of all things Jesus Christ the form of that living God O you Paraclete the Comforter three persons and one God three in trinity and one in Unity I am kept and defended in the power of God the father with me, the power of God the Son be with me and the power and virtue of the holy ghost save keep and defend me from all mine enemies in both bodily and ghostly

---

[347] This name may be derived from the Greek Kabeiroi, the twin spirits who were famous metal-workers, and presided over the orgiastic dances at Samothrace in Greece in honour of the goddesses Hekate, Demeter and Persephone.

[348] The rest of the page is blank, and the prayer on the following page is in the second hand.

Lord God I beg thee that by thy passion heart blood against mine enemies to dwell with me and make my path good and by these names of Y.S.V. that our Lord God spake to Adam when he received wisdom to name all the creatures of the earth and by the holy spirit of god and virtue of this word or name Ruematon good Lord god deliver me by all the works that ever you did & by all the words that ever you spoke on earth and by the virtue of thy perfect breathing protect thou & deliver me By and in the virtue of the holy trinity good lord God forgive me and have mercy upon me both now and ever Amen Amen Amen So be it o Good god so be it o father of heaven so be it o blessed trinity fiat fiat fiat.

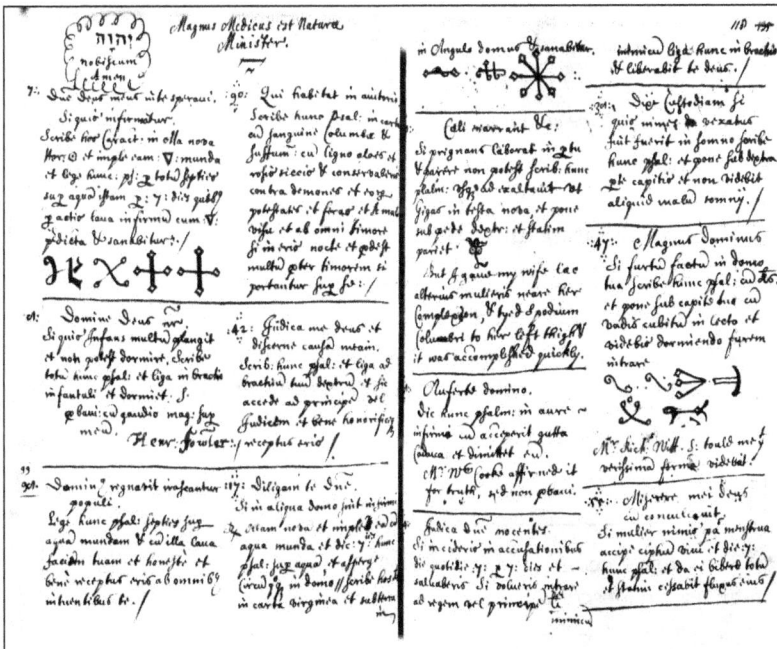

55 - First of several pages of Latin charms in the MS here using the Psalms. The cloud contains the Hebrew IHVH (Tetragrammaton) and the words nobiscum amen, so literally meaning 'God be with us, Amen'

יְהוָֹה
nobiscum
Amen

Magnus Medicus est Naturae Minister[349]

---

7 Domine deus meus in te speravi[350]

Si quid nifirmatur

Scribe hoc Caracter: in olla nova Hor:☉ et imple eam :▽: munda et ligi hunc Psalm per totum septied su per aquam istam per :7: dies quibque per actid laua infernal cum :▽: predicta & sanabitur.[351]

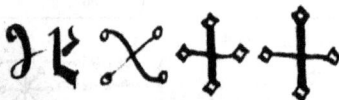

56 - Characters to be engraved on the cooking pot in the preceding charm using Psalm 7

---

90 Qui habitat in adiutori[352]

Scribe hunc Psalm in carta cum sanguine columbae & suffumum cum ligno aloes et rosis siccis & conservabitor contra demonis et eoy potestates et feras et Amabo visu et ab omni timori si in evis nocte et podest multum poter timorem si portantur super se:[353]

---

[349] "The Great Doctor is the Servant of Nature". Magnus Medicus was also a term used to describe Christ the physician, i.e. the great doctor.

[350] Psalm 7:2 "O Lord my God in thee have I put my trust."

[351] "If something has been weakened. Engrave this Character: in a new cooking pot, in the hour of the Sun, and fill it with clean water and read this Psalm completely seven times over that water during :7: days. Upon completion of this, wash the weakened [thing] with the prescribed water & it will be made whole again."

[352] Psalm 90:1 "He that dwelleth in the aid (of the most high)."

[353] "Write this psalm on papyrus/paper with the blood of a pigeon & fumigate with lignum aloes and dried rose & you will be protected against demons and their powers and their wild and evil appearance even if [they are] unavoidable at night and you will go forth more powerful against

7 Domine deus meus[354]

Si quid infaus multum plangit it non potest dormivi Scribe totum hunc Psalm et liga in brachio in fautuli et dormiet. S. Baui cum garulio mag: super meum.[355]

---

42 Judica me deus et discerne causam meum[356]

Scrib: hunc Psalmet liga ad brachium tuum dextrum et sic accede ad principium vel Judicum et bene honorificique[357]

Henry Fowler[358] receptus eris[359]

---

98 Domine regnavit irascantur populi[360]

Lige hunc posal: septies super aquam mundum & cum illa caua faciem tuam et honesti et bene necroptus erid ab omni by inturntibud te.[361] (118)

---

17 Diligam te Domine.[362]

---

much that is feared if this is carried with one." The same charm is found in The Book of Gold, Rankine & Barron, 2010:164.

[354] Psalm 7:2; "O Lord my God."

[355] "If a child cries a lot and can't sleep. Write this entire Psalm and read it on the arm of the little child and it will sleep. I have tested it myself and now I am happier and elevated."

[356] Psalm 42:1; "Judge me o God and distinguish my cause."

[357] "Write this psalm and read it on your right arm and thus reach a high position or appraisal both good and honourable." This charm is also found in The Book of Gold, Rankine & Barron, 2010:99.

[358] This may refer to the Henry Fowler who was a physician and the mayor of Gloucester in 1671.

[359] "You will have received this [charm] from Henry Fowler."

[360] Psalm 98:1 "The Lord hath reigned, let the people be angry."

[361] "Read this psalm seven times over clean water & with that wash your face and you will be honestly and well spoken of and looked upon by all." Again this charm is found in The Book of Gold, Rankine & Barron, 2010:179.

[362] Psalm 17:2 "I will love thee O Lord."

Si in aliqua domo suit infirmi ♃ ollam nobam et implius ead cum aqua munda et dic :7: hunc Psalm super aqua et asperge circul quoque in domo // scribe host in carte virginea sub terra in Angula domus & sanabitur[363]

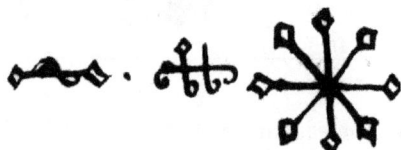

57 - Characters to be written on the pot for the preceding charm using Psalm 17

---

18 Caeli enarrant &c:[364]

Si prignans laborat in pertu & parere non potest scribe hunc Psalm utque ad exultavit ut Gigans[365] in tista noba, et pone sub pede dextra: et statim pariet[366]

58 - Presumably this figure is also drawn on the tile for the preceding charm using Psalm 18

But I gave my wife lac altrius mulieris near her Completion, & tied a podium colubri to her left thigh & it was accomplished quickly.[367]

---

[363] "If in any house there is someone ill ♃ , take a new cooking pot and fill it with clean water and say :7: [times] this Psalm over the water and sprinkle [or: asperge] it round, also in the house // write these [characters] on virgin parchment [to be buried] under the earth in a corner of the house & he shall be restored to health." This is also found in The Book of Gold, Rankine & Barron, 2010:55.

[364] Psalm 18:2 "The heavens show forth (the glory of God)."

[365] Verse 6

[366] "If a pregnant [woman] is at hand & she cannot give birth, write this psalm until 'exultavit ut gigans' on a new piece of clay [or tile] and tie it on her right leg, and she will immediately give birth." This is a simplified version of the charm in The Book of Gold, Rankine & Barron, 2010:57

[367] "But I gave my wife milk from another woman near her completion & tied a pigeon's leg to her left thigh & it was accomplished quickly."

95 Adferte domino[368]

Sic hunc Psalm in aure infirmi cum accepevit gutta caduca et dimittet eum.[369]

Mr & Mrs Cooke affirmed it for truth, sed non probavi.[370]

34 Judica domine nocentis[371]

Si incideris in accusationibus die quotidie :7: per 7 dies et saluaberis si volueris intrari ad regem vel principio ci inimicum liga Rune in brachio & liberabit te deus.[372]

38 Dixi Custodiam[373]

Si quis minis vexatus fuit fuivit in somno soribi hunc Psalm et pone sub dextra perte capitis et non vidibit aliquid malum romny.[374]

47 Magnus dominus[375]

Si furtum factum in domo tua scribe hunc Psalm cum deus et poni sub capite tuo cum vadis cubitum in lecto et videbis dormiendo furem nitrari.[376]

---

[368] Psalm 95:7 and 95:8 both start with this phrase meaning: "Bring thee to the Lord."

[369] "Thusly write this psalm on the ear of someone ill while they have received a fallen drop and it will send him forth."

[370] "But I have not put it to the test."

[371] Psalm 34:1 "Judge thou O Lord that wrong me."

[372] "If you will fall into accusations, say everyday :7: [seven times] for seven days and you will be saved if you want to go in [gain entry] to the king or prince [take] unfriendly [?] chicory, bind it to your arm & God will set you free." This seems to be derived from the charm for the same Psalm in The Book of Gold, Rankine & Barron, 2010:87.

[373] Psalm 38:2 "I said, I will take heed."

[374] "If someone was tossed from a pinnacle while he was sleeping, write this Psalm and put it under the right-hand side of the pillow for his head and he will not see anything bad in his sleep." Again this is derived from the charm in The Book of Gold, Rankine & Barron, 2010:94.

[375] Psalm 47:2 "Great is the lord."

[376] "If theft is committed in your house, write this psalm when the second [night begins] and put it under your head when you go to the bedroom in your bed and you will see while sleeping the thief entering." A simplified

59 - Characters to be written with Psalm 46 in the preceding charm

Mr Rich Nitt S: told me that verissimam formam videbat.[377]

50 Miserere mei deus[378]

Cum conculcuit si mulier nimis pa menstrual accipi ciphum vivi et die :7: hunc Psalm et da ei bibrud totum et statim cissabit flugus eius.[379]

57 Si veri atique iustitiam[380]

Si vis solueri veneficia et nicautationes et facinacoem coisus dic 7: hunc Psalm et nullus nocebit tibi per asiliam.[381]

66 Deus miseriatur nostri[382]

Ad curandum dimoniacum dic hunc Psalm super aqua mundam 7 et potari eum facies et fanabitur.[383]

---

version of the charm, with less symbols, to that found in The Book of Gold, Rankine & Barron, 2010:178.

[377] "he had seen a true form."

[378] Psalm 50:3 "Have mercy on me, O God."

[379] "When one is wounded or a woman has too much of a menstrual flow, take a cup with a drink [in order] to live, and say :7: [seven times] this psalm and give him it to drink entirely and immediately his flow [of blood] will stop." A similar use is found in The Book of Gold, Rankine & Barron, 2010:110, but with a different methodology.

[380] Psalm 57:2 "If in very deed you speak justice."

[381] "If you want to solve poisonings or incantations [enchantments] or having eaten anything that would do you ill, say :7: [seven times] this psalm and nothing that is directed at you will cause harm." As seen in The Book of Gold, Rankine & Barron, 2010:120.

[382] Psalm 66:2 "May God have mercy on us."

[383] "To cure demoniac possession say this Psalm over clean water :7: [seven times] and drink it and wash your face with it."

Ego vero fumigo illum cum hipati Lucy super prunas si est mouchur frendit fomit: gr: et hunc est rigula cerissima :3: probavi

Cum gaudio et riumentia magna[384]

60 - Image of fish to emphasise the use of the fish in the Book of Tobit as described in the preceding charm for Psalm 66

Friar Conch was caused to shave the per his head & to anoint the sufferer with the blood of a red Cock :3: times & Pherbo[385] to ease the pain Then he did use to write these names upon the bread & seep it all night in water & let the patient drink it at :5: mornings et subterra Crustam ut putreseit sic morbus[386]

Raba. Tabza. Acbaras. Calva, Salva, peipinamo precepit. Abde Deeanus Sacra. Uno.

The Friar had it from an Egyptian as he affirmed examined

61 - Figure, unclear use

---

[384] "I in truth fumigated this by daylight with liver on burning coals [a reference to the apotropaic use of fish liver by Raphael in the Book of Tobit 6:7 and 6:16], if it is a demon the smoke will cause it anger and to grind its teeth and weaken. This is most truly powerful. :3: [three times] have I tried [tested] it with joy and great laughter."

[385] Feed or nourish.

[386] "and put the crusts under the earth and as they putrefied, so did the disease."

76 Voce mea ad dominum clamavi[387]

Si quid ligatus furvit Scribe hunc Psalm In lamina vitria et delur eam cum ▽ benedicta et dabiberi legato et soluetur & maleficio gratia dei.[388]

---

114 Dilexi[389]

Scribe hunc Psalm utque custodieus parvulos et suffumiga eum mastice et lingo aloes et liga in brachio infantis et liberabitur ab atrophia Corporis[390] (119)

---

50 Miserere mei deus secundum[391]

Magnum misericordiam him. Scribe hunc Psalm utque salutis mei[392] et liga circa ventrum patientis et restringit fluxum rufum ventris sui, it ought to be written on the parchment of a lambskin[393]

This I had at the high commission novi historiani[394]

---

[387] Psalm 76:2 "I cried to the Lord with my voice."

[388] "If someone has been bound, write this Psalm on a glass plate and erase it with blessed (Water) and by drinking it, the curse is lifted & dissolved by the grace of God" As also seen in The Book of Gold, Rankine & Barron, 2010:148.

[389] Psalm 114:1 "I have loved."

[390] "Write this Psalm so that it may protect the little ones and fumigate it with mastic and lignum aloes and tie it to the arm of the child and he shall be delivered of atrophy of the body" A simplified version of the charm given in The Book of Gold, Rankine & Barron, 2010:200.

[391] Psalm 50:3 "Have mercy on me, O God, according (to thy great mercy)."

[392] Verse 16.

[393] "Write this psalm until salutis mei [my salvation, line 16] and tie it around the belly of the patient and restrict the red flow [blood flow] of his belly, it ought to be written on the parchment of a lambskin" As seen in The Book of Gold, Rankine & Barron, 2010:110.

[394] "Of a historian I was acquainted with"

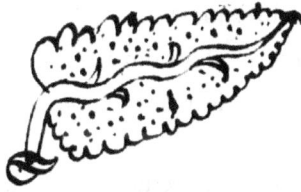

62 - Leaf image, purpose unclear

63 – Turnip, to be used in the charm below

Boil it & make a plaster & lay it on the old scar & give the patient pounded Caledony[395] in his drink

This poor charm did make me wonder. I cured my cousin Mr Sam Armstrong's leg which was for 14 years.

I hail it from an old poor soldier.

---

[395] Possibly Celandine from a corruption of its Latin name of Chelidonium.

Horologium Carnurlitarum[396]

Use it as I told you dic[397] :3: Psalm 102

Tu exsurgens domine misereberis Sion quia tempus miserendi eius quia venit tempus[398]

Fac voluntate & credulitate credeus in opera nic derisor.[399]

Carmen explissimum contra Spasnum[400]

Istem carmen sequitum contra spasnum explissimum est a multis inuctum to utrutis & tam partibus trausuarinis qui in astis. Nam apud Mediolanum et nulami in lumbardia lope quo dus leonellus filius regis Anglici mepsit filium dium Mediolan. Anglici ibidi spasmo vixabant (ppt) apotacomi coiuorper forein & calorim patrie & miniam replecom conde quidum mihi & filius deum Regnacili de Grayale Schirland iusta Chesterfield qui fuit apud Mediolam cum duo leonello & Ruit sicum carmen figurus & quidum armigum a spasmo mixatum ita caput suum vitro trahebat & feni cosque ad cullum suum ad madum balishe qui pedolori & augustia fene rapiravit. Et quo wiso des miles accipit carmen in pergamen scriptum in bursa poitum & collo pacieute apposuit dicentibe circumstautib eveni duica cum ave maria & ut mihi iurabit fidelite infra 4er horas coel quinque sanitati urstilutus est. Et postea muetes alios a spasmo ileum libavit eum magna fama de ille carmiur in illa Cuitate exereuit. Ileum in Cuitate lincoly fait quidam Ro qui muctis amis vexatas fuit a spasmo in libys suis in noctibus per vetorque bat pules suos ad cullum suum & libir eius ereserre incipiebaut ita quod fere non poluit ire qui cum isuum carmen super se portam il de cetreo ut digit a spasmo non istraxatus.[401]

---

[396] "Carmelite Sundial." Probably refers to Horologium Sapientiae, a Carmelite treatise included in Additional MS 37790 (Amherst Manuscript).

[397] "Say."

[398] Psalm 101:14 "Thou shalt arise and have mercy on Sion: for it is time to have mercy on it, for the time is come."

[399] "Do this willingly & believing and [there will be] believers in your work, not mockers."

[400] "Spell that is most effective against cramps."

[401] "This spell that follows is most effective against cramps from many [causes] such as infections and the uterus and in such a degree that it was brought here from distant parts. For near Milan and Nola in Lombardy, it happened that two sons of an English county, through a matchmaker,

Ilium ap London quidem muliter pregnans ita vexabit a spasmo qui fere perierat que huit lapidem qui pelitot dicite & nihil ei valiut tandem cum istud super se portadat amplius ei non nocebat spasmus per certo.[402]

Ileu apud villa de Huntingdon fiumt homo quidem quid entem sec pacifum spasimus apo imto peles am bor subib vitro guheudo a Pra cervare voluit nua wie ita que oportuit de udcessilate cadere ad Prave cum impetus super facie rius. Qui umo eum isliul carmen sique super se portam et amodo a Spasmo libatus est.[403]

---

married two daughters of Milan. The Englishmen were tortured there by cramps through the drinking of a foreign substance and they were hot and developed redness, as was indeed conveyed to me & with the two sons was Reginald Gray of Sherwood near Chesterfield & he rushed down himself for the incantation and figure & a certain remedy against cramps was mixed and brought in glass to his head accordingly & wild through sharp pains he was cared for and the evil banished that caused him to be in misery and to breathe constrictedly. And having seen it two soldiers received the spell written down on parchment [?] and placed in a leather bag & fixed securely around the neck and saying while standing nearby and coming out with saying the Ave Maria & in such a way he swore to me truthfully that within four hours the sharp pains were cured and within five [hours] his health was restored. And after that many others with severe colic were freed from cramps and great fame was within that community for her [him?] that performed the incantation. Whenever in that community there was someone or multiple people tortured by cramps and was not free to sleep at night, such a thing was fastened to their neck, and in their freedom would begin to help in such a way that this evil could not strike, which could no longer afflict with cramps those over whose door this incantation had been said."

[402] "There was a certain pregnant woman from London tortured with severe colic who passed away and while she lived had a stone over which prayers were said & she did not get better, but would she have carried this [parchment] upon her, even much larger colics would not have harmed her for sure."

[403] "To the Villa of Huntingdon came a man who sought relief from spasms that caused him to be as if nailed to the ground with his skin or clothes [?] and he wanted it cut out of his life; as has been said it was made necessary with the disability making him fall on the ground, and sometimes an attack causing him to collapse right onto his face. When he carried this enchantment with him on his shoulder, and had it over his door, he was delivered from the spasms forthwith."

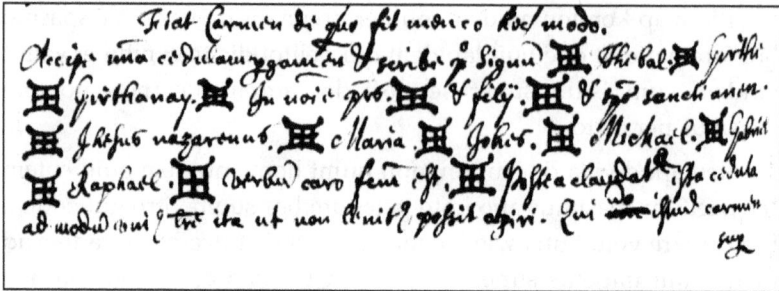

64 - Charm given in following text

Fiat Carmen di quo fit menco hoc modo[404]

Accipe una cedulam pergamen & scribe primo Signum ✠Thibal ✠Girthi ✠Girthanay ✠In nomine patris ✠& filii ✠& spiritus sancti amen ✠Jesus Nazarenus ✠Maria ✠John ✠Michael ✠Gabriel ✠Raphael ✠verbum caro feni est[405] ✠Postea claudat ista cedula ad modum vuius erit ita ut non lenitus possit agiri. Qui uno istud carmen (120) super si houisti ni dei omnipotente nomine gissevit & crededit sum dubio a spasmo no ent agranatus[406]

---

[404] "Let there be a spell from God that shall be unto the doctor in this way."

[405] The original version of this charm for cramp dates to the surgeon John of Arderne (1307-1392) in the fourteenth century. Verbal Charms in British Folk Medicine, Forbes, 1971:309. "In nomine patris + et filii + et Spiritus sancti + Amen. + Thebal + Enthe + Enthanay + In Nomine Patris + et Filii + et Spiritus sancti + Amen. + Ihesu Nazarenus + Maria + Iohannes + Michael + Gabriel + Raphael + Verbum caro factum est"

[406] "Take a small sheet of parchment and write on it first the Sign ✠Thibal ✠Girthi ✠Girthanay ✠In the name of the Father ✠& the Son ✠& the Holy Ghost ✠amen ✠Jesus of Nazareth ✠Maria ✠John ✠Michael ✠Gabriel ✠Raphael ✠the word is for the esteemed ending [?]✠After that close this sheet so that it will be like a cone and cannot be carried on one's person in smoothness [i.e. wearing the parchment on one's body should be uncomfortable, perhaps so it will not be forgotten]. Upon this once sing the incantation (120) and if on top of this you write the name of the all-powerful God & believe, then I would doubt very much that the cramp would not be lifted."

Istud heatur in nimemicia perpetuum deum, qui virtute dividit vobis pictris & herbis & secrete severtus in onis noscaut carmem ni forte virtute a deo datam amiltat[407]

Quia iudi quidum mulicrem spasum pacietrum & dalusist si anulus auvrum hus lapidem pelitate pulcherium & pedeam tria voba carinis Thebal &c sculpta in circle anuli & nichilei ysiceibatus Et statim cum habuat istud carmen super si clausum libata est absque mora Et sic perus quon dicit per ee cor que wobri ego solebam feribri carmen pedem cum evis grecis ne a laycis perceperit.[408]

Ego deus Magist Elohim Ardern Cirurgius aliquando manus in Newark iupta Lincoln: & postia apud London ista pe scripta misa & immabilia alia de isto carmine midi & audivi . Et si forte aliqui aliquo islunt utiu carmen hutrunt vocatur tauun tautam lauds per cuis operacae sunt adepti & hoc veputo quia irrementus illiut occupabant.[409]

Experimentum contra Paralisim & Epilepsiam est morbum cadeum quo lestor deum multi sunt curali[410]

---

[407] "This is completed in the beloved name of the Eternal God, who bestows power upon your pictures and herbs and secrets which are understood with difficulty, and who knows the incantations that would not have their powerful force if not given by God and who will send it forth."

[408] "Because there was a certain woman with a spasm that needed to be subdued & it was to desist if a ring was affixed with a beautiful stone & carved three times for [in the name of] God in Theban & engraved in the circumference of the ring & with this one may not be helped. And immediately when one has this, an incantation is to be [said] over it according to custom if that which is closed up is to be freed. And so this was said in order to get rid of that which harmed by going to the heart. I have tested this as is my custom and written the spell on a sheet with Greek ink so that laypeople may not perceive it." [I.e. with invisible ink]

[409] "I, master surgeon Arderne, by God Elohim, from a manuscript in Newark under Lincoln: after the script was sent to near London & among countless others [i.e.: spells] I saw and heard this very incantation. And if ever any spell has been called by anyone from anywhere with so much complete praise, it is this one by those adepts that have worked it & this one I think is powerful because it has been empowered by the very ones that have mastered it."

[410] "By experimenting against Paralysis & Epilepsy which is the falling disease, many have, with the grace of God, been cured."

Rex Sanamude est avence, herbe peralis cum ovacoed nica brisus vicibus incantates & collo paciente suspende dicredo cauden oromi & succus eay potui det per eto dicus continuos & sanaber. Ideo: Audem[411]

Alevura portala nou sunt urigere Regam viribem donec deponat vel si sub cermiali paciente ipey non potest erigi Rega super iacente

Itm vugat corigia vel ceforum pamu laudi de succo revence & super carus midani erige & erl effeuviat. Ideo: Audem[412]

Ad sanguinum struiganus Medicina Rea & qabala[413]

God all thou were in Bedlam born And followed in under flown London & staunchedly shown to stand still, also verily staunch this mans blood. & dicat quinquis per ur & ave maria in honorius plagiary Christi. Io: Audem[414]

Contra Podagram[415]

Quidum in Anglia curant quibque podagrum cum sigillo beatae maria distim peralum cum optimo aceto. Io: Audem[416]

Contra perdiconim visus[417]

---

[411] "And the King of the Healthy World has advanced by dangerous herbs and gentle prayers alternated with incantations & and when lying down, suspend from the neck the entire prayer you say and have him drink liquor [liquid?] for 30 consecutive days & he shall be healed. To that end: may I be brave."

[412] "The regaining of new health cannot be in any way than anointing by the power of the [heavenly] King, while it is applied little bit below the heart, or, when the patient cannot be otherwise than lying down, fumigate over him by the power of the [heavenly] King. This way it spreads from the heart or head by praising God with the flow of the [bodily] juices & he shall rise above the hollowed-out state & flow full of [life-]force. To that end: may I be brave."

[413] "To cause the blood to coagulate – Duty-bound [compulsory?] Medicine & Qabalah."

[414] "& say [this] five times across him & Hail Mary in the name of the suffering of Christ. To that end: may I be brave."

[415] "Against gout."

[416] "A certain man in England cured anyone suffering from the gout with the seal of the blessed Mary, and I give the patient the most excellent vinegar to drink. To that end: may I be brave."

[417] "Against the deterioration of the sight."

Qui septimo dic in dextro vie ni nono die in sinistro April brachio facit se mimic non perdet visum.[418]

Qui in fini May in 4° vel in 5° die se focevit mimic de quo brachio voluevit nunquam habit febriem.[419]

Ives luut dies in anno prohibite & plusque prohibite in quibus si quid se faciat mimic ho vel bestia nifra tres dies moritur vizt. A kal; Aprilis. A kal: Augusti. A kal: Decembris.[420]

Now: que qui in 3° die Aprilis se freevit minim non habit vam capitis nisi gumuid quotus hoc faciat . Et qui in io die May se freevit mmm nullam febrem habit neque tysim. Et qui 2ii° [4] die meus Sept se faciat mmm viz in die sei lambti non habit ydrophisim freuesim nae eticam vo est, quia hunc venenum agitur & aer veneosus erit usque ad Me dium.[421]

Prima luna January, prima luna June scita luna Octob portat perictim mortus siquib minuat illary. Io: Audem[422]

(121)

---

[418] "He that is seen on the seventh day with the right and on the ninth day of April with the left arm to make an image of himself he shall not lose the sight."

[419] "He who in May on the 4th or 5th day from the end makes an image of himself with whichever arm he wants will never have the fever."

[420] "With regard to boundaries there are three days in the year that are prohibited & more than prohibited. In those days whatever you make an image of, human or beast, will die within three days, viz. on the kalend [15th] of April, on the kalend [15th] of August and on the kalend [15th] of December."

[421] "He that makes an image of himself on the 3rd day of April shall not have pain in the head unless if he that made it drinks a lot. And he who on that day in May makes an image of himself will neither have the fever nor typhoid. And he who on the 22nd day of the month of September makes an image of himself and washes himself that day shall not have dropsy [oedema] and any symptom shall be curbed because that poison will be driven out & the air shall be wholesome with God at me [my side]."

[422] "And he who carries on the first moon of January, the first moon of June and the first moon of October an image, such an image, whatever ails him shall diminish. To that end: may I be brave."

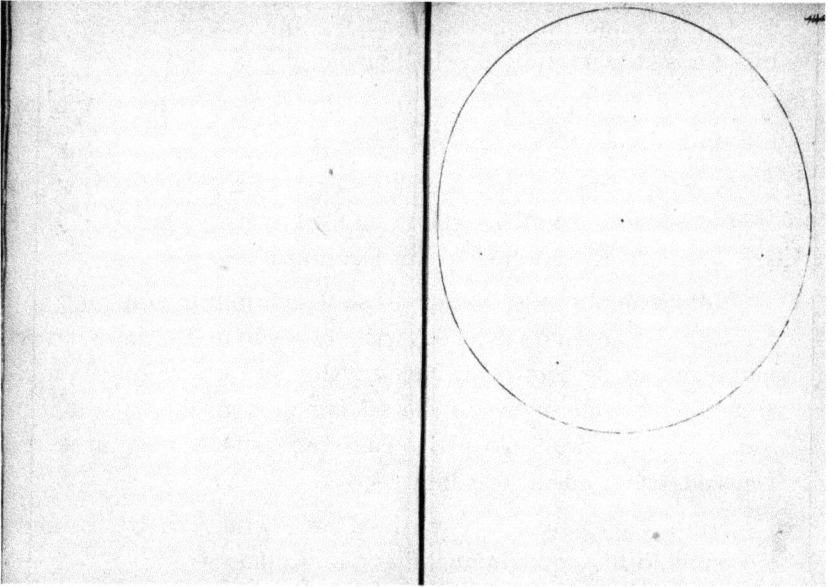

65 - This large empty circle at this point in the MS suggests an image which was never completed

(121)

Here beginneth the Book of the 7 Images of the days That Philosophers that were blessed knew and understood whereby to have their desire Being a Science high and plain But should not be showed nor taught but to good men and secret Therefore take heed, Beware and prove. Viz.

The first Image Is of the Sonday And shall be made of Gold or of (   )[423] That is one part (   )[424] and the second part Copper Or of yellow wax And write on the Image these names following The ☾ Increasing In August or in April, The Sign is ♌, The Angels Michael Dardiell Hartapiell[425] The angels of the Air *Varcan* King His ministers Tus Andas Cinaball As you shall find before In the Considerations folio.

If thou wilt bind mens Tongues Make the Image in the hour of ☾ In the full And say this Conjuration following

I Conjure you Angels above us by the Seal of the ☉, *Ga, Ganar, Gaions, eillon, amacyon castub, con,* And by the maker of Heaven and Earth and all parts of the world And of the winds which are between Heaven and Earth And by him which is King of all Kings, *Farsaell Sardardicas itala, Cassiel* I conjure you by these names *Salane taaletaa cassa alum, vardab, elec, elos, udo, calud,* He that brought ( )[426] *yassaell, dardiell, Hela raphiel Cranael,* see you fulfil my asking in all things

The second Image is for Moonday It is made of Silver of or white wax and must be made on Moonday on the first hour as I take it[427] (the Second hour of the day). You shall find before you In the considerations for Moonday what Angels govern. If you will make (   )[428] make the Image on the second hour of Monday In the heat of Cancer And in the month of July or March And these

---

[423] Blank space.

[424] Blank space.

[425] Turner gives Huratapal.

[426] Blank space

[427] This phrase, "on the first hour as I take it" has been added as an inclusion and the following remark bracketed. This is correct for lunar attributions as the first hour of Monday would be the lunar one.

[428] Blank space.

be the names of the winds, *Cancer, habetell*[429] *abundant* and his helpers be *Calon*[430] *mulcala abrera.*

I Conjure you Image by this conjuration, I conjure you Angels unto whom is given the Seal of the Moon *Somucha somoha, herb, cehafa Cassal nata* I Conjure you that you fulfil my asking And heartily pray and desire you *Gabriel Michael* that you be helpers and not hinderers from this time until my petition be fulfilled. (122)

The third Image is for Tuesday and must be made of red brass or red wax. In the hours of ♂ In the month of April or December and this work is worshipful and precious when you work you shall name the names of the Angel to whom is taken the Seal of ♂ *Saliel Cariel armail* and the names of the winds *aturbi, abelit, anaabbus,* and his helpers *Carinal imiual pasas,* Saying

I Conjure you Princes of the Angels unto whom is taken the Seal of ♂ *Mastas vraci festinavit famtiell yoasel aramael* by the names of *Charoal, achiell damis, hiaions horeb* the lord of the high *allam aiton, baal, connens,* the lord of worship *alcomehamade, clahima, chadema* the lord of Heaven and Earth and there is no other Lord, *Saltiel anvarial harama lib, benhic,* and to his helpers that they help fulfil that which I have asked, and thou wilt destroy him. To have the bloody flux Or to do it away. For harm make the Image of Red brass and bury it in the earth when the[431]

The fourth Image is of Wednesday The angels names are Michael veriell Seraphiel. The names of the winds, Siaar, phallus Sambas farma, make this in the month of July or October of lead and grave in it these names Conjuring the image to make hate between man and woman.

I Conjure you Angels by the maker of Heaven and Earth without him is nothing living He is the mighty maker and commander and in his Heart is virtue He is the almighty King, under his authority is taken the Seal of ☿. I Conjure you Michael Seraphiell Minarell by these names, Serie adonay Sabaoth, him that is Lord of heaven and Earth And by the goodness of him that is

---

[429] Habatal is the name of an angel in Liber Juratus.

[430] Calion is also the name of an angel in Liber Juratus.

[431] Sentence cuts off here leaving a half blank page.

your strength and keeper that is only <u>almighty</u>, all in all that is and ever was and ever shall be, I conjure you Michael (   )[432] veriell that you fulfil my asking. (123)

The fifth Image is of Thursday. The Angels names are Lathaxiell, parante mal assassaiel and these be the winds that be ordained upon the image, heal and his helpers, yesse yenesaight naadol, make the image of Brass that hath the colour of Saffron, Or of yellow wax, make it on the Thursday In the month of March in the height of ♓ or in January in the height of ♐. If to make love, write on the heart of the woman the name of the Man, And say viz

O Lord God Creator of all things put the good will of the daughter of AB in the good will[433] of the son of CD and put the good will and great love and make them as steadfast as thou didst Adam to Eve, and between Tobias and Raphaell and between Michael and Gabriel, Of the which one is fire and the other is water and one grieveth not the other but there is between them good accord, and make it as steadfast after the same manner as thou has the Angel of the which the one is fire the other snow And the Snow quencheth not the fire, Nor the fire consumed not nor wasteth not the Snow So make these two accord together, That is B the son of A and D the daughter of C and I Conjure you Angels by the name to whom is given this work Diffialofon alexa haila aliaml axel halt athay itna Saphea acolcrostel xoni relfato stifellore the which knoweth the secret of the beginning and ending of all things the which shall never die flie serape hee ecrissell nmellich with their helpers & that they may soon fulfil my bidding in this Image that I have made and make it stable. Then bury the image, They shall both accord and agree together.[434]

The Sixth Image is of Friday The Angels belonging to this Image the these Anael Ragnel Salgmel, and them under are Lambores and his helpers letraraamsag. Make this Image on the Friday In the House of ♀ in white wax in the Month of May In the height of ♋ Or in the Month of October And the name of the Man

---

[432] Blank space here, presumably the name Seraphiell should be here.

[433] Will is repeated here.

[434] The voces magicae in this conjuration and the others in this section are similar in style to those found in the Notary Art.

upon the Heart of the Image And the name of the woman And hang the Image before the Stars And smite it with a twig or wand of Olive Tree And Conjure the Image, viz

I Conjure you Angels Anael kargiel Samuel baffala haasa hafea guthaca adtcalea arkinlia alka allea onat akaba sana saniorie mami tartais reat malatrin aachnine soaea jendoad, d, d, a, a, by him which is Cedas and Galba the lord of Angels and winds the high afferie Adonai Helay sardaday nota historiae Alaba God the Creator God the fair And there is no other And he is mighty ex ra cia ya anuel i cia ubar auiel ybarbel sabqueel By this Conjuration I Conjure upon you Angels by the strength of ♀ that is right fortunate I Conjure upon you that you fulfil my asking my cause and my lust Joining the Son of the Man A to the daughter of the woman B, That his heart burn in love with the man as Eve burned for Adam in all things Airoa Aireal attear kacciael Tolteche his heart will burn this Image before the Gate of the house when they go each day and hour. (124)

The Seventh Image is for Friday being a worshipful Image of all Images ♄ being the highest of all the planets. The Angels are Cassiel Matreton Gaoel and the winds, Menera Altibam alstas anatnabie. If thou wilt bind Tongues of enemies and make truce between men that are at debate, Make the Image and grave upon it the names aforesaid In the Gate of the city or Town and bury the Image within it and all things of the City or town shall be done If thou wilt make discord bear the Image In to the City town or house and bury it in the midst thereof. If thou wilt make discord between Man and Man or woman, Make the Image of Clear pitch and make the head of the Image (   )[435] a hinds head and put them back to back and write in virgin Parchment these words that ensue and put them between the ribs of the Image. It breeds discord and causes fighting and murder and debate never to be recalled, viz.

I Conjure you ye cia mitharens atanael Angels assigned to the seal of ♄ be helpers to me in things commanded ye, Denel amomium affia and haabach rabit that you come and fulfil my request by the name of the lord the blessed Phial yan yagina bonor ya yaffia Tassa Ju fiabib anagodin Clirobas liayaod ayn achi adin her Saday adominor Sabaoth adonay eloy eloe gnae healfola seriaie alila yesus agnibora ore, all the companies of Angels Saffiell

---

[435] Blank space.

micraton satquiell princo memeta affla obnala alis saipaleppe fulfil you my desires by the holiness of this Conjuration that is hear upon you.

It is all faulty, grossly, (   )[436] finis septem imaginum[437] (125)

Charms for diverse Diseases

For a prick with a Thorn: Our blessed Saviour And Lord Jesus Christ was pricked with the point of a Thorn It never rankled nor never swelled Nor never would no more do Nor never shall this Say this iii [3] times then say i [1] Pater noster, i [1] Ave & i [1] Credo.

For those that are Mad, Man or Beast The Hair being cut off lay Betony to the Mould of the Head. Then write these words in a piece of Cheese *Antanbragon Tetragrammaton* And give the party so diseased.[438]

For the Falling Sickness write with the blood of his little finger[439] These verses following In a long Scroll of Parchment And let him wear it about his Neck. *Jasper fert Mirum thus Melchior Balthasur Aurum Hec quicunque secum portat tria nomina regum soluitur amorbo domini pietate caduco.*[440]

For to stay Bleeding Say as followeth. The Babe that was born in Bethlehem, And Baptised in the stream of Jordan, The water was wild, The Child was mild The water was wood[441] The Child was

---

[436] Blank space.

[437] "Complete the seventh image."

[438] This charm and many of those following are to be found in Book of Receipts and Chirurgery, Lady Ayscough (1692). They were later reproduced by Charles Dickens in Household Words Vol 5 (1852).

[439] This charm is found in A Right Profitable Book for all Diseases, Levens, 1582.

[440] "Caspar with his myrrh began these presents to unfold, Then Melchior brought in frankincense, Balthasar brought in gold. Now he that of these holy Kings, these names about shall bear, The Falling Ill by grace of Christ shall never need to fear."

[441] The original text has "rude" here, this is probably a corruption or miscopy, as it makes no sense.

good, Jesus Christ stop the blood of AB That it may stand as stiff in every vein, As the water was wild & wood Still it stood, when Jesus Christ was Baptised therein[442]

+ In the name of the father + and of the Son + and of the Holy Ghost + amen.

For A Fever + Ralga + Galam + Cacula + Melcoy talen + Tetragrammaton + Deus + fiat +

For the Toothache Say, Abraham laid him down to sleep on the mount of Allis like Jesus seeth, when thou sleepest or wakest Abraham awake Good lord I cannot Sleep for the Toothache which is in my teeth. The Toothache grieveth me so sore, That I shall never sleep no more, Rise up Abraham go with me There shall no toothache grieve thee, Nor no other man, That this pray thrice came.

For them that may not Sleep write in a Bay leaf these iii [3] words iii [3] times *Ismael Ismael Ismael adjuro te per Angelum Michaelem ut soperetur iste homo vel isto femina*.[443] Lay it under their heads they not being aware thereof And they shall Sleep.[444]

For the Ague Deus deus homo omnipotence genitis pater hominum creatore solus bonus + Jesus Christus natus + Jesus in honore trinitatis + Jesus nazarenus + mortuus + resuscitates dic 5 **Pater** nosters, 5 aves in honore vulnerum Christi 5.[445]

---

[442] This charm is derived from one found in A Book of Experiments out of Dyvers Authors, MS Bod e Mus 243 (1622). It is also found in Harley MS 211, fo. 85v, as a late C15th CE charm.

[443] "Ismael Ismael Ismael I bind thee by the Angel Michael so that thou mayest put to sleep this man or this woman."

[444] This is based on a fourteenth century charm for fever, being identical in every detail except for the addition of the name Michael. Verbal Charms in British Folk Medicine, Forbes, 1971:297.

[445] "For the Ague God, God, omnipotent forebear of man, father of men, sole and good creator + Jesus Christ born + Jesus in honour of the trinity + Jesus the Nazarene + dead + resurrected. Say 5 Our Fathers, wish ardently 5 [times] in honour of the 5 wounds of Christ."

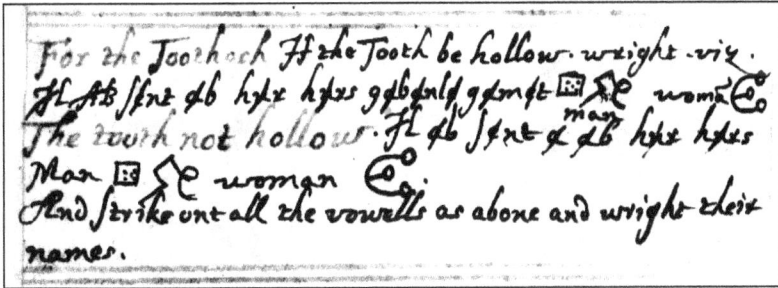

66 - Charm for Toothache, text given below

For the Toothache If the Tooth be hollow, write, viz,

Il AB sent ab hur hurs gabanle gamet[446] man

 woman

The tooth not hollow Il ab sent a ab hur hurs man

 woman

And strike through all the vowels as above and write their names

---

[446] Although it is not clear from the font, the e's are also struck through. The word man or woman is not included in the charm, but is indicating which character to add to the end of the phrase. This may be the first recorded example of reduction sigilisation where the vowels are being noticeably removed.

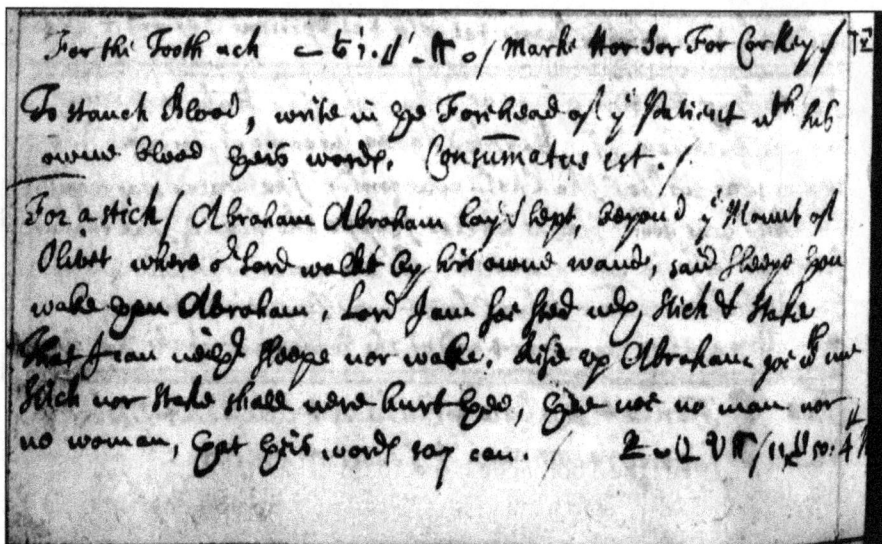

67 - Several healing charms in the second handwriting in the MS

[447]For the Toothache [charm symbols] Mark Her Sore For Cankry.[448]

To staunch Blood, write in the forehead of the patient with his own blood this word, Consumatus Est[449]

For a stick[450]/ Abraham Abraham lay & slept, beyond the Mount of Olives where our lord walked by his own word, said help God wake you Abraham, Lord I am sore sweat with stick & shake

That Jesus willst sleep nor wake. Lift up Abraham go where no stick nor stake shall ever hurt him, Give not no man nor no woman, that this would say can [charm symbols] (126)

---

[447] This section is in the second handwriting.

[448] Malignance or soreness.

[449] John 19:30, "It is finished".

[450] Old name for a stitch.

For the Toothache. Gellum Galum: Cahely, finally Cay, write these words in verses thrice & read the first verse 3 times and then prick in every letter a hole through.

For the biting of a mad dog:

Lemas Lamus Remus Ramus Oxilioge

For an Ague. / Take a Crust of Bread & write these three words following & after they be writ eat them

Calinda Calindan Calindant.

Another./ write these words upon a piece of Bread, & let the party eat every day and of the word[451] (127)

For the Antimonial Cup [452]

Take the venom of a toad ¼oz

Arsenic 1⅛oz

Teeth of Lizard as many as you can get;

The shavings of mule (beaten to death) hoof 3oz

Put these in a crucible calcine[453] them;

then project upon <u>copper</u>: =x

For to make optic glass

Take a pound of copper 4 ounces of lime half an ounce of lime glass and half an ounce of the file due of Iron. First melt down your copper then put in all the parts of the thing together then cast it in what form you please.

When you have cast it as smooth as you can polish it with a pumice stone and pour on athel[454] oil & smooth too if you polish it

---

[451] This is a corruption of the technique of banishing fever by writing Kalendenta on a piece of bread, with the second and subsequent lines losing a letter off the end until it reached just the K (forming a downward triangle), and eating a line each day (giving the final piece with the K to a dog to eat), copying the reduction principle seen in Abracadabra charms which reduced to an A on the bottom line. See Verbal Charms in British Folk Medicine, Forbes, 1971:295.

[452] Antimonial cups were cups with antimony included in the casting, which reacted with wine to produce an emetic to encourage vomiting. This seems an extreme form of such a device.

[453] I.e. reduce to ash.

then after polish it dry very well with pottery made well with a little water[455] (128)

For theft or **anything thou desirest**. Say the iiiith [4th] Psalm Cum invocarem &c And when you come to the verse, be angry and sin not[456] Say it thrice Afterwards say Kyrilayson Christilayson Kyrilayson[457] Our father &c Ave maria &c Credo &c Then write their Greek names in parchment + Agla + Cad + Iskiros + Mediator + Elyson + Panton + Craton + Cisas In the name of + Thou + In the name of + Jesus + Christ + the life eternal

Then roll them in virgin wax and put it under your head and Sleep and you shall see whatsoever you desire + **finis** + **Amen** + **fiat**

Take Ants eggs and the blood of a white Hen, anoint your face therewith and you shall see wonders. (129)

To have Conference with Spirits:~:

To speak with any person that is dead Go into the Churchyard on a Friday at night at 12 or 2 of the Clock And walk round about in the Alley 6 times And when you come to a Corner Stand still And say the lords prayer And the Creed And before you have gone 6 times about you shall meet them that you would speak with As they were wont to go.

To have Conference with the fairies In the House where those use when you intend to work be the last up. The night before the new or full of the Moon Then sweep the Hearth very clean And set a bucket of fair water on the Hearth so go to bed. And be you the first that shall come down the next Morning And you shall see as it were a fat or Jelly upon the water. Take it forth with a Silver Spoon

---

[454] A tree also known as the salt tree.

[455] The end of the section in the second hand.

[456] Verse 5.

[457] This is clearly a corruption of the Greek liturgical refrain Kyrie Eleison (Lord have mercy) which antedates Christianity. Thus "Kyrie Eleison Christ Eleison Kyrie Eleison", is "Lord have mercy, Christ have mercy, Lord have mercy".

and put it into A Silver or Tin vessel and so keep it And when you will work the night before the new or full of the Moon, If there be a Table in the Room Set a new Bowl full of new Ale upon the board And iii [3] new white cloths with iii [3] new knives with white hafts. This done make a fair fire of sweet cloven wood Then sit in a Chair with your face towards the fire Then take your foresaid stuff forth and anoint your Eyes therewith And sit silent And see all the house be quiet and at rest And when you have sitten so a while you shall see iii [3] women come in, But say nothing but nod your head at them as you shall see them do to you And they will go to the Table and eat and drink, when they have done let the first pass And the second But the third you may take and ask what you will of her. Probat.

To have Conference with a Fairy Stroll underneath an Elder tree when the Sun is at the (highest) hottest Sanctified Rushes And stand under the Tree and say, *Magram Magrano* Three times and you shall see a flower spring like yellow Gold or Gold yellow And when you have it you shall want nothing. There will also appear a fair woman Demand of her what thou wilt have And thou shalt have it.

To have familiar Spirits Take a Fowl called a Lapwing Kill her and save her blood[458] in a Silver or Pewter vessel and Stop it that no Air come into it and in 6ii [8] days it will be turned to worms And in 6ii [8] more it will be but one worm. Then take of walnuts and Almonds and make a paste thereof and with a Stick or your little finger make a hole and put the worm therein and in 6ii [8] days it will be a lapwing again Then take the blood of her Right wing and anoint thy Eyes therewith, Then look forth of thy Chamber window toward the East And thou shalt see all the Spirits of the Air in order. Then call one of them and ask his office and he will tell thee, If he be for thy term If he be not command him to send one that is And he will do it. Then say unto him *Vade Christus sit Mater te et me,*[459] *In nomine Patris + et Filii +* &c.

---

[458] Obviously a female lapwing.

[459] "Go, Christ, may the Mother be with you and me."

To have Conference with Spirits Take Pedra di dura fruit[460] On the day of St John Baptist[461] Or in the vigil of St Peter[462] Or in the third day after and burn it and cast it into a secret place And after the third day come thither and you shall find as many Devils as by them And thou shalt see them and bind them saying as followeth.

When our Lord descended down from Heaven to deliver the People In the name of the same Lord I Conjure you Spirits that you do whatsoever I command you And that you do no hurt to any creature And thereto I charge you + In the name of the Father + And of the Son + And of the Holy Ghost + Amen +

Then ask or bid them do what thou wilt and they will perform it.

To see marvellous things Take the fat of a black Cat ungelt[463] and the fat of a white Hen And anoint your Eyes And you shall see marvellous things. If you would have any other to see them let him set his foot upon yours And he shall see it.

To see strange sights Make an ointment of the Gall of a Bull and the fat of a Hen And anoint your Eyes. (130)

To have Conference with familiar Spirits Do as followeth[464]

In the day and hour of ☿ take a white howlet[465] and kill it under the right wing Saying these words

Fuua Handa Musdali faon dyiaga Samiel Rostalagath This fowl I do kill in the name of you all Commanding you by the name *Rufangoll* your Superior by whom you do all secrets in Earth amongst men, And by *Hemeolon* your prince I adjure you that you do your humble obedience unto me AB at all times henceforth and with your power unknown give virtue and strength to this my purpose constraining all inferiors under you to serve me at all times days hours and

---

[460] The rock of a hard fruit, i.e. a fruit stone like a cherry or plum.

[461] June 24th, the old Midsummer.

[462] June 29th.

[463] I.e. not neutered.

[464] This following section is found in Folger Vb.26 fo.138-140 (c.1580).

[465] Owl.

minutes And at all times and in all places without hurting of me my body or Soul or any other living Creature.

Then reserve his blood in a Clean vessel, And of his fat In another clean vessel.

In the day of ♃ consequently following and in the hour of ☿ kill a lapwing as you did the Howlet under the right wing saying these words.

Dala Dangolath Emenguill Saluagan Arsdorth Sedmaon Pandolath, This fowl I kill in the name of you all Commanding you by this name *Rufangol* your superior by whom you do all secrets on Earth amongst men And by *Hemeolon* &c ut suya with his blood and fat.

In the day of ♀ in the hour of ☿ ensuing Kill a black Hen as you did the lapwing under the right wing against the Heart, Saying

Eloofe Pendagell Etheluill Enan Dirath Ruiaminta Edlodell, This fowl I kill in the name of you all &c

Then reserve his blood and fat ut suya

In the day of ♄ in the hour of ☿ next following kill a black cat under the right side against the Heart saying

Felofell Gariguam Samion Eligamill Reumdath Fesoraell Hermadafin This beast I kill in the name &c.

Reserve the blood and fat as before.

In the day of ☉ in the hour of ☿ kill a wart[466] or mole under the right side saying

Odanan Opathan Deothan Hermiadall Fernola Gauiham Tlodalath This beast I kill &c.

Reserve his blood and fat &c.

In the day of ☾ in the hour of ☿ kill a bat under the right wing saying as followeth

Ramasael Kaeldath Riarnfa Fesaloell Reralath Dupanfalon This fowl I kill &c Reserving his blood and fat &c

In the day of ♂ and in the hour of ☿ take a Raven and kill her under the right wing saying

Ohorma Sedelpha Oremaell Soquidaell Myiasalet Rendos Lymaxill This fowl I kill &c

Reserve the blood And fat in clean vessels

---

[466] Possibly rat?

Take the fat of all these aforesaid fowls and beasts of each of them 5ii [7] drams[467] mix all well together with a slice of Bay tree upon the palm of thy hand clean washed with Rose water, Saying in the tempering of them these 5ii [7] words *Julia Hodelsa Inafula Sedamylia Roauia Sagamex Delforia*[468] Inferiors and servants to the Empress and Princess of all fairies Sibyls and all amiable creatures delighting in the company of human people *Lady Delforia* as you be present amongst men invisible at all times as soon as I shall anoint my eyes with this ointment And that you be as familiar with me as you were with King Solomon that mighty prince And as you were with Prince Arthur that valiant prince And as you opened and showed to king Solomon the hidden natures and properties and virtues of Metals precious Stones Trees and Herbs and the secrets of all Sciences underneath Heaven Even so I command require and adjure you *Julia Hodelsa Inafula Sedamylia Roauia Sagamex* with the Empress *Delforia* to do the like to me at all times without disdainfulness by their names whereby I do bind you *Gath vasagath ulagar Jeramilia Roboracath Regath Segath* even as you fear the just judgement of *Readufan* upon pain of Hellfire and everlasting damnation.

This is done at the [conjunction] of the ☾ in the hour of ☿ put the ointment in a vessel into the midst of the Fairy Throne. But first take ii [2] or iii [3] drams[469] of each blood And write these 5ii [7] names in virgin parchment *Julia Hodelsa Inafula Sedamylia Roauia Sagamex* and *Delforia*. All these names must be written 5ii [7] times, Three times with a pen made of the third feather of the lapwing of the left wing, And iiii [4] times with the feather pen of a Raven made of the (131) fourth feather of the Right wing with these Characters following

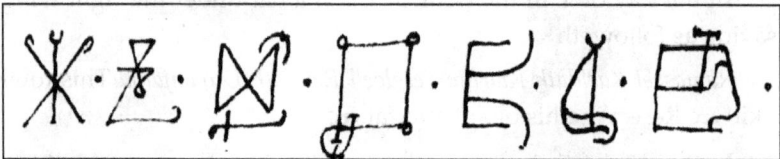

68 - Characters of the Seven Fairy Sisters, described in the preceding text

---

[467] 7/8oz.

[468] The seven names here are for the Seven Fairy Sisters mentioned in several MSS. see e.g. Folger Vb.26 (c.1580) and Folger MS 2250 (c.1600).

[469] I.e. ¼ or 3/8oz.

Then lap it about the vessel and seal it fast with virgin wax repeating these 5ii [7] names *Julia Hodelsa Inafula Sedamylia Roauia Sagamex* and *Delforia* In sealing of it.

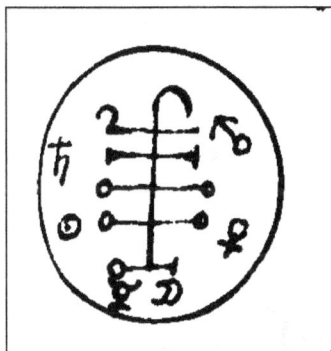

69 - Seal for working with the Fairy, described in the following text

The Seal must be made of Copper as this figure, But first before thou do put this into the Fairy Throne provide iiii [4] Hazel rods of one years growth Cut them in the day and hour of ☿ the ☽ increasing shave them white Then write upon every one of them The 5ii [7] names in the hour of ☿ *Julia* &c repeat these 5ii [7] names iii [3] times at every wand, First to the E[ast] then to the west then to the S[outh] last to the North, Saying the 5ii [7] names *Julia Hodelsa Inafula Sedamylia Roauia Sagamex* with *Delforia* the Empress of all Fairies Sibils all other amiable creatures delighting with the company of Christian people Hear me I call you every each one by name, And by the mighty names of Ligation wherewith Solomon did include you in a ball of Glass *Pannath Davion Segamilion Sugarnyell Darusa Jerasami Ariamilath* that you come at this present and make perfect this ointment That as often as I shall anoint mine eyes therewith I may see you perfect being without fraud or collusion truly showing to me all secrets of Herbs Trees Stones Metals privy talks of People Even as you fear the just Judgement of God upon pain of Hellfire and everlasting damnation whose names here included Sealed with the Seal of King Solomon the mighty prince with which sealed he Sealed the vessel wherein he bound you fiat fiat fiat

Making this Pentaculum over the vessel upon the ground within the same Throne with a Hazel Rod of one years growth

70 – Pentaculum described in preceding text

This do iii [3] days iii [3] times a day every day. This done or ended take it up and put it into a secret dark place iii [3] other days That ended put it into the Sun to rectify 6 other days Let it remain not moved.

But first before you anoint or presume to anoint thine eyes therewith Be in clean life the space of 5ii [7] days, Then anoint thine eyes therewith and look towards the East. Then shalt thou see diverse creatures most beautiful to behold in garments of diverse colours Then speak to one of them which thou likest best beckoning thy hand towards him with saying these words.

O thou beautiful creature and gentle virgin by what name soever thou art called By God the Father I call thee By God the Son I command thee By God the Holy Ghost I choose thee And by the obedience thou owest to thy Lord God, I adjure thee to be obedient unto me forever henceforth as thou dost hope to be saved at the dreadful day of Judgement In which he shall say Come ye Blessed and inherit my fathers Kingdom And go ye Cursed into everlasting Damnation In Hellfire to burn forever, Even as thou dost fear the Last Judgement of God upon pain of Hellfire and everlasting damnation Give me true answers of all such things as I shall ask or demand of thee. To this I swear thee By God the Father the Son and the Holy Ghost to be true to me at all times even as thou wilt avoid the heavy wrath of God Sitting in his high Throne to Judge everyone according to right And also I Command thee by all the power that God hath over all Creatures, In Heaven, Earth and in Hell, Hereafter to meet with me at all times thy Self alone quietly, whereupon depart at this time And the peace of God be between thee and me now and forever. Amen

Then at all times she will meet with thee at what time thou anointest thine Eyes. Of this assure thy self to be most true, But when thou talkest with her Talk not long Neither yet demand her name Her Parentage nor yet her kindred or for what she is for fear of Indignation Nor yet whether she be Spirit or woman Let that talk go But demand things necessary for thy purpose. Beware you offer her no discourtesy at any time of polluting thyself, when thou hast talked enough with her wash thine Eyes with Rose ♒ [water] or some other Sweet ♒, when she doth depart Say these words following.

Go in peace thou beautiful Creature of God to the place appointed of God Signing thy self with the sign of the Cross. Finis
[470] (132)

---

[470] The section also found in Folger Vb.26 ends here.

Against Thieves:

Bless the Ground with the Sign of the + And say all the good that be here I bequeath to the keeping + Of the Father of Heaven + And of the Son + And of the Holy Ghost + Three persons and one God. If any Thieves come to steal it The Holy Ghost let them And cause them to abide here unto the time I come to them Also + In the name of the Father + And of the Son + And of the Holy Ghost + That I may escape all mine enemies And Thieves where and whatsoever they be Also by the virtue of + St Matthew + Mark + Luke + And John + which do agree in one very faith I here bind you Thieves without any sealing As St Bartholomew did bind the Devil with his Hoary beard in a chain, Thieves Thieves Thieves stand here In the virtue of the Holy Trinity And in the virtue of the death and resurrection of our lord Jesus Christ And go not away Thieves go not away + In nomine Patris + et filii + et Spiritus Sanctus + amen +

Bartholus Bartholum with thy grey beard

Stand by me for I am afeared

St Peter on the one side St Paul on the other

The Father The Son And the Holy Ghost in the Midst

Away all villains into the woods

If you take away any of my goods

Stand you still here until I come again + In the name of the Father + And of the Son + And of the Holy Ghost + Amen +

In Bethlehem was Jesus born

And Christened in the flood Jordan

Between two beasts was he laid

In that shed was neither wolf nor thief

But the blessed Trinity

The self same God that there was born

Defend me and my goods from harm

In the name of the Father And of the Son And of the Holy Ghost Amen

Matthew Mark Luke and John

Four Evangelists all in one

As you write the Trinity
Of our Saviour most truly
My Good which in this Circle be
I wish they might be safe with me
And that such Thieves as will me wrong
Be they weak or be they strong
Matherion before And Botherion[471] behind
So those thieves you do them bind
As St Bartholomow bound the Devil
To defend him from all evil
With the hairs of his grey head
And also eke his hoary beard
So you Thieves see you stand still
As the spindle in the Mill
That from hence you do not start
Until I say you shall depart
By Alpha and Omega height
The first of day the last of night
And by that blessed Trinity
Three in one One in three
See you Angels with me tend
That my goods you safe defend
Until the morrow Morn of day
I bid the Thieves to part away
So Thieves Thieves Thieves stand you still
And be obedient to my will.
Fiat fiat fiat amen.

---

[471] Two of the demon bishops mentioned previously, though Betherion has been corrupted slightly.

Wheresoever I go or Ride for to fett[472] about this place

To God the Father And the Son all those for to let

If any here do come my goods away to fett

With the Father and the Son I bind them And by the ☉ and ☾ and by the 5ii [7] Planets and by the virtues aforesaid and all the Saints in Heaven I bind him by their virtues so that he shall not depart until I bid him go. In nomine Patris &c Say it iii [3] t[imes].

The right Spell for thieves[473]

In the name of the father and of the son and of the holy ghost Amen.

Defend this my house ground and goods this night and all other times from all thieves Witches also spirits Elves and all other evils and I charge thee thou spirit that hast the charge especial of open as of secret things and by the virtue of the omnipotent power of Almight god maker of heaven & earth and Creator of all mortal flesh and of all other things visible and invisivle and I charge thee thou spirit by all the holy names of God the most highest + Elo Ely Sabaoth Adona[y] Saday Tetragrammaton Alpha et Omega and by all the names of god that may be spoken or not spoken also I remind thee thou spirit Which are called Banalum by all the aforesaid naming & by the virtue and power of them that if any thief or thieves hitherwards to me within this place where I go with my goods belonging to me or else also I charge thee Banalo[474] by the great virtue and power of almighty God and of the Virgin mary Gods mother and by all the powers of St. Peter and St. Paul and by all the holy company in heaven and by the Angels and ArchAngels that if any thief or thieves hitherwards come they may be struck down both blind and that still stand to or they are kept as stiff as any staff. (134)

---

[472] Fetch.

[473] This section is written in the second hand.

[474] The name of the spirit is varied here from the earlier Banalum.

Against witchcraft:~:

Take Oil of Pompilion[475] ii [2] d[rams][476] But first make the parties water Seeth[477] in a pan Then put in the oil Then take an Iron Red hot and put it into the water Saying In the name of the Father and of the Son And of the Holy Ghost Avoid all witches and wicked persons from this party from this time forth forevermore. And say it iii [3] times. But in any case shut the doors and windows And let nobody come in while that you be about your business, And keep the party so close that nothing may see her while you be about your business. And let her say her prayers.

I sign thee with the sign of the +. In the name of the father and of the Son and of the Holy Ghost, Jesus, Job and Peter rid this evil from this Ground. Say this all at iii [3] times iii [3] several Mornings one after another together with iii [3] Pater nosters iii [3] aves and iii [3] Credos for one that is forspoken.~.

Solutio seratu[478]

Fac Imaginid hominis (it Caput sic ut Caput Canis) in manu clasem tenenter fieb 2:a facie quae dul facta fuevit intendius non transfixit senum aliquo it ad illa ne serane tangat it statius aqua itur.[479]

If any be in danger of witchcraft let them carry about them Chervil, Stickwort[480] or Pomegranate & be free. (135)

---

[475] Another name for Poplar bud oil.

[476] I.e. ¼oz.

[477] Boil

[478] "Softened Wax."

[479] "Make an image of a man (stretch the head so that it is the head of a dog) and holding it in a closed hand, say twice: on the face which was made soft and stretched out do not transfix anything of age in the way anything of wax stays untouched by water." This Latin seems to have been miscopied in places.

[480] Another name for Agrimony.

Experiments: To go Invisible:~:

At such time as Men sow Beans. Take a Bean And put it into the Heart of a black Cat being ready Roasted Then bury it in a dunghill Or in *Alio loco Saturnaliter*[481] and when they be ripe Carry one about thee And thou shalt be invisible.

To make all in the House dance write these words in virgin Parchment Epos nepos cestpofas celiphna kendala, And say, I Conjure thee virgin Parchment by virtue of these names written in thee That all the Men & women in this House do Dance when I do rehearse their names.

To go Invisible: Take a piece of Lead And write therein *athatos Itiros theon pantocraton* And put it under your left foot.

To go Invisible: Take the water of Fennel and go unto a Ants hillock Saying 9 times putting down the water on the hillock Conjuro te Belzebub hostem domini nostri Jesu Christi ut redeam in Lapidem per quem eum invisibilis.[482]

[483]If you wish with any that you in fair art, put your right hand in your left or rest in your before & say with good delivery as following, Jesus aute trauferus et mediul illam ibat in quo + ceep crolit gogum geragum garbe garbo (136)

Experiment of the herb Valerian:

First kneel down of both your knees your face to the East And make a Cross over the Herb, In the name of the Father and of the Son And of the Holy Ghost Amen. Then Say A Pater noster Ave Maria And Credo in deum Also St Johns Gospel &c. This must be done secretly alone upon the Friday Or Thursday, The Moon being at the full And before you do speak any word to any Creature. Also

---

[481] "In the way of Saturn, in another place."

[482] "I conjure Thee, Beelzebub, enemy of our Lord Jesus Christ, so that I obtain a stone which makes one invisible."

[483] This next short piece is written in the second hand. The words seem to be a mixture of Latin and barbarous or corrupted words.

you must say before you take him quite out of the Ground as followeth.

I Conjure thee herb that art called valerian for thou art worthy for all things in the world In pleasancy in pleache[484] in chapmanhead[485] In Court before Kings rulers and Judges, Thou makest friendship Thou Comfortest the Man that desireth the love of Lords and Ladies And right of Kings and Queens. So grant thou that they that bare thee his will, So mayest thou be called valerian, For God hath given thee might that thou mayest well be likened to Mortagon[486] Of the unworthy thou makest worthy, The sorry thou makest blythe[487] And the poor rich, For thou doest great Miracles, Thou art well likened to Mortagon to the which all Spirits of the Earth and the Ghosts of Hell do hang to thee and obey thee, And all Princes thou overcomes. For whosoever hath thee whatsoever he desire he shall have + In the name of the Father + And of the Son + And of the Holy Ghost + Amen +

I Conjure thee in the name of the + Father + the Son + And the Holy Ghost + I pluck thee +

I Conjure thee In the name of the Father And the Son And the Holy Ghost And by Mary the Mother of our Lord and Saviour Jesus Christ That bare him that is God and Man And by the holy breasts that she gave him suck with And by all the right that Mary had by her Son And by the Crib that he was laid in And by his death And by his uprising And by the show that he showed to Mary Magdalene And by his Ascension to Heaven And by the Holy Ghost that he sent down to his Apostles And by the Assumption of our Lady St Mary And by his worthiness And by all the dreadful day of doom And by God Almighty and by all that in God is And by all that Men say of God And by all that in Heaven and in Earth And in the Sea is And without the Ground is + I Conjure thee by + Mathion + The name of God our lord which Moses bore in his forehead + I Conjure by + Sopher + and by + Ipomachion + by + Gechel + by + Emanuel + by + Alpha + and + ω + and by + Adonay +

---

[484] A hedge or vine border.

[485] A chapman is a merchant, chapmanhead is a term for trading.

[486] A herb described in medieval texts as being Martial with the power to break iron. See Sloane MS 1091. Mortagon has been identified as the Martagon Lily (Lilium martagon L.), see Plant Names of Medieval England, Hunt, 1989:182.

[487] Cheerful or carefree.

And by all the names of God + I Conjure thee by the holy Patriarchs and Prophets By the Apostles By the Evangelists By the Martyrs And Confessors And by all holy women and virgins, And by the hours of the day and of the night And by all the Fruit that giveth smell and grow bloom blow and wax + I Conjure the valerian by the + Father + And by the Son + And by the Holy Ghost + And by Jesus Christ + Leo + Agla + Promomagentus + Lapis + Fermamenti + Pax + Lux + Omnia + Fremitates + Alua + usion + Tetragrammaton + Thenus + Creator + Salvator + Consolator + Ordinator + I Conjure thee by + Abednigo + Misack + Sidrak + Staux + and per mortalis + Amen + I Conjure thee valerian by the name of + Aminadab + which the Sea heard and saw the wind in the Heavens Thunder by the which many Devils fell in + I Conjure thee by the Conjurations and Adorations that Alexander and Alysaunder[488] And Aristotle made on thee That thou a great power and might had and may have. So that what Man or woman I give of thee unto in meat or drink That thou them guide and rule till the time that my will be fulfilled And also whosever beareth thee upon him before King Prince or Judge Lord or Lady or any other person Man or woman That he may be liking and lusty to them all And that which he doth desire or ask by the worthiness of the valerian might forthwith and surely it may be granted to him that beareth thee + Amen + Agies + Agies + Agies[489] + Kirelison + Christeleson + Kirelison + Paternoster &c + Ave maria &c + Credo &c + The blessing of the father + The blessing of the Son + And the blessing of the Holy Ghost + be on thee valerian + Then say St Johns Gospel and keep it clean in a fair cloth + finis + (137)

To gain the love of a woman when the moon is in the South gather valerian saying these words over it *Miserere mei Beatus vir qui non intilliger*[490] and say iii [3] Pater nesters iii [3] Aves and iii [3] Creeds – Put it under thy Tongue and Kiss her And she will love thee

---

For love Burn valerian to powder and give some of it to her to drink And she will love thee.

---

[488] Name given to Alexander in a Medieval Romance c. 1275.

[489] This is clearly a corruption of the Greek Agios (or Hagios) meaning 'Holy' and often used in conjurations in threefold form.

[490] "Have pity on me, Blessed man who does not understand."

Experiments of the Herb vervain

To gain the love of Man or woman Go to the Herb vervain when it is flowered near the full of the Moon And say to it + The lords Prayer + Then say + In the name of the father + vervain I have sought thee In the name of the Son I have found thee + In the name of the Holy Ghost + I will gather thee + Then say + I Charge thee vervain by the virtue of our Lord Jesus Christ And by the holy names of God + *Helion* + *Heloy* + *Adonay* + and by all the holy names of God That when I carry thee in my mouth that whosoever I shall love or touch that thou make them obedient unto me And to do my will in all things + fiat + fiat + fiat + Amen +

For love Take vervain in thy Mouth And Kiss any Maid saying these words *Pax tibi sum sen sum conterit cor in amore me,*[491] And she shall love thee.

To make peace betwixt Enemies Go between men that are at debate having vervain about thee and say *Ratifaxat* and thou shalt make peace betwixt them.

For speedy deliverance let the woman have vervain about her being in travail with Child And say this word *Grespas* and she shall be delivered.

For weariness in Travail[492] Put vervain in his Shoes and say this word *Mestias*[493] and he shall not be weary of travailing that day.

To catch fish Carry vervain about thee And say *venite*[494] and all fishes shall come about thee.

---

[491] "I am peace[ful] unto thee, and if I am not, may he strike my heart with love."

[492] Hard work or toil.

[493] Possibly a corruption or miscopying of Messias (Messiah).

[494] "Come".

To hive Bees Rub the Hive with vervain And hive the Swarm in him Saying these words *venite nomen armm*[495] And they shall love it. (138)

For sore Eyes Make a paste of vervain And put it into A mans Eye that is sore Saying this word *Lucem fac domine*[496] and it shall heal him.

For Theft Take vervain gathered in the Month of May And mix it with Gold or Silver In Monday before Sun rising In the waxing of the Moon And touch whosoever thou hast in suspicion of theft And if he be Guilty He shall confess it unto thee.

To go invisible Let iiii [4] Masses be said over vervain And bare it about thee And thou shalt go invisible.

To know whether the Sick shall live or die Put vervain into the Sick mans Hand And say this word *Archinclms* and you shall find whether he shall live or die.

To know whether the Sick shall live or die Take vervain in thy Right Hand And take his Hand in thy Hand the Herb being between your hands so that he know it not And ask him how he doeth And what he thinketh of himself If he say he hope he shall recover, He shall recover, If he say he shall die, He shall die.

To gain the love of great persons Carry vervain about thee.

To know whether a Maid be virgin Cause her to sit down upon the Herb unwittingly. If She be not a Maid She will not nor cannot.

That thy Enemies hurt thee not Carry vervain about thee.

---

[495] "Come in the name of Armm".
[496] "Make light Lord."

For Theft Touch all the suspected with this Herb And the Thief shall weep.

Gather vervain In the Monday night before Holyrood day.

Experiments Of the Herb Called Elitrapa:[497]

Gather this Herb in August The Sun going into Leo And roll it in a Bay leaf together with the tooth of a wolf.

That none shall have power to speak against thee in any wise Bear it about thee.

For Theft Put it under thy head in the night And thou shalt see the Thief and all his conditions

For to prove a womans Honesty Put it in the Church under the Seat whereas she sitteth. If she hath used more men than her Husband She shall not be able to go forth of the Church unless it be taken away. This last hath been proved and is most true. (139)

Experiments of the Herb yarrow:

For Gold that is hidden. Take the juice of Yarrow and powder of Alum And powder of Copper And the filings of fine Copper, All being mixed together fill an Elder Stick therewith the pith being taken out very clean, Then Close up the ends with wax And lay it over the place where you suspect Gold is hidden And if there be thrice so much Gold as will way the stick It will devour it in 8 hours. (140)

Experiments for Love:~:

Write in an Apple these names following + Guell + blatirell + Gliaell + and give it her to eat. **Probat.**[498]

---

[497] This name does not correspond to any known herb, but may be derived from Elaterium, a name used for the Wild Cucumber.

[498] "Proven".

Write in an Apple these words + s x R gausuite ++ J Tetragrammaton J B scelfagus in gioth ynyod +++ agios B + simid

Write in an Apple Raguell Lucifer Sathanus And say I conjure thee Apple by these three names written in thee That whosoever shall eat thee may burn in my love until such time she hath fulfilled my desire.

Write in an Apple Hely + Helyas, Thy name and her name and give it her to eat. Fiat.

Write in an Apple, Causma abroth sordaye, with your name, fiat.

Write in an Apple, guell + B satyrell, give it her to eat.

Write in an Apple on a Friday before it fall to the ground, The womans name and these names following rerxcvmclisa lucifero a p p e n a Raguell Lucifer Sathanus, I Conjure you by these three names That every one that eateth thee fulfil my will.

Write in an Apple before it fall from the Tree + *Aleo* + *Deleo* + *Delaton* + And say I Conjure thee Apple by these three names which are written in thee that what woman or virgin soever toucheth and tasteth thee may love me and burn in my love as fire melteth wax till my will be fulfilled.

Write in an Apple before it fall to the ground on a Friday *reacamo lise Lucifero* and the name of the woman. Probatum.

Write in an Apple, *Chiuas Eathmus Sifance* And give it her to eat, et amabit te.[499]

---

[499] "And she will love you."

Write in an Apple *Saglaff dather mos fileimes* and give it to a woman In the new of the moon, et amabit.

Write in an Apple before it fall from the tree these 3 words with the blood (   )[500] *Lucifer Sathanus Rusal* And say Conjuro to porno per omnes damones qui tentaverint Adam et Evam in Paradisa ut quecunque mulier dete gustanerit in amore meo andeat.[501]

Write on a Red Apple with the blood of a Rearmouse[502] or Bat 3 *l 1 s A r e e 2* and give it to a maid to eat.[503]

Write in an Apple with the point of a Knife, On the one side *Tabora* and on the other side *Odul Ochara* and give it to be eaten either to man or woman And he or she shall love thee

---

Write in an Apple your names And these three names *Gosmer Synady Heupide*, And give it to eat to any man that thou wouldst have after thy will and he shall do as thou wilt

---

Cut an Apple in iiii [4] parts and on every part write + Sathiel + Sathiel + Obing + siagel + and say + I Conjure thee Apple by God the living only and true by that holy God that hath created thee and by the iiii [4] evangelists and Gospels And by Samuel and by Mary and by all Time that thou shalt not stand still until I shall have the love of the woman which shall eat of thee + In the name of the father + and of the Son + and of the Holy Ghost + Amen + Let it be so + &c

---

[500] Blank space suggesting the type of blood was to be filled in later, or possibly that it was the person's blood.

[501] "I conjure thee furthermore by all the demons who tempted Adam and Eve in Paradise so that whichever way through you the woman will taste love for me and desire me."

[502] An old word for Bat.

[503] A similar charm is seen in MS Gaster 1562.

Write with the point of a knife in an Apple that Groweth these words *Dedica lupa druca dedia Calpa Draco*[504] And give her to eat that part with the names And eat thou the other part

---

Write in an Apple these iii [3] words + Satuell + Latuell + Datuell + And say I Conjure thee Apple by these iii [3] names that be written in the book of life that she that eateth this apple may me so fervently love That she have no rest Until I have had my will of her.[505] (141)

Write these letters in thy left Hand, *h l d p n a g u st*, carry them in the morning before Sun rising and touch whom thou wilt and she shall follow thee, fiat.

Write this sign in thy Left Hand and touch whom thou wilt before Sun rising and say unto them follow me. You may try it upon a Dog or Bitch.

71 - Charm described in the preceding text

Write this in thy Left hand and touch whom thou wilt before Sun rising and say follow me

72 - Charm described in the preceding text

---

[504] "Consecrate the skin[?]/ head[?] of a wolf consecrate the head [?] of a Dragon."

[505] A similar charm is seen in MS Gaster 1562.

Write these letters in thy left hand before Sun rising, *h b n f m g b s*, and touch her or him et sequitur.[506]

Write these letters in thy left hand before Sun rising, *h l n p m q u m*, and touch her neck privily et amabit.[507]

Write these letters in thy left hand, *b u x s a p p*, and touch her therewith and she shall follow thee.

Write these letters in thy left hand and no woman shall deny thy request, *l s j x t t c e ff s v q 2*

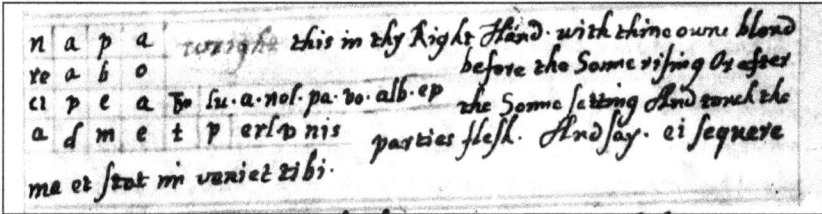

73 – An attraction charm recorded here in the MS. The table has the letter sequence:

n a p a

re a b o

cl p e a bo lu a nol pa vo alb ep

a d m e t p erl v nis

The words at the side say:

"Write this in thy Right Hand with thine own blood before the Sun rising Or after the Sun setting And touch the partie's flesh. And say, ei sequere me et stat mi veni et tibi"[508]

Write these letters in thy hand, *c m n b s p*, and touch whom thou wilt, et amabit.

Selized zelarge belarge et belarge, touch a woman upon the breast in the hour of Venus And she shall love thee entirely.

---

[506] "And he/she does follow".

[507] "And she will love [you]."

[508] "He will follow me, and stand, and come to me and you."

Take iii [3] hairs of her head And a thread spun upon a Friday of a pure virgin and make a Candle therewith of virgin wax iiii [4] square And write with the blood of a Cock Sparrow the name of the woman And light the Candle whereas it may not drop upon the Earth, And she will come to the Candle.

Take a nutmeg and sweat it iii [3] or iiii [4] days under thy right Armhole. Grate it and mingle it with the ashes of a Green Frog and give it to a Maid, et amabit te.[509]

Take the Navel string of a Boy new born the which the Midwife cutteth away, dry it to powder and give her thereof to drink. There is none such.

Take a red Frog and bury him in a Hillock Then take the bones and lay them on a Tilestone Red hot till he lift over himself on the other side So let it lie till she is so likewise Then make powder thereof And strew them on her clothes whom thou lovest, And she shall love thee.[510]

Take the Tongue of A Sparrow and close it in virgin wax under thy upward clothes the space of iiii [4] Fridays, then take it and keep it in thy mouth. *Sub lingua tua*[511] then kiss thy love. Et ipso te amabit.

Write these words with the blood of a white Pigeon, *Oli mele cee ele el*, lay them in Green cloth of Silk ad carry it with thee and thou shalt have the love of all people.

---

[509] "And she will love you."

[510] This is probably derived from Agrippa's Three Books of Occult Philosophy.

[511] "Under thy tongue". This may be a reference to the Song of Solomon 4:11, "honey and milk are under thy tongue".

Write these names in virgin parchment, *Grasayt* x *Crux* x *Pluto* x *Craton* x *l* x *t* x *lio* et vide crepusculum.

Make an Image of her you love Of virgin wax And Christen it in Holy water Saying, I Baptise and Christen thee In the name of the Father and of the Son and of the Holy Ghost, And write the name of the woman In the forehead of the Image And thy name in her breast And write upon her head Venus. Then take iiii [4] new needles Prick one of them in the Back of the Image right against the Navel And in her Right side another In her left side And the other above the Navel And write in her left side *Sieate*, And on her Right side *gratuell* And at her navel *Almederie* And at her back *Mammoye*: Then say. I Conjure you Spirits by the power of the Father which is divine And by the power of the Son which is human And by the power of the Holy Ghost which is Latitude of the world That you will come speedily and make no tarrying either in Hell or in the Sea Or in the world before you have fulfilled my will and pleasure, Come therefore from the East from the South from the west And from the North And rest not day nor night until I have my pleasure as I will with her And I Conjure you again by the power of *Lucifer Belsebub Astiroth* and by him which hath any power in love or to love that you rest not in any place until AB be enforced to love me, I conjure you holy Angels of the East west North and South *Lathinos Imbroson Samabathon Samyn Anthreson vene fatha Thini Reanet unn tend Belissemd Monoy Tymon* and by all the names of the most high God And by all the powers and orders of the Heavens and Earth that you increase love between AB and me and that she may be obedient unto my will and accomplish my desire. Then make a fire in her name, The coals being kindled lay them abroad and write in the Ashes her Image and a little Mustard seed and a little Salt upon the picture. Then lay up the coals again, As the composition leapeth and swelleth so shall her Heart And she shall be kindled in thy love that she might be with thee.

Make an Image of virgin wax In the forehead whereof write her name And in the right front venus and in the left front saturnus and in the back Jupiter. Then take red thorns and make fire and say, I Conjure thee Image By the virtue of the Father and of the Son and of the Holy Ghost that as thou dost waste so may this woman waste her love from all other men saving me. And I Conjure thee Image and Planets whose names are written in thee by the virtue of God and all holy Saints that you tempt this woman Ab whose form and name thou art made for That she shall not sleep nor take no rest in any place Neither Stand nor Sleep nor wake nor do anything else but that she come with all speed to fulfil my will and pleasure.

Always work this In the day and Hour of Venus.

Write these letters in virgin wax, *l s c u c ♌*, and carry it in thy right hand and ask what thou wilt and thou shalt obtain it.

Write this character in virgin Parchment And what woman you touch with it shall love thee

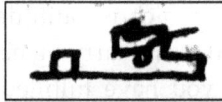

74 - Character described in preceding text

Write these names in virgin wax or virgin parchment, *Asmo Tolana Tanaell Eliboll Erusia H b ri k y k y k*, then say, I Conjure you Spirits by your God which you obey that this woman be made to fall in love with me this night and to make her Heart to lie inflamed with me and suffer her not to wake nor sleep eat nor drink until she hath fulfilled my desire. Then lay the wax or parchment under the Chamber door that night before she go to bed. And when you lay it there say iii [3] times, Let it be done. (143)

Write these words with thine own blood And lay them in the bed of a woman, Badull arbrculus arbarculare, and say, I Conjure thee by the prince of Devils that thou neither sleep nor sit eat nor drink until thou hast fulfilled my desire.

The King of venus shall be of lead made in the hour of venus to have love of all men, And to make a woman to follow thee whether thou wilt. Fast Friday till Even[ing] And in the night with the blood of a Calf In a green place make this character And the name of the Angel *Abamatra* in the skin of a bear and as often as thou show this to any woman she shall do thy will.

♀ ·ιουο ♌

*75 - This character is written beneath the preceding charn,
so assumedly this is the character referred to*

Say unto a woman in her left Ear, *veneto melchy mobelchy* follow me. Fiat.

Write these words with the blood of a white Cock or Hen, *vadull Abarculas*, and cast it in the bed of woman And say, I Conjure thee A by the prince of Devils that thou sleep not sit not eat not nor drink not until thou hast fulfilled my will.

Take the hairs of a woman whose love thou desirest And keep them till the friday following And that day rise before ☉ rising. Then with thine own blood write thine own name and her name in virgin wax or parchment And burn the Hairs and letters together to dust on a red hot Iron and give it her in meat or drink And she shall be so much taken with thee that she shall take no rest &c.

Take the Heart of a Turtledove and seeth it in water then put it into a heap of Salt until it be dry. The powder thereof will get the love of a woman Or if you rub it about your lips and Kiss her She will be enamoured.

Take ii [2] Cramp Rings[512] of Gold or Silver lay them both in a Swallow nest that buildeth in the Summer let them lie there i2 [3] days Then take them and deliver the one to thy love and keep the other thy self.

Watch a Mare And as soon as the foal is fallen Take the lump of flesh that growth in the forehead of the foal, It is called *Hipomides* and is not but of a Horsecoal dry and pulverise and give to whom you love.

Take a lace or Girdle and anoint it with Asperis oil[513] and give it her to wear whom thou dost affect, et amabit.

---

[512] A ring worn as a cure for cramp.

[513] Unknown substance – asperis is latin for 'harsh' or 'difficult'.

Take a Bat let him bleed with a Glass or Flint and with the blood write this letter J and touch a man or woman and they shall follow thee. For trial touch a Dog and he will follow thee.

Take A Nutmeg and prick it full of holes and you shall see it wear a dew upon it such a one take Put in your armpit ii [2] days that it may take your Sweat (tu pone meum in Spermate proprio)[514] so let it soak therein then dry it on a Tilestone and it will fall to powder the which put into a womans potion or potage but drink not of it yourself and she will do your pleasure without any doubt.

In March when Toads do engender Kill ii [2] that are engendering and put them in a box full of holes and put it in a Pissemire bank[515] when all is consumed Get the bones take them and cast them into a running water And you will see one of the bones will go against the Stream Another will stand upright in the Stream And another will Sink, These iii [3] keep. Put that that Swimmeth against the stream in a Ring and she that taketh it at your hands faciet tecum in lecto.[516] Put that that standeth upright in a Ring and give it to a woman et iuit tecum quocunque vetii,[517] And grate that to powder that sinketh and she that drinketh thereof shall hate thee.

Write in virgin wax these letters *A z bi l p g g t s e q c R c u* and have it with thee, and ask what thou wilt and thou shalt have it.

76 - Letter sequence for preceding charm

(144)

---

[514]"You [must] put [it] in the proper seed of bear-wort."

[515] Pissemire is an old word for ant, thus pissemire bank = anthill.

[516] "It will make her come to your bed."

[517] "and it will go with you to any kind of [her] forbidden place."

Experiments for all Games:~:

Take the good Stone called Solsequium[518] (The Marigold or Turnesoll) for all gaming Before the Sun rising And kneeling towards the East Say as followeth.

I Conjure thee Solsequium by the virginity of our blessed lady St Mary the Mother of God and by the Maidenhead of St John the Evangelist And by the Maidenhead of St Catherine **Also** I Conjure thee By all thee by all the Apostles And by the four Evangelists Matthew Mark Luke and John and by all Martyrs and Confessors and by all virgins And by all the Joys of our Lady St Mary And by all the four Elements Fire Water Air and Earth, And by these holy names of God *Helli Helli Helli Lamasabacthani*[519] *uetu Adonay Eloy Semhamephoras* And by the name which Aaron bore on his forehead And by the Planet under which thou art And by the Character and Seal of the same And by all the holy names of God whatsoever they be **I Conjure** thee Solsequium that thou let me not be overcome of any Creature Neither that I lose at any kind of Game Or Games but that I may have the victory of all Mankind whatsoever I desire to play with all while thou Solsequium art about me Or in my Mouth *Non veniet in mematitia superbi nec manus Proditoris moreat me finis Solsequii.*

Make an Image of Gold unto thine own likeness In the hour of Sol ascending In the which Image write the name of the Angel of the Sun with his Characters And write in the same Image This Character of the Sun $\rightthreetimes$ The which done bear it very secretly about thee, Hung about thy neck, upon thy Heart.

Take the longest feather in a Swallows wing And write with the blood of a Bat In virgin Parchment *Abat Abac Fala aio abac abasack* And hold it in thy left hand And touch the Dice Saying *Abac Ida adita abac abac abracala abasac.*

---

[518] Literally 'Sun follower', so probably heliotrope as the appropriate stone for this description.

[519] This is clearly derived from "Eloi, eloi, lama sabacthani", or "My god, my god, why have you forsaken me", Jesus' words on the cross, and one of the very few Aramaic phrases not translated in the Bible. See Matthew 27:46 and Mark 15:34.

Write these words with the blood of a Pehen[520] In virgin Parchment *Gasone tartenero* And bind it fast to thine Elbow or thereabouts of thy right hand And reckon what chance thou wilt and thou shalt have it. (145)

Write with the longest Feather of a Swallows wing and with the blood of a Bat In virgin wax or Parchment viz *Daforson adabrant maric.*

Write in virgin Parchment *Asac alac anaza*

Take the Tongue of a Kite or Gleade[521] and do him no more harm but let him go again And write on the Tongue and wrap it up in a Cloth of Green Say And cause a Mass to be said over it of the virgin Then hang it about thy neck near thy right shoulder.

Take iii [3] leaves of Mowseeare[522] and write these names therein *galga cala effia* and bind them to your little finger. Probatim.

Take iii [3] leaves of Ribwort[523] and write on the first *san x can* on the second *Cota* on the third *tellebray* and win at Cards.

Take iii [3] leaves of Mowseeare and write therein these iii [3] names *Galga Gayla Offatale:*

---

[520] Peahen.

[521] The old name for a Red Kite.

[522] The plant Mouse-ear Hawkweed.

[523] A type of plantain (Plantago lanceolata).

Write these words in virgin Parchment with the blood of a Turtledove and put the Parchment on a linen Cloth sown round that it may go about thine arm that shall throw the dice.[524]

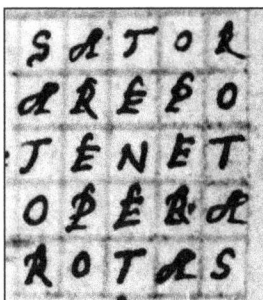

77 - The SATOR magic square, used in the preceding charm

Take virgin Parchment and cause to be said over it iii [3] masses of the Trinity And iii [3] of the blessed virgin St Mary and iii [3] of the Passion And make this figure put it in a Red Cloth and bind it to thy arm and play

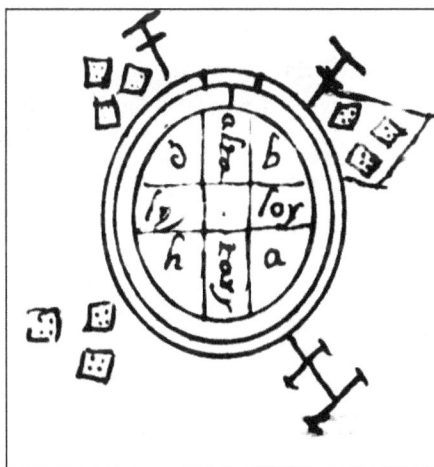

78 – Gambling figure used in the preceding charm, note the dice mainly show four dots for Jupiter, associated with fortune

---

[524] An earlier version of this charm is found in MS Bod e. Mus 243, where the result is given as obtaining what thou wilt.

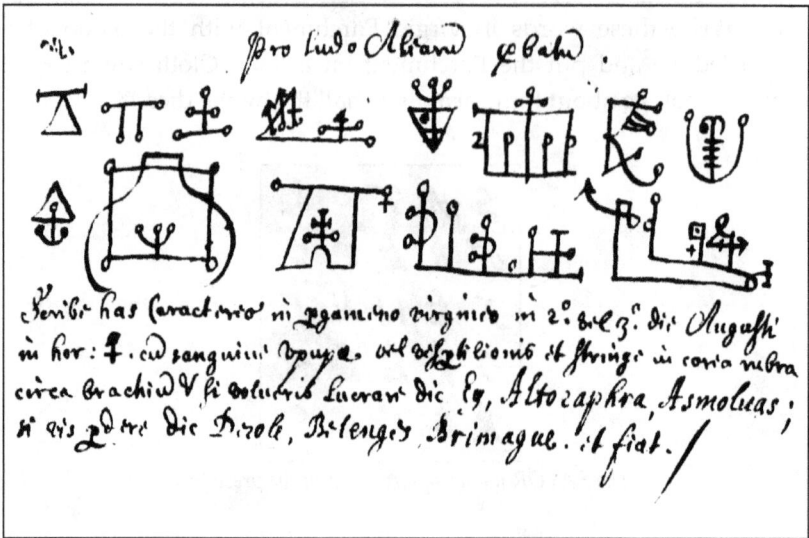

79 - Characters and text for the following charm

Pro ludo Aliand[525] [symbol] Bahu[526]

Sevibi has Caractirio ni ygamino virgine in 2° 8re 3° die Augusti in hor ♀ ad sanguine upupe ure vesytilioius it stringi in coria rubra circa brachiul V si volucris lucrari dic *Ey, Altozaphra, Asmoluas*; si eis yd ere dic *Dorole, Bilenges, Brimague, il fiat.*[527] (146)

---

[525] "For the game of the stranger"

[526] The following section is in the second hand.

[527] "Write these characters on a virgin parchment on the 2nd or 3rd day of August in the hour of Venus with the blood of an hoopoe or roller [another type of bird] snared with red leather round its claw & when worms have been acquired for it, say Ey, Altozaphra, Asmoluas; when it comes forward, say Dorole, Bilenges, Brimague, so mote it be!"

Toothache[528]

Mars, hur, abursa, aburse: 3 times

Jesus Christ for mary's sake

Take away this toothache

Write these words 3 times and as you say the words let the fire[529] burn one paper, then another, and then the last I saw the experiments and the party immediately cured (147)

---

[528] This note added in to the book is in the hand of Elias Ashmole

[529] The word is unclear in the text and this is the most likely choice, particularly as it is recorded as such elsewhere.

80 - Table of Planetary Hours and Page from an Ephemeris, stuck into the back of the book

(148)

Ann Savadge in Rosemary Lane[530]

---

[530] This reference is written in the hand of Elias Ashmole. The MS ends here.

Bibliography

Manuscript Source Material

Additional MS 36674, C16th

Bodleian e. Mus 173, 1623

Folger Vb.26, 1580

Lansdowne MS 1202, C17th

MS Laud Misc 19, C17th

Sloane MS 3824, 1649

Sloane MS 3825, 1641

Sloane MS 3846, C17th

Sloane MS 3851, C17th

Sloane MS 4042, C17th

Sloane MS 4061, C17th

Wellcome MS 1026, 1692

Wellcome MS 4669, 1796

Printed Source Material

Agrippa, Cornelius (2005) *The Fourth Book of Occult Philosophy*. Maine, Ibis Press

Agrippa, Cornelius (2005) *Three Books of Occult Philosophy*. Minnesota, Llewellyn Publications

Aubrey, John (1890) *Miscellanies Upon Various Subjects*. London, Reeves and Turner

Boas, F.S. (1928) *Elizabethan Drama*. In *Year's Work in English Studies* Vol. 9.1:152-167

Briggs, K.M. (1962) *Pale Hecate's Team: An Examination of the Beliefs on Witchcraft and Magic amongst Shakespeare's Contemporaries and His Immediate Successors*. London, Routledge & Kegan Paul

Briggs, K.M. (1959) *The Anatomy of Puck: An Examination of Fairy Beliefs among Shakespeare's Contemporaries and Successors*. London, Routledge and Kegan Paul

Briggs, K.M. (1953) *Some Seventeenth Century Books of Magic*. In *Folklore* Vol 64.4:445-462

Coletânea (2007) *São Cipriano, O Bruxo (capa aço)*. Rio de Janeiro, Pallas

Davies, Owen (2003) *Cunning-Folk: Popular Magic in English History*. London, Hambledon & London

Davies, Owen (1997) *Urbanization and the Decline of Witchcraft: An Examination of London*. In *Journal of Social History* Spring 1997:597-617

Davies, T. (1774) *The Lives of Those Eminent Antiquaries Elias Ashmole Esquire and Mr William Lilly, Written by Themselves*. London, T. Davies

Debus, Allen G. (2002) *The Chemical Philosophy: Paracelsian Science and Medicine in the Sixteenth and Seventeenth Centuries*. Devon, Dover.

Dendle, Peter & Alain Touwaide (2008) *Health and Healing From the Medieval Garden*. Suffolk, Boydell Press

Dickens, Charles (1852) *Household Words Volume 5*. New York, Angell, Engel & Hewitt

Eamon, William (1994) *Science and the Secrets of Nature: Books of Secrets in Medieval and Early Modern Culture*. New Jersey, Princeton University Press

Flint, Valerie I.J. (1991) *The Rise of Magic in Early Medieval Europe*. New Jersey, Princeton University Press

Forbes, Thomas R. (1971) *Verbal Charms in British Folk Medicine*. In *Proceedings of the American Philosophical Society* Vol. 115.4:293-316

Gaster, M. (1910) *English Charms of the Seventeenth Century*, in *Folklore* 21.3:375-78

Gettings, Fred. (1981) *Dictionary of Occult, Hermetic and Alchemical Sigils*. London, Routledge & Kegan Paul

Gibson, Marion (2003) *Witchcraft and Society in England and America, 1550-1750*. London, Continuum

Grattan, Thomas Colley (1836) *Agnes de Mansfelt: A Historical Novel*. London, Saunders & Otley

Gray, George John (1861) *Athenae Cantabrigiensis, Vol 2, 1586-1609*. Cambridge, Jonathan Palmer.

Grell, Ole Peter & Andrew Cunningham (2007) *Medicine and Religion in Enlightenment Europe*. Surrey, Ashgate Publishing

Henning, Basil Duke (1983) *The House of Commons 1660-1690 Volume 1*. London, Secker & Warburg.

Hunt, Tony (1989) *Plant Names of Medieval England*. Cambridge, Cambridge University Press

Johnson, William (1657) *Lexicon Chymicum cum Obscuriorum verborum et Rerum Hermeticarum*. London, Gulielmi Nealand

Karr, Don & Stephen Skinner (2010) *Sepher Raziel: Liber Salomonis*. Singapore, Golden Hoard

Kittredge, George Lyman (1929) *Witchcraft in Old and New England*. Harvard, Harvard University Press

Klaasen, Frank (2011) *Three Early Rituals to Spoil Witches*. In *Opuscula* Vol 1.1:1-10

Klaasen, Frank (2003) *Medieval Ritual Magic in the Renaissance*. In *Aries* Vol. 3.2:166-199

Knighton, C.S. & Richard Mortimer. (2003) *Westminster Abbey Reformed: Nine Studies, 1540-1640*. Surrey, Ashgate

Martin, Charles Trice (comp) (1976) *The Record Interpreter: Abbreviations, Latin Words used in English Historical Manuscripts and Records*. London, Stevens & Sons Ltd

McLean, Adam (1982) *A Treatise on Angel Magic*. Edinburgh, Magnum Opus Hermetic Sourceworks 15

McLean, Adam (ed) (1982) *The Steganographia of Johannes Trithemius*. Edinburgh, Magnum Opus Hermetic Sourceworks 12

Menghi, Girolamo & Gaetano Paxia (2002) *The Devil's Scourge: Exorcism During the Italian Renaissance*. Maine, Red Wheel Weiser

Mowat, Barbara A. (2001) *Prospero's Book*. In *Shakespeare Quarterly* Vol 52.1, pp1-33

Ogilvie-Thomson, S.J. (2000) *The Index of Middle English Prose Handlist XVI: Manuscripts in the Laudian Collection, Bodleian Library, Oxford*. Cambridge, D.S. Brewer

Olsan, Lea T. (2003) *Charms and Prayers in Medieval Medical Theory and Practice*. In *Social History of Medicine* Vol 16.3:343-366

Peterson, Joseph H. (ed, trans) (2009) *Arbatel, Concerning the Magic of the Ancients*. Florida, Ibis Press

Peterson, Joseph H. (ed) (2001) *The Lesser Key of Solomon*. Maine, Weiser Books

Pollington, Stephen (2003) *Leechcraft: Early English Charms Plantlore and Healing*. Norfolk, Anglo-Saxon Books

Rankine, David & Harry Barron (2010) *The Book of Gold: A 17th Century Magical Grimoire of Amulets, Charms, Prayers, Sigils and Spells Using the Biblical Psalms of King David*. London, Avalonia

Rankine, David (2009) *The Book of Treasure Spirits*. London, Avalonia

Rankine, David & Sorita d'Este (2007) *Practical Planetary Magick*. London, Avalonia

Redgrove, H. Stanley (2003) *Roger Bacon: The Father of Experimental Science and Medieval Occultism*. Kessinger

Roberts, Ernest S. & Edward J. Gross (1901) *Biographical History of Gonville and Caius Colledge 1349-1897* Vol. 1. Cambridge, Cambridge University Press

Scot, Reginald (1990) *The Discoverie of Witchcraft*. Dover Publications

Skemer, Don C. (2006) *Binding Words: Textual Amulets in the Middle Ages*. Pennsylvania, Pennsylvania State University Press

Skinner, Stephen (2006) *The Complete Magician's Tables*. Singapore, Golden Hoard

Skinner, Stephen & David Rankine (ed) (2009) *A Collection of Magical Secrets*. London, Avalonia

Skinner, Stephen & David Rankine (2008) *The Veritable Key of Solomon*. Singapore, Golden Hoard

Skinner, Stephen & David Rankine (2007) *The Goetia of Dr Rudd*. Singapore, Golden Hoard

Skinner, Stephen & David Rankine (2004) *Practical Angel Magic of Dr John Dee's Enochian Tables*. Singapore, Golden Hoard

Smith, Horace (1826) *Brambletye House; or, Cavaliers and roundheads, a novel, Volume 3*. London, Henry Colburn

Thomas, Northcote W. (1905) *Crystal Gazing: Its History and Practice , with a Discussion of the Evidence for Telepathic Scrying*. New York, Dodge Publishing Company

Thomas, Keith (1971) *Religion and the Decline of Magic*. London, Penguin

Thompson, C.J.S. (1927) *Mysteries and Secrets of Magic*. London, John Lane

Wheeler, Edward J. & Crane, Frank (1889) *Current Opinion Volume 3*. London, The Current Literature Publishing Co

Yates, Frances A. (1983) *The Occult Philosophy in the Elizabethan Age*. London, Ark

Index

A

A Book of Experiments out of Dyvers Authors 23, 284

A Key to Helmont 14

A Right Profitable Book for All Diseases 23

a Windor, John..............15, 16, 114

Abednigo 164, 302

Abraham..101, 109, 140, 159, 220, 244, 284, 286

Acts 89, 93

Additional MS 36674..20, 21, 22, 251, 252

Agrippa, Cornelius..7, 18, 20, 21, 22, 23, 24, 27, 28, 35, 37, 97, 156, 180, 181, 210, 254, 255, 257, 258, 310

Alexander the Great 77, 302

Almutel 183

Aloes 104, 171, 258

Altar 133, 197, 201, 211

Alum 255, 305

Amber 256

Anael 169, 176, 177, 281, 282

Andragias 244

Anglicus, Gilbertus 7

Apollonius............................... 56

Apple.................305, 306, 307, 308

Aquarius................................. 258

Aratron......................64, 65, 66

Arbatel..18, 22, 35, 54, 56, 57, 73, 78

Archangels..142, 145, 152, 153, 155, 210, 212, 217, 223, 230, 231, 240, 241, 244, 245, 246

Archimedes 77

Arderne, John............................. 7

Aries 52, 53, 183, 258

Aristotle 77, 302

Asariel..................................... 235

Ash 255

Ashmole, Elias..17, 24, 26, 38, 319, 321

Astrologater 8

Athanasius Creed 142

Aubrey, John 23, 24

Ave Maria..42, 147, 229, 273, 288, 300, 302

Ayscough, Lady.... 22, 23, 27, 283

B

Bacon, Roger....................... 14, 15

Bacon, William 14, 35, 248

Balsam..................................... 258

Balthazar 229

Baratria................................... 151

Baron 20, 222, 223

Bartholomew, Saint 296

Bealphares..224, 230, 231, 232, 233

Bedelum................................. 256

Belzebub..............52, 154, 155, 300

Belzibub ... 154, 155, *See* Belzebub

Benjamin 103, 255

Beryl 133, 134, 136, 216

Betherion..147, 148, 297, *See* Boytheon

Bethor 64, 65, 66, 67

Black Poppy............................ 255

Bodleian e. Mus 173.......... 14, 212

Book of Receipts and Chirurgery 22, 23, 27, 283

Boytheon..........................143, 144

Brimstone..........179, 247, 251, 256

Bubb, Captain..12, 13, 18, 21, 50, 51

C

Cabereon............................. 19, 20

Caesar, Julius.............. 77, 92, 220

Caius, Dr John 21

Camphor 255, 257, 258

Cancer 218, 258, 279

Capricorn................................258

Carmelion 19, 261
Cassia 104, 257
Cassiel, Archangel..178, 179, 279, 282
Charlemagne, King 52
Charles I, King 7, 12
Cherubim..40, 111, 142, 223, 230, 231, 239, 240, 242
Chervil 299
Cinnamon 257, 258
Codex Gaster 1562 216
Conuociell.............................. 244
Copper 69, 118, 279, 293, 305
Coriander................................ 254
Costum.................................. 258
Crystal..97, 113, 114, 115, 127, 133, 134, 136, 138, 210, 211, 212, 216, 217, 218, 220, 221, 237, 238, 239, 240
Cyprian, Saint 35, 39, 40, 52

D

Dalatel 53
Daniel..52, 62, 81, 87, 93, 140, 164, 192, 220, 250
de Abano, Peter 156
De Occulta Philosophia..7, 18, 181, 254, 255, 257, 310, 324
Dee, Dr John..15, 16, 21, 25, 26, 114
Delforia 292, 293
Dentalion .... 153, *See* Donskion
Deuteronomy 89
Dickens, Charles 27, 283
Discoverie of Witchcraft..7, 13, 22, 193, 216, 224, 237
Dominations..210, 212, 223, 230, 231, 240, 241
Dominions............142, 239, *See* Dominations
Donskion 151, 152
Dryads.................................... 74

E

Ebrion...........20, 261, *See* Oberion

Ecclesiastes 73
Elizabeth I, Queen 15, 21
Elves 125, 298
Euclid 77
Euphorbium 255, 256, 258
Evans, Ellen 11
Exodus...................... 197, 203, 253

F

Fayreford, Thomas 7
Fletcher, John............... 13, 21, 50
Folger Vb.26..17, 19, 20, 22, 222, 290, 292
Forman, Simon.................... 20, 21
Fourth Book of Occult Philosophy.. .... 7, 18, 156, 180
Frankincense..154, 227, 241, 255, 256, 257, 258, 283

G

Gabriel, Archangel..20, 62, 108, 133, 138, 142, 169, 170, 171, 229, 244, 246, 250, 274, 280, 281
Gaddesden, John.........................7
Galbanum 258
Galen 76, 77
Gauntlet, Arthur..9, 10, 11, 12, 13, 14, 16, 17, 18, 19, 20, 22, 23, 24, 25, 26, 28, 38, 41
Gemini.................................... 258
Genesis 74, 79, 196
Gilleflowers 255, 256
Gold..21, 22, 23, 68, 69, 71, 92, 104, 105, 115, 152, 155, 170, 201, 224, 229, 254, 279, 289, 304, 305, 313, 315
Gostu .... 255, *See* Costum
Gray's Inn Lane............................ 38
Griffith, Sarah.......................... 25

H

Hagith 64, 65, 66, 69
Harley MS 6482...................... 216
Harvey, Gabriel........................ 20

Hazel Wand..............237, 253, 293
Hempseed................................ 254
Henbane............................254, 255
Henoch.................................... 74
Heptameron..18, 20, 22, 156, 170, 179
Heptarchia Mystica..................... 21
Hercules................................... 77
Hermelie 15, 114, 116
Hermes..56, 61, 77, 89, 93, 114, 258
Hesiod....................56, 77, 93
Hilton, Walter 10
Hippocrates......................... 76, 77
Hodelsa............................292, 293
Holy Oil 195, 197, 202, 203
Homer.....................56, 77, 93
Humphreys, John..9, 17, 18, 24, 25, 26, 28
Hyssop 159

I

I Corinthians 84
I Kings.................................... 87
II Chronicles........................87, 197
II Corinthians............................. 87
Inafula 292, 293
Iron 118, 153, 253, 287, 299, 313
Isaac..101, 138, 140, 159, 192, 220, 244
Isaiah 64, 76
Iscarath................................. 150

J

Jacob..50, 101, 108, 129, 130, 138, 140, 159, 163, 220, 228, 244, 248
James I, King 8
Jasper.............................229, 283
Jekyll, Lord 14, 26
Jekyll, Sir Joseph 21, 26, 33
Jesus..40, 42, 43, 44, 46, 47, 51, 52, 53, 57, 63, 73, 98, 101, 105, 106, 108, 113, 114, 115, 116, 117, 118, 127, 131, 133, 135, 136, 138, 140, 142, 144, 147, 148, 149, 150, 152, 153, 154, 155, 159, 160, 210, 212, 217, 220, 223, 229, 230, 231, 232, 235, 236, 237, 238, 239, 240, 241, 244, 245, 246, 248, 249, 250, 251, 252, 262, 274, 283, 284, 286, 288, 296, 299, 300, 301, 303, 315, 319
Job..................................... 90
John Baptist..62, 71, 142, 145, 148, 149, 210, 290
John, Gospel........58, 71, 76, 99, 286
Joshua 71
Judas................................. 78, 198
Judges 196
Julia............................ 17, 292, 293
Jupiter..67, 176, 184, 189, 211, 218, 240, 241, 255, 256, 257, 258, 266, 291, 311

K

Key of Solomon 7, 20, 22, 251
Kings of Collen............... 210, 229

L

Lansdowne MS 1202........... 22, 23
Lapis Lazuli 255
Laud, William 10, 11, 12
Laurel 39, 189, 255
Lazarus.................................. 220
Lead 118
Legge, Dr Thomas 21
Leo 52, 53, 223, 258, 302, 305
Leo, Saint 52
Libra 183, 258
Lignum Aloes..227, 249, 255, 256, 257, 258, 264, 270
Lignum Balsam 255
Lilly, William..9, 11, 12, 13, 15, 16, 17, 18, 24, 25, 51
Lodestone 256
Lucifer..151, 152, 153, 154, 155, 239, 306, 307, 311
Luke, Gospel..59, 62, 76, 77, 89, 91, 108

M

Maherion .... 147, *See* Mayrion
Mahiron .... 144, *See* Mayrion
Mandrogrora 255
Marion .... *See* Mayrion
Mark, Gospel 43, 315
Mars..68, 173, 184, 189, 211, 257, 258, 319
Mary Magdalene 221, 301
Mary, Queen 21
Mastic..174, 227, 249, 255, 256, 257, 258, 270
Matherion....147, 148, 297, *See* Mayrion
Matthew, Gospel..58, 59, 62, 76, 81, 87, 88, 91, 315
Mayrion 143, 144
Mechtildis, Saint 204
Melchior...........................229, 283
Melton, John............................... 8
Mercury..160, 174, 184, 190, 211, 256, 257, 258, 262, 280, 290, 291, 292, 293
Merlin...................................... 204
Mermaids................................... 83
Michael, Archangel..62, 142, 169, 239, 244, 274, 281, 284
Misach...................................... 164
Miscellanies Upon Various Subjects 23, 24
Moon..70, 142, 156, 158, 159, 160, 162, 171, 183, 184, 191, 201, 205, 211, 214, 216, 217, 218, 224, 235, 257, 258, 261, 280, 288, 300, 303, 304
Mortagon 301
Mortlake 15, 16, 25
Moses..41, 89, 93, 105, 109, 152, 154, 163, 196, 198, 220, 248, 250, 253, 301
MS Bod e Mus 243 284
MS Gaster 1562 ....307, 308
MS Laud Misc 19 .... 10, 11
Musk 255, 256
Myrrh 104, 229, 255, 256, 258
Myrtle......................256, 257, 258

N

Nigromancia............................... 14
Notary Art................................ 281
Nutmeg 256, 258, 310, 314
Nymphs, Water Elementals.... 74, 77, 85

O

Oberion 19, 20, 261, 262
Och 64, 65, 66, 68, 71
Of Occult Philosophy 20, 22, 180
Olive Oil................................. 134
Olympic Spirit..................... 64, 72
Onele 134, 135, 136
Ophiel....................... 64, 65, 66, 69
Opoponax 255, 258
Orpheus 77

P

Paracelsus 7, 77
Parsley...................................... 254
Pater Noster..42, 147, 229, 283, 300
Paul, Saint........................... 61, 296
Pentacle..160, 161, 165, 166, 192, 193
Pepperwort...................... 257, 258
Phaleg....................... 64, 65, 66, 68
Philo... 59
Philosopher's Stone 69, 75
Phul 64, 65, 70
Pisces 218, 258
Plato... 77
Pomegranate............................ 299
Pontius Pilate 147, 235
Poole, William 25
Potentates....................... 210, 223
Potestates..65, 142, 212, 231, 239, 240, 242
Powers..................................... 210
Principates..142, 212, 223, 230, 231, 239, 240, 242
Psalm..21, 22, 43, 142, 192, 264, 265, 288

Psalm 101................................. 272
Psalm 102................................. 272
Psalm 103................................. 109
Psalm 110................................... 93
Psalm 113................................... 59
Psalm 114................................. 270
Psalm 118................................... 91
Psalm 119................................. 203
Psalm 16..................................... 59
Psalm 17................................... 265
Psalm 18................................... 266
Psalm 22................................... 227
Psalm 31..................................... 76
Psalm 34.............................44, 267
Psalm 38................................... 267
Psalm 42................................... 265
Psalm 43................................... 142
Psalm 45................................... 104
Psalm 46................................... 129
Psalm 47................................... 267
Psalm 49..................................... 59
Psalm 50..............87, 159, 268, 270
Psalm 51......46, 128, 146, 222, 229
Psalm 54............................... 42, 76
Psalm 57................................... 268
Psalm 58................................... 142
Psalm 6....................................... 42
Psalm 64..................................... 44
Psalm 66................................... 268
Psalm 67................................... 193
Psalm 7.............................264, 265
Psalm 71..................................... 42
Psalm 76................................... 270
Psalm 77................................... 142
Psalm 8....................................... 43
Psalm 80................................... 103
Psalm 90................................... 264
Psalm 91.................44, 46, 99, 130
Psalm 95................................... 267
Psalm 98................................... 265
Ptolemy...................................... 35
Pygmies 60, 67, 74, 85, 125
Pythagoras.......................... 56, 77

Q

Quicksilver 69

R

Ragarad 150
Raguel, Archangel 140
Raphael, Archangel..62, 142, 173, 174, 177, 244, 269, 274, 281
Red Coral 256
Red Roses.................................. 256
Revelation................................. 197
Ring 150, 204, 207, 314
Roauia 292, 293
Romans....................................... 61
Rosemary Lane........... 24, 25, 321

S

Sachiel, Archangel..171, 175, 176, 177
Saffron..176, 190, 254, 257, 258, 281
Sagamex 292, 293
Saganes.......................................74
Sagittarius................................ 258
Samael 169, 171, 172, 173, 177
Samson 196
Sanders..................... 255, 257, 258
Sathan..14, 46, 83, 89, 90, 93, 144, 150, 151, 152, 153, 154, 155, 244, 248, 249, 250, 251
Saturn..66, 179, 184, 189, 204, 211, 255, 257, 258, 300
Saturnion 244
Satyrs...85
Savadge, Ann..12, 24, 25, 26, 27, 28, 321
Scale of Perfection...................... 10
Scorax 19, 261
Scorpio 218, 258
Scot, Reginald..7, 13, 22, 193, 216, 224, 237, 326
Seal of Secrets 19, 79
Searle, John 13, 14, 44
Sedamylia 292, 293
Sepher Shimmush Tehillim 22
Septuagint................................. 22
Seraphim..40, 111, 142, 223, 230, 231, 239, 240, 242

Severion 19

Shelborne, Sarah..*See* Skelhorn, Sarah

Sibilia.........237, 239, 240, 241, 242

Sidrach 164

Silver..70, 155, 171, 224, 254, 261, 279, 288, 289, 304, 313

Skelhorn, Sarah 9, 10, 11, 17, 18

Sloane MS 3824..17, 22, 143, 144, 151, 153

Sloane MS 3825 17

Sloane MS 3846..14, 15, 16, 19, 22, 24, 25, 114

Sloane MS 3851..8, 12, 14, 17, 18, 19, 20, 21, 22, 23, 25, 31

Sloane, Sir Hans 14, 26, 33

Solomon..20, 39, 134, 155, 165, 166, 197, 217, 223, 246, 249, 250, 253, 262, 292, 293, 310

Somers, Baron John .21, 25, 26, 28

Spenser, Edmund 20

Sperion ....147, 148, *See* Spiron

Spiron..............................143, 144

Steganographia 253

Storax..19, 255, 257, 258, *See* Scorax

Sun..39, 63, 68, 71, 73, 116, 142, 156, 158, 159, 164, 170, 183, 184, 200, 201, 202, 203, 204, 211, 213, 217, 224, 235, 241, 242, 257, 258, 264, 289, 294, 304, 305, 308, 309, 315

Susanna.................................. 140

T

Taurus 258

Te Deum Laudamus 110, 143

Teltrion..............................143, 144

The Art of Juggling or Legerdemaine 13

The Book of Gold..21, 22, 265, 266, 267, 268, 270

The Fair Maid of the Inn 13

Theltrion .... 147, 148, *See* Teltrion

Theltryon .... 147, *See* Teltrion

Theurgia Goetia 253

Thimyam................................. 255

Thrones..142, 145, 210, 212, 230, 231, 239, 240, 241

Tin...................................... 118, 289

Tobit 62, 269

Turner, Robert..18, 73, 170, 177, 178, 179, 183, 190, 192, 203, 208, 209, 279

U

Uriel, Archangel...... 169, 178, 244

V

Valerian........................... 301, 302

Venus..150, 177, 184, 190, 211, 257, 258, 309, 311, 312, 318

Vervain.................... 303, 304, 305

Virgin Mary..142, 145, 147, 148, 149, 150, 152, 153, 210, 217, 223, 235, 241, 244, 246, 250

Virgo..258

Voces Magicae.................. 29, 281

W

Wellcome MS 4669.............. 20, 23

White Poppy................... 254, 255

Withers, Oliver................... 15, 16